Montage

THE INDIA LIST

Mrinal Sen

MONTAGE
LIFE. POLITICS. CINEMA.

With Photographs by Subhash Nandy

Seagull
BOOKS

LONDON NEW YORK CALCUTTA

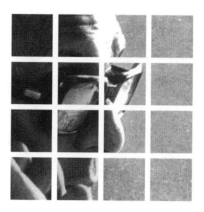

Seagull Books, 2018

First published by Seagull Books in 2002

Text © Seagull Books, 2002, 2018

Photographs © Subhash Nandy, 2002

ISBN 978 0 8574 2 498 3

British Library Cataloguing-in-Publication Data

A catalogue record for this book is available from the British Library

Typeset by Seagull Books, Calcutta, India

Printed and bound by Maple Press, York, Pennsylvania, USA

Contents

MONTAGE

An Uncertain Journey

My first few encounters with Calcutta led me to many things but not to cinema. I came to cinema fairly late. And I came to it through writing and the whole affair was purely accidental. That is a different story. An uncertain journey finally led me to cinema in the mid-fifties.

My first film *Ratbhor*, made in 1956, was a big disaster, the biggest of all big disasters. I hate to talk about it. Having made it I felt terrible, I felt humiliated.

Nil Akasher Niche [1958] was my second film. The story dates back to the 1930s. It was over-sentimental, technically poor, visually unsatisfying. But the one aspect of the film which I still stand by and find relevant even today is its political thesis which upholds the notion that the struggle for Independence is inseparably linked to the liberal world's crusade against fascism and imperialism. That was perhaps precisely why, despite my own reservations about it, someone like Jawaharlal Nehru appreciated the film.

3

Baishey Sravan, my third film made in 1960, made me feel great. It wasn't really a great film, but I felt good nevertheless.

Baishey Sravan explores the relationship between a man and his wife who is a much younger and very attractive woman chosen for him by his widowed mother. This relationship is the film's primary preoccupation; how it develops and then eventually collapses without the apparent presence of 'another'. Without the aid of any catalyst, as it were, to cause and/or to accelerate the process. The first part of the film, therefore, is concerned with these three characters. The man, his pretty young wife and his widowed mother. At a point in the film, the mother dies and from then on, the film focuses entirely on the married pair. Set in a remote village, the film captures a variety of experiences causing both happiness and despair to the couple, until very slowly but inexorably, the Famine of 1943 creeps into the film.[1] The camera remains indoors, picking on the cracks appearing in their relationship, and moves outside only once. A long shot of the starving villagers abandoning the village in search of food. Outside, the famine grows uglier (and this our camera deliberately avoids), inside, all is quiet but oppressive ... Till the very end it remains the story of these two people—embittered and unable to endure the harsh reality of the famine, they hurl against each other in impotent fury and rage. They breathe only the stench of corpses. There is nothing to salvage them, to pull them out of the filth, and this is what the film focuses on. My intention was not to capture the physical details of the famine nor to present the statistics of the afflicted people who simply starved and dropped dead. To suggest the slow but inevitable liquidation of every last vestige of human decency was what I had aimed at. Yet the man was no villain and the woman was all grace. It was a cruel time and a cruel film.

Understandably, such a film can hardly be a financial success. Although it was a failure at the box office, *Baishey Sravan* granted me a firm foothold in the world of cinema; I was recognized as a 'regular' filmmaker. And, for reasons of my own, I henceforth made it a point to constantly break new ground, cast off the shackles of conformism and evolve new modes of expression. Risky propositions all, very risky. Even now. In every sphere, in any discipline.

Talking of cinema, a highly conformist society like ours is most likely to breed conformist viewers. More often than not, they are found to go in for what I would term, 'stock' responses. I repeat, 'stock' responses. It is unfortunate but only too true.

In the early 1960s there was a little-known man in Films Division [Government of India's film-production house] called Promod Pati, who defied the prevalent principles, norms and laws of the establishment and let loose a burst of madness on the screen. The results were varied but I was fascinated by the youthfulness and verve of the filmmaker and by the fair amount of gay abandon that he seemed to display.

Soon afterwards, the French New Wave made its influence felt in our country. And I sensed a certain madness in the air. A madness and a freshness. I felt an irresistible urge for change. It seemed to be the best time for me to playfully and yet meaningfully defy the existing barriers, barriers that mainstream cinema would seldom cross. I made *Akash Kusum* in 1965. It was all about the 'exploits' of a modern young man, in a desperate bid to overcome the problems of wealth or the lack of it. It may be broadly defined as a comedy.

The evident innovations in *Akash Kusum* were done mostly out of necessity and partly out of sheer playfulness. And, at times, also to shock the conservative Indian audience. A small number liked the film; others thought it was self-indulgent and the rest found it pointless—mere gimmickry.

I did not allow myself to be cowed down but proceeded along my own charted course—steadily, happily, clumsily, desperately. And later, things came to such a pass that for another film of mine made in 1970—*Interview*—I seriously considered introducing a card in my credits, reading 'Screenplay, Direction & Gimmicks by Mrinal Sen'.

How and where do you draw a line and say, 'This far and no further or you land into the area of gimmicks?'

To make an honest statement, *Interview*, for what it was worth, called for a very different treatment. There was hardly any plot-driven, calculated 'story'. It is all about a young man's day-long search for a pair of suits in the city, which he will need for an interview. All the city laundries are on strike. Everything therefore occurs in a mad rush, typical of life in a metropolis. And the film is a variegated blending of fictional narrative—just a touch of it—newsreel coverage, an almost *cinema verité* type of documentation and, finally, a provocative session of dialogue between the young man and the invisible 'me', followed by a sudden flight into quixotic fantasy. Certainly not every storyteller's cup of tea. And within the format provided by the subject, I made full use of the fact that cinema was a continuously growing phenomenon—a hybrid art, thriving on cross-fertilization. I went wild. I released everything that was maddening, restless, nervous, vibrant, buoyant and even flippant within me in a desperate bid to break the frontiers created and closely guarded by the conservatives. And I shall not deny that I did get carried away in the process, and even displayed a certain amount of infantile enthusiasm. In retrospect though, I wish I had avoided it.

It was in the early 1970s that the very air in Calcutta seemed to crackle with anger. Anger and unrest.[2] That was when I made three films in three successive years—*Interview*, *Calcutta 71* [1972] and *Padatik* [1973]. They were, justifiably, angry and restless. And in varying degrees, both passionate and blatant. Here, when I use the word 'blatant' I mean it and write it in a positive sense. That was when my team and I could not escape the pressure of our times. That was when we affirmed our condition of rebellion. All this perhaps reads like a pamphlet but that was our reality then.

The third film, *Padatik*, was different from the first two both in content and form because here, without losing their focus on the continuing battle against all kinds of social, political and economic oppression, the characters do a bit of soul-searching as well. The question asked was, 'Is everything all right on the anti-establishment front? Isn't it time to examine and question the validity of the mandates of leadership? Isn't it proper to challenge the establishmentarianism in the leadership? And, if necessary, "to go against the tide"?'

All these three films, like most of my earlier ones, were simultaneously loved and hated—both for the conceptual texts and their modes of expression. I remained as controversial as ever. My unit members and I were always prepared with our arguments, never too tired or uncomfortable to present our case. I remember, whenever I felt defensive, I used to come up with a quote from Niels Bohr, a stalwart in the world of twentieth-century physics, which went something like this: 'A truth attains a quality only when it becomes controversial.'

The mid-1970s and the years that followed were a period of transition for me. It was also when I had one of the most exciting experiences of my lifetime—the making of my one and only Telugu film, *Oka Oorie Katha* [1977].

Hindi–Urdu writer Premchand's last and perhaps cruellest story, 'Kafan'—which is the basis of *Oka Oorie Katha*—was set in a village in Uttar Pradesh in North India. While writing the script I had imagined a typical Bengal village as the setting, in East India. Whereas the film was ultimately shot in a remote village in Telangana in South India. Not an easy job at all! My unit and I had to familiarize ourselves with many features of an alien lifestyle and culture—outfits, food-habits, local customs, rituals, modes of physical expression and so on. Not so simple a task—there was so much to get to know and fall in love with—unless you can develop a kind of respect for the circumstances in which your characters live, love, desire and ultimately perish. The problem of the language and its nuances remained with us till the end. But what I found strikingly similar—whether in the north, south, east or west—was the spectre of poverty and exploitation. Which was what the story was all about. And that was precisely why, even though we had plenty of foreign elements to encounter and to come to terms with, we never felt that we were working in an altogether alien milieu. The culture of poverty and exploitation is the same everywhere, and there too, we did not fail to do justice to the characters and the locale.

I had a similar experience in the mid-1960s: I invaded a village in Odisha and made an Odia film, *Matira Manisha* [1966]. A simple story of a peasant family in a remote village, where the rule of the patriarch and that of the village mahajan play equally dominant roles.

Having made *Matira Manisha* in Odisha, I thought I had done a good job. But, as was always wont to happen with me, *Matira Manisha* raised a controversy. A group of hardcore academics felt that I had taken undue liberty with the text. This, according to them, was nothing short of sacrilege.

I must confess that I am genuinely unaware of having done anything that can be construed as libellous. Without committing any offence to the social milieu of the 1930s—the era in which Kalindi Charan Panigrahi located his novel—I had merely invested the story with contemporary sensibilities. My questions, I believe, are pertinent enough: Is it obligatory on my part to treat the text as a fragile artefact, preserved in a glass case in some museum? As a person not unaware of the contemporary situation, is it not my prerogative to recreate the story? To redefine it, to reinterpret it? And, in the process, to provoke, to criticize and to challenge? I think these are issues of great importance to the activists in the areas of social anthropology and aesthetics.

In time, my home state, West Bengal, had a new government. The government of the Left.[3] A significant change came over a large section of the ruling front and a quite perceptible change at that. Much less self-criticism and much more self-complacency. And the latter, predictably, gave rise to a withdrawal of tolerance primarily on all ideological fronts.

Around the same time, I came across an important document by one of the foremost creative Marxists in Europe, a wounded and humiliated Elio Vittorini. In a letter to Palmiro Togliatti, that giant among the European Marxists, Vittorini had written: 'The point is not to pocket the truth, but to chase the truth.'

I was intrigued by the obvious connection—Vittorini's angry statement made years ago when he was attacked by his friends of the orthodox variety and the change that had gradually come over things at home.

I felt confused. I withdrew into my own thoughts, and seeking silence, questioned myself as I had done often in the past, 'Am I going in the right direction?'

So it has been. Checking and double-checking—on my journey through life.

Now, I felt compelled to combat this self-complacency. I scraped together enough courage to face the reality of this new situation, to confront it, to come to terms with it. In the process, I realized that within each of our given situations, we are all, in small or large measure, incorrigible peddlers of fantasy. And that fantasy is our safest and only escape route.

Ek Din Pratidin, made in 1979, marked the beginning of a new phase in my career as a filmmaker and this phase lasted for quite a few years thereafter. My main aims and concerns are remarkably unchanged even today. I am always trying to delve into the interior, into that realm which lies hidden behind the facade of the outside world; to discover mysteries, frustrations, confusions, contradictions; to identify the terrible sense of isolation, even emptiness and, of course, the hidden strength which lies behind this apparent despair.

On the physical plane, *Ek Din Pratidin* ended on a note of despair. The films that followed—each one moving in its own orbit—were similar in that they shared this despair on the physical plane, but deep within, possessed a certain strength. I thought I had arrived at a moment of truth.

The response in the domestic circuits was good, but the militants among my long-time admirers felt that I had mellowed considerably and that I had been receding from the political scene. They were extremely unhappy that the films did not carry 'messages'. They found *Ek Din Pratidin* much too despairing, *Akaler Sandhane* [1980] utterly defeatist, they discovered in *Khandahar* [1983] the story of feudal hangover. And in *Kharij* [1982] they expected that, on his return from the crematorium, the father of the deceased boy-servant, would slap the young employer across his face.

9

Unperturbed, I continued my work and even today, I think I have succeeded in staying the way I want to be. I say a clear 'No' to fragile optimism, I confront, I fight, I survive on tension. And as I survive, I look beyond. And I dream. And what is true of me is also true of my characters.

And, in this context, on the technological front, I find it obligatory to use my tools with restraint. I repeat, restraint. Not because I am ageing and therefore mellowing. I am ageing, true, but with age and experience I am becoming more careful, more austere.

As I look back, I realize that through experiences and experiments, through failures and errors and also successes, I have tried to understand my medium and myself. I have been constantly changing. I have been correcting my own conclusions. I am doing so. Even now.

[*Edited version of a paper read at National Institute of Advanced Studies, Bangalore,* 1994.]

Notes

1 The Bengal Famine of 1943 killed more than 2.1 million people across undivided Bengal in British India, and led to mass migration and a general slide towards economic inequality in the region. Mrinal Sen's *Akaler Sandhane* (1980) deals with a film unit trying to shoot a film about the Bengal Famine in contemporary rural West Bengal.

2 A reference to the militant Naxalite movement and its brutal repression in rural and urban West Bengal during the early 1970s. The events greatly impacted cultural and educational life in Calcutta.

3 In the 1977 election to the West Bengal state legislature, the Left Front led by the Communist Party of India (Marxist) won a landslide victory and formed the government.

Unfamiliar Faridpur

My ancestral home is Faridpur.[1] That is where I spent my childhood and my youth. Faridpur—an unknown little town belonging to the ancient landmass of undivided India. In reality, it was poised uncertainly between being a city and a village. Today, Calcutta is my home. Today, Faridpur is foreign to me.

After 1971, there were frequent invitations to visit Bangladesh. There was no way of refusing. There was no other place that offered me such affection, such love, such anticipation. And besides, the place was only an arm's length away. Whether it be by Indian Airlines or Bangladesh Biman, by the time one seated oneself and adjusted the seat-belts, it would be time to land; that's how short the flight was. Who can resist the call of a place that is so close to us?

This is something no one can hold against me. It was only during those few years after the war for freedom that I stayed away, even though this was unintentional. I would think to myself, they've just about taken over the country. Let things get sorted, let them settle down a bit, I'll go once they've got everything organized.

The first time I went back to Bangladesh, to Dhaka, my wife Geeta —a true-blue 'ghoti'[2]—was with me. Her every step was accompanied by exclamations of surprise and astonishment. As though, despite having lived in a house for so many years she had never ever, even for a moment, visited the eastern wing. It was as if a door had been flung open that day. And there were no limits to our explorations. That four-day visit flashed past in a series of meetings and banquets and felicitations. Day and night. Talk, talk and more talk. Endless conversations. To make and to pay attention to.

By the time I got my bearings, it was time to return. That's why we never got around to visiting Faridpur. Not then, and not the next time. My wife was with me then, too. Finally, on the third visit. Once again, my wife was with me. Faridpur was on this bank of the Padma. On the other side, Dhaka lay way beyond a cluster of villages and settlements. At that time, it used to be an entire day's journey. I'd been there many times during my childhood, ever since I can remember. The moment the sun rose and the first rays of light splashed across the sky, we would pile into a horse-drawn carriage and set off for the jetty—Topakhola. At least a couple of miles away, if not more. We would arrive at Topakhola and then board the ferry—called *Damdim*. At first there would be the narrow canal which would gradually widen out. We would leave the jute and paddy fields behind us and then, at one point, in about an hour or so, we would be confronted with a view of the Padma. Ever so slowly we would suddenly be mid-river where the eye could see nothing but churning waves on either side. Then one could notice, away in the distance, a two-tiered ship. An *Emu* or an *Ostrich*. Standing absolutely still amidst incredibly turbulent waters, waiting for *Damdim*. It was really quite an experience. And every time it would be just the same. But the excitement and the novelty—of changing over mid-Padma from the *Damdim* into an *Emu* or an *Ostrich*—never diminished.

It would be evening by the time we reached Narayanganj. On the way we would pass Bhagyakul, Taarpasha, Louhajang. And aboard the ship, twice a day, we would be served meals of coarse rice and chicken curry. Unbelievable, heavenly. I used to ponder at length then—and I do so even today—on how, despite travelling on this ship which served such delicious chicken, it was still possible for so many people in this country to remain vegetarian? What kind of austerity was this? But then again, who knew? Maybe they were the only ones who had been able to discern the unique flavour of the dal on board!

From Narayanganj, it was only a short way by train. To Dhaka. And by the time we reached Dhaka, the evening would have begun to darken into night. This meant that it would take an entire day to reach Dhaka from Faridpur. Getting back was the same. It would take the same amount of time. One whole day.

This time, however, the moment I reached Dhaka I decided that I would go to Faridpur, even if for only a few hours. Especially now that it took only four hours by car to get to Faridpur from Dhaka. But first, the automobile, with all its passengers still inside it, would have to be transported across the waters by the ferry. To the other side of the Padma. To Faridpur.

The year 1940. I still hadn't left Faridpur. I would, later that year. I would go to Calcutta to study. I had just about crossed over from childhood into adolescence. Or perhaps, I was emotionally poised between the two. I was born into a large family, with many brothers and sisters. Ours was not an economically affluent family, nor was it poor. My father was a lawyer—independent and upright, without any trace of arrogance. After years of successful practice, he was accepted as the leader of the Bar in our small town. Throughout his career in the courts of law, he made it his mission to lend active legal support to militant political activists—'freedom fighters', as they are called now—very few of whom, for obvious reasons, could escape death by hanging. My father was disbarred for a period of six months when Mahatma Gandhi was arrested immediately on his return from the Round Table Conference in England in the early 1930s, and, as a mark of protest, my father and his colleagues boycotted the court sessions. The following day, the district magistrate singled out my father and disbarred him temporarily.

My mother, too, defying social constraints, had done her bit for the revolution by singing one of Rabindranath Tagore's songs at a public meeting attended by Bipin Chandra Pal, one of the famous Lal–Bal–Pal triumvirate.[3]

I had spent my childhood and my growing years in a place that was a combination of the urban and the rural. Now, I was off to a strange and unfamiliar land. Now, I was off to Calcutta.

Ma was crying softly and scurrying about on various errands. I noticed Baba hovering around me constantly, looking grave. The older children had already flown the nest. My sisters had got married and left for their new homes and my brothers were pursuing their careers—one was in Assam, beyond Dibrugarh, another in Batanagar and yet another in Jamshedpur. I don't recall noticing any great change in the expressions of those younger than I, who were still studying in school. Perhaps because we were a large family. Though our bonds were very strong, we were not given to outward expressions of emotion. Except for my mother, who was just like any other mother in any other household. She was busy putting my things together, this and that, so many odds and ends, pausing only occasionally to wipe away her tears with the edge of her sari. And my father, gently running his hand down my back and saying, 'Take care.'

I don't know what came over me suddenly. My last night at home. Making certain that my father was within earshot, I asked my mother, 'Ma, have you ever noticed any exceptional quality in me? Have there been any signs? You know . . . like great personalities display in their childhood? Any flash of genius?'

My mother was dumbfounded at this question. Either she was unable to grasp it, or she had understood it but was struggling to frame an adequate response. I am sure that if my father hadn't been present she would have given me a piece of her mind. And Baba, trying hard to

pretend that he wasn't listening, smiled despite himself. He said, 'Here, hop on to my back,' and kneeling promptly on the floor, turned into a 'horse' for me.

This was one of Baba's favourite games. A game we had both outgrown, even then.

Somewhere in-between his solemn facade and serious personality, he had managed to preserve the child in him for a very long time. And now, perhaps this also served as an effective means of evasion. My father had certainly been able to realize that until then their son had not really proved himself to be anything above average. And he was not the kind of person to make emphatic promises about the future. And to be quite honest, what had I shown him anyway that would enable him to answer my question? Nonetheless, in a spot of fun, I rattled off a newly borrowed phrase to my father. Perhaps it would also help reassure my mother to a certain extent. I said it with a certain offhand air that was intended to fool people into thinking that the words were my own. Actually it was a Bertrand Russell quote read out to me by Amal-da —an extremely erudite student and a fount of knowledge. I hero-worshipped him in my youth. The line was: 'Everyone is a genius up to the age of ten.'

Baba stared at me through his glasses, his brows creased in a frown. Ma was still watching him. And at that very moment I understood that Baba had just granted me a 'benefit of the doubt'. And it was with that benefit of the doubt that I came to Calcutta and spent the first few months feeling homesick. But that was just during the first two-three-four months. After that, with each passing day, I began to fall more and more in love with Calcutta. For a variety of reasons—social, political, cultural. Right through the days of famine and violence and war. Terrible days. Awful days. But memorable ones all the same.

I would, of course, keep going back home regularly oh holidays. I remember clearly the last time I went back. It was sometime in 1942. That was my very last visit, for that particular phase of my life.

In the days that followed, the waters of the Ganga and the Padma hardly mingled and may have even retreated from each other's paths. After an interminably long time, after forty-seven years, came the day my wife and I were both travelling from Dhaka to Faridpur, now just four hours away by car. I was carrying with me an absence stretched over forty-seven years and the almost complete loss of all my childhood memories. My oblivion and my wife's wonder. The ferry crossed the Padma and halted near the ghat. I could no longer recall the name of the station, just the fact that it would never stay in one place. The whole year through it was completely at the mercy of the Padma—sometimes it would drift far off to the left or to the right or be pushed backwards and forwards. I remember it then took us about an hour or two to reach the city by car. The car moved at its own pace. And the rural landscape rolled past on both sides.

I still didn't know where we were going or to whom, or where we would finally arrive. I only knew that we were on our way to Faridpur after forty-seven years. And during those forty-seven years my mind had not suffered even the tiniest pang of separation. My wife asked me at one point, 'Can you recognize anything?'

I pursed my lips in thought and then shook my head. 'No.'

Our companion for the ride, Abul Khayer, was beaming with anticipation and excitement. His entire attitude radiated the promise, 'Wait and see where we're going, which Faridpur I'm taking you to.' I came to know that we were not going to take the well-known and oft-travelled route of my childhood days; that the jetty Topakhola was now at the other end of the city. We were approaching from the opposite direction, from the direction of Gowalchamot.

Gowalchamot!

You mean Rathtala?

Suddenly, visions of the Faridpur 'rath-er mela'[4] rose up in my mind. And I remembered the wet roads, washed clean by the Ashadh rains. I remembered how all of us would walk to the mela each year and how I would come home, invariably drenched to the skin. And be scolded by my mother, without fail. And then, seven days later when I would start my tantrums, eager to go for the Ulta Rath, she would frighten me with 'How do you think you'll get back home? Won't your head be *ulta* as well? How will you walk then? And all that way?'

As a child I used to really believe what she said, imagining that that's what happened on the way back from the Ulta Rath. And that it happened to everyone who went. Once I grew up, my mother stopped telling me such cock-and-bull stories and the urge to walk that long way by ourselves also died out gradually.

The Rathtala at Gowalchamot was quite far from the city.

'This is the same Rathtala,' one of our companions pointed out. I stuck my head out of the car window for a look.

'Can you recognize anything?'

My wife asked me, 'Well? Can you?' As though it was an attempt to try and jog the latent memory of an amnesia patient.

No, I couldn't recognize anything. Houses had sprung up everywhere, shops had been set up and the Rathtala had shrunk greatly in size.

I asked, 'Is Jagabandhu's ashram still there?'

'But of course. Although nothing is the same any more. It's still standing, that's about it.'

The name Jagabandhu had suddenly leapt to mind; I hadn't really been trying to remember. And besides, every now and then in Calcutta at *Gita*-reading sessions, there would be mention of this great man, and I had seen his picture a few times in the local dailies as well. I would remember Jagabandhu then. And I had seen his picture on the walls of Nabendu Ghosh's[5] house, both in Calcutta and in Bombay. Nabendu-babu was a disciple of his. Fragment by fragment, the pieces began to fall into place. Some words. Some images.

Just that much and no more—just as much as I had seen. Nothing else. It was like looking through the lens of a camera; one can see only so much and within a specific frame.

I asked, 'The canal's up ahead. And that wooden bridge. Isn't that so?' I was told that the wooden bridge had been dismantled before it collapsed of its own accord and a concrete one constructed a little away from its place. This bridge was a permanent one and very wide too. And almost fifteen years old. Yes, that's what I was told.

By then, our car had moved onto the bridge.

My wife could not contain her excitement. She asked me, 'Did you remember the canal? And the bridge?'

I did know about them but I remembered them only this very instant. How strange!

I thought of *Lost Horizons* [1937]. And Ronald Colman came to mind.

We crossed the bridge and I asked, 'Which way now? Right through the fish market?'

My wife was amazed. She said, 'It's as though you have memories from a previous lifetime.'

It was exactly like that. Unloved and unwanted, dregs of memories from the very depths of my unconscious were being magically brought up to the surface, one by one—image following image, event following event. There had been no preparation, no conscious attempt. Silently. Silently they floated up to the surface and then stayed embedded in my mind, imprinted on my soul.

The car, of course, did not turn to the right but continued straight on. That was where, at one point of time, a certain section was demarcated as the red-light district. Our guardians had strictly warned us to avoid the neighbourhood. Nonetheless, turning a deaf ear to their instructions, a group of us youngsters had visited the place; all of us together. Sheer curiosity. Once or twice we had even spied a respectable young man or two visiting the same neighbourhood. Others, just like us, would see them too. And the whispers of gossip would break out immediately and snowball into a scandal within the city. Now, however, the place is a respectable residential area. Unfamiliar. The car turned into a lane. It was all so new to me. In a little while, the car stopped in front of a house. And it was not just the master of the household but a small group of family members who stood waiting for us, on the threshold. We stepped out of the car. The place seemed very new to me—tidy, civilized, respectable.

After the welcome and the pampering and the eating were over, we set off in search of the past. On foot. I said, or, rather, instructed, 'Please let us lead the way. The rest of you can follow us. Let me choose which way to go. Even if I happen to go off in the wrong direction. At worst, we will take a little longer to get back to the road that leads to my house. The town is hardly large enough for us to get lost in.'

By then, many of Faridpur's inhabitants had collected in a crowd, to accompany us as we walked along. And since it was a holiday, everyone had plenty of time on their hands. Very soon, the crowd following us assumed the form of a small procession. Led by my wife and I. Although we were walking in unison, my wife too was in a sense obedient to the paths I was choosing to explore. Everyone was quiet. Even if people spoke, it was in whispers. And amid this mute procession I was the only one who continued speaking. And I did nothing but reminisce aloud. Bit by bit, skeletons of memory were being fleshed out and appearing before my eyes; it seemed as though they and I were walking side by side, hand in hand. And my 'running commentary' continued, like a stream of consciousness, but it was still all extremely disjointed, random, restless.

Here is the Asthir house, and there, the garden in front. I can't see the jamrul tree; probably not there any more. It was the same tree I had once fallen off. Not because the branch broke under my weight. But because I was unable to maintain my balance as the sudden tremors of an earthquake shook everything. I had not broken or sprained any limbs. But I remember how the neighbourhood had suddenly resounded with the sound of conch shells being blown in all the houses; many people rushed out to stand in the open. We came to know later that no damage had been done to any of the houses in the city. The next day's newspapers announced that the successive tremors had resulted in many people in Bihar being rendered homeless and that the damage was terrible. More stories about the devastation in Bihar began to trickle in over the next few days. The elders in the city organized first a meeting and then small processions through the streets to collect money for the earthquake victims. Money, clothes and food were collected from homes and sent off, although not to Patna but somewhere else. Or perhaps it was all taken to the Faridpur Ramakrishna Mission. I can't remember too clearly. For us youngsters, the whole thing, of course, had taken on the air of an unexpected festival.

A little further and there was the immense field of Norail. Still untouched. Still a field. The elders could not play there; they were banned. We children would play there—football, hockey, badminton, hadudu, danguli and so much more. All of us would play and there were days when I would return home injured. And if I ever sprained or twisted any of my limbs there was always Ma's potent remedy—*chun-holud* [lime and turmeric]. She would warm the mixture of turmeric and slaked lime and apply it, then cover the area with a banana leaf and tie the whole thing up. I remember once when I had an upset stomach, my mother ground the mixture into a paste and made me swallow some of it.

The very thought of the Ramakrishna Mission brought to mind the tall, graceful and elderly figure of Prakash Maharaj, the head of the ashram, where every evening puja would be performed in an atmosphere that was appropriately solemn and austere. We children would sing. The devotees and the others who came regularly for darshan—everyone was asked to join in. And once or twice a year we would all sit in a line on the verandah and partake of the ashram's prasad which consisted of khichudi. Ma used to say that the ashram's prasad never made anyone ill, hearing which I would happily gorge on it. Also every now and then I would see Prakash Maharaj accompanied by the other sannyasis, going from door to door, collecting alms. I had heard from my father that Prakash Maharaj was a man of many parts; he was secretly helping the nationalist freedom fighters in many ways. Even after the country was partitioned, Prakash Maharaj had apparently stayed on in Faridpur.

I moved on. And the procession followed soundlessly at my heels.

I stopped a little short of Ambika Majumdar's[6] house. Isn't the house there any more? Such a large house, that huge compound, all those trees. I turned questioningly towards Khoyer-saheb. Where is it? 'There it is. We can't possibly have moved it elsewhere. Look carefully. It's just been obscured by the trees.'

Yes, that's right. A few trees had spread their branches and hidden it from sight, as though standing guard over a special moment in time, sanctified by tradition.

Sometime in 1916 or 1917, before I was born, Ambika Majumder used to be the president of the Indian National Congress. He was a famous and formidable personality. Respected by all, he was then at the very forefront of the Independence struggle.

I asked, 'Who lives here now? Any relatives?'

No, the house was now the Faridpur University Hostel. Apparently I wouldn't be able to recognize anything if I entered the place. It had been a large house to begin with but it had been extended further and widespread repairs had been carried out.

But Ambika Majumder's math, the site where he had been cremated?

'What do you mean? Where can it go? The memorial of such a great man. Who would have the audacity to lay even a finger on it?'

I looked carefully now, and noticed it standing proudly a little distance away, barely visible through the trees. It was no immense structure but even today, after all this time, it was still bearing witness to the past.

I remembered that one of Ambika Majumder's sons, Kiron Majumder, used to be a teacher in our school. He used to teach the girls, not us. And during the vacations he used to tutor his second son Gobinda and me, at home. Gobinda and I were classmates. 'Kiron-sir' was a terrific teacher but he had an equally terrific temper. And once he started teaching, he would never stop; he had absolutely no regard for mundane matters like time. I'd been walloped a couple of times as well. Even Gobinda was not spared.

Kiron Majumder's third son Mukunda had turned out to be the one with the rebellious streak; he was an absolute daredevil. One day he said, 'Just watch me. I'm going to teach my father a lesson.'

On full moon and new moon nights, Kiron Majumder would regularly visit the math and stay there till late at night, praying all by himself. Those inclined to gossip would, of course, claim that he was actually addicted to alcohol. But that is a view that could hardly be endorsed by the middle-class frame of mind and value system.

Mukunda wanted to lie in wait for his father, late one night, when he was on his way back from the math, and then frighten him by pretending to be a ghost. He would perch on one of the topmost branches and keep a lookout for his father. And the minute the gentleman walked past he would leap upon him out of nowhere. It goes without saying that he would be appropriately dressed in ghostly garb for this late-night surprise.

Gobinda and I wholeheartedly seconded this motion. But one detail that Mukunda had hidden from us, had not breathed a word about, was that when he would ambush his greatly respected grandfather's 'irritable' son, he would be wearing not even a stitch!

And he did just that. As a result, for the next couple of months, our teacher did not venture anywhere near the math, especially at night.

I remembered the Mukunda episode as I walked on but didn't mention it to those around me. Later, in private, I recounted it to my wife adding a few exaggerations and colourful details of my own.

Most youngsters possess a tendency to 'cheat' their elders and seniors. I am afraid that I must confess to possessing that trait myself.

I was a little older then, studying in the tenth standard. Shyama Prasad Mukherjee[7] was coming to Faridpur. And he was being accompanied from Calcutta by the president of the Hindu Mahasabha,[8]

Manmatha Mukhopadhyay. Two national leaders coming from Calcutta to Faridpur! The town was abuzz with excitement and anticipation. The event was publicized continuously from morning to night. There was no end to the discussions about this event in all the schools and colleges. Every political outpost was also in a similar state of tense expectation which threatened to mount to dizzying heights. Heated discussions that at any moment would cross all limits and defy all logic took place throughout the town. One of our schoolteachers—who taught us history, and lectured on the Marathas excellently, referring to Chhatrapati Shivaji as 'Shibji'—got so involved in the party's activities at that time that he stayed away from school for a couple of days. He left a message saying that he would make up for the absence later.

Many people gathered at the meeting. Even those who were not supporters of the Hindu Mahasabha were present. And most of them were my seniors. I was well aware of the actual intent behind their attending the event. I had followed them in. I had just recovered from a major illness and my mother had been unwilling to let me out but had finally given in to my tantrums. Before I left, she handed me an umbrella with an extremely sturdy handle. It had been drizzling outside.

Shyama Prasad stood up to deliver his speech. The entire place resounded with earsplitting applause that seemed to go on and on. Our history teacher got on the dais and raised his hands to silence the enthusiastic audience.

An extraordinarily eloquent speaker. The clarity and sincerity of his speech and thoughts greatly impressed his listeners. At one point, he made an extremely loaded statement: For the Municipal Corporation elections, Subhas Chandra Bose had allied himself with the Muslim League.[9] This extremely wrong move was naturally 'prejudicial to the interest of the Hindus'.

Immediately, a round of applause broke out and there were loud cries of 'shame, shame'. And simultaneously, my seniors let out a collective roar.

I saw a small group of the organizers run agitatedly in their direction. I spotted our history teacher among them.

Both sides were waiting for attack and both sides were equally busy preparing to flex their respective muscles. Within seconds, the whole thing degenerated into a blur of pushing, shoving, fisticuffs, punching —a chaotic free-for-all ensued.

I could no longer contain myself. Our teacher was almost within reach and, with his waist bent slightly and his head lowered like a charging bull, he was grappling with a member of the opposition whom he had pinned in a fierce bear hug. Who was it? It was my own dear Mejda, one of my elder brothers. Everything else disappeared from in front of my eyes except our teacher's shiny pate, as though thrust deliberately in my direction. Without a moment's thought, I gave in to temptation and landed a resounding blow on his head with the stout handle of the umbrella my mother had handed me. Before the full import of my impulse could strike me, I was grabbed by the waist and bodily removed from the midst of the chaos and confusion, and set down in a safe place, away from the melee. It was a friend of my brother's. He said, 'You've done your bit. Now scram.'

Three days later, I bumped into the same teacher at the market. He had come to buy fish. Here, in this very fish market. His head, or rather his bald pate, was criss-crossed with strips of medical plaster. The moment he saw me he said, 'Just look at what those chaps have done, Mrinal. Didn't even think for a moment before assaulting an old man. Be very careful. And don't go anywhere near those goondas.'

In the mean time we had covered quite a bit of ground. The procession had also increased in length. I was still leading it; my obedient wife followed and was, in turn, followed by a group of my Faridpur fans.

I stopped in front of Ismail-saheb's house. It was his second daughter who today, was the famous Feroza Begum. Then I had been very young, childhood far from over. Ismail-saheb was a lawyer in the city. Although he would address my father as 'dada'—elder brother—he would not really treat him with much deference. Nonetheless, we were always frequenting each other's houses and the two families were very close. We would celebrate festivals of both communities with equal enthusiasm and enjoyment. And I was personally attracted to the family for a reason different from all of these. The elder daughter Lily was my younger sister Rani's classmate and friend. She was very beautiful and a rather sweet girl. When there was a fresh outbreak of Hindu–Muslim violence in Calcutta, Bombay, Ahmedabad, Benares, and when the communal unrest spread like an epidemic throughout the country and reached even our Faridpur, I determined that the only permanent solution to this widespread frenzy would be to organize mass inter-community marriages. Acting, of course, on the principle that charity begins at home. Having pondered over such things I had secretly promised myself that I would grow up and marry Lily. No one knew about this, not even Lily; I was the only one, and every time I thought about the betterment of Hindu–Muslim relations, this resolution would leap to mind. How old could Lily have been then? Twelve? Thirteen? And I was two years older.

Lily came to know of it much later. She had married Bangladesh's famous Kamrul Hassan. Both of them had come to Calcutta and were staying at Khaled Choudhury's lair.[10] Lily telephoned me, 'Do you remember me? I am Lily, from Faridpur.'

I replied nonchalantly, 'You obviously have no idea, but I was actually supposed to marry you.'

Breaking into peals of laughter, she asked, delighted, 'Is that so? Really?'

It was only later that I came to know that she had known about it for quite some time. Then I realized, recalling her laughter, that Lily would have made a very good actress.

Tamijuddin-saheb's house no longer possessed its former glory. During his lifetime and my childhood, the house had had a completely different air. At the back, there used to be a pond of truly exceptional proportions. It was lined with ghats. Which were also huge. One was reserved for Tamijuddin-saheb and his relatives and the other was for the public. We would go there, all of us together, to bathe in the pond and then spend hours splashing about in the water. And on the opposite bank Tamijuddin-saheb would sit in his lungi, rubbing oil all over himself. So slowly, it seemed to go on for ever. Calmly and patiently. Tall and well built, he had glowing rosy complexion. After Partition, Tamijuddin-saheb spent most of his days in West Pakistan. He was the first president of the Pakistan Constituent Assembly.

Today, despite the blazing sunshine, the house, the pond, the very air about the place—somehow seemed to be shrouded in shadow.

We walked on. Not more than a hundred yards. I turned around once and instructed, 'Not one word. Don't you dare. I know. I can tell. We are very close to home.'

My wife asked, 'Really?'

'I can smell it,' I replied

My wife pulled the anchal of her sari closer. As though about to cover her head. After all, she was about to enter the home of her in-laws'. How could she do so without covering her head with a *ghomta* [headscarf]?

Why is this place lying here so neglected? So unkempt? This was a plot of land just after Tamijuddin-saheb's house.

Suddenly, visions of the past floated before my eyes. This place was used to park pushcarts and bullock carts. Some Hindi-speaking families used to live here too. The men would operate the carts and the women would make dung cakes and then go from door to door, selling them.

Kari came to mind. I could recall her clearly. A young girl of sixteen or seventeen—well built with perpetually dishevelled hair and a strange but beautiful wildness. Not at all demure like my sister. She could bubble over with loud peals of laughter and run as fast as a hare. And she could yell like a startled swan. She and her sister, my sister and I used to play in front of our house. Sometimes we would let a few others from the neighbourhood join us as well. They were all girlish games. We would play together, fight occasionally, sometimes come to blows. But even that would always be a match among equals. Ma was not very happy about my friendship with Kari. She would say, 'That girl's head is crawling with lice.'

Was that really so?

Ultimately, I did arrive in front of our house. I took a few steps forward and then paused. My wife, looking at me. And behind us, a crowd of almost a hundred. All of us were undergoing a strange experience; all of us assailed by an extraordinary emotion. Each and every one of us. Unbidden, tears welled up in my eyes. Before us, a few people standing scattered in front of the house. They were the new residents. Standing silently. One of them clutching a bunch of flowers. A middle-aged lady standing with a handful of flowers. Garbed like an ordinary housewife. The flowers were for us. The flowers were their welcoming gesture. A strange silence still held us in its grip.

The mistress of the house finally spoke up. She asked me, 'Was Reba your sister?'

I started. My wife, who knew everything, was taken aback too.

Were she alive, Reba would have been almost sixty today. Almost ten years older than the lady before us. At the tender age of five she slipped and fell into the pond. She drowned. She had been so precious to all of us. She had been Jashim-da's favourite too. Jashim-da, who was like one of the family. Reba.

I thought of my father. He left this place in 1948. When he had sold the house and was preparing to move away, he had requested the buyer to preserve the little memorial for Reba beside the water's edge. The buyer had kept his promise. The house had then passed into the hands of the people who now lived in it. They hadn't moved it either.

Reba's memorial was exactly the same as I remembered it. Even her name could be read clearly. Not a patch of moss; it had not been allowed to grow.

People thronged from all sides. People of Faridpur. Watching me, watching my wife.

Both of us seated on either side of Reba's memorial.

One of the boys from the house came towards us. Arms filled with flowers. Which he scattered all over the memorial. A middle-aged lady came forward. She gently pulled the *ghomta* over my wife's head. My wife grasped her hands and burst into tears.

I remembered. Reba had once drawn aside Jashim-da—the poet Jashimuddin,[11] Sadhu-da to us—and asked him perplexedly, 'Jashim-da? When do flowers bloom? And when the water hyacinth?'

[*'Faridpur Aaj Bidesh'* (*2001*). *Translated by Sunandini Banerjee*]

Notes

1 A town in modern-day south-central Bangladesh. After the Partition of British India in 1947, Faridpur became part of East Pakistan and, eventually, that of Bangladesh, following the Bangladesh Liberation War of 1971.

2 A person from West—not East—Bengal. The dialect, folk tradition and cuisine of a 'ghoti' are distinct from those of East Bengal or modern-day Bangladesh.

3 Bipin Chandra Pal (1858–1932): along with Lala Lajpat Rai (1865–1928) and Bal Gangadhar Tilak (1856–1920), formed the Lal–Bal–Pal triumvirate of assertive anti-colonial nationalists in British-ruled India in the early twentieth century. They advocated the Swadeshi movement of boycotting imported items and using Indian-made goods.

4 A popular fair during the Rath(a) Yatra, or the annual Hindu Chariot Festival, which takes place in parts of eastern India in the monsoon month of Ashadh, between June and July. Generally, three wooden chariots carrying the deities Jagannath, Balaram and Subhadra are pulled through the streets of a city or town. Seven days later, in what is called Ulta [reverse] Rath(a), the chariots retrace their journey back to their original abode or temple, where they reside for the rest of the year.

5   Nabendu Ghosh (1917–2007): born in Dhaka, an acclaimed Bengali author and screenwriter of classic Bollywood films of the 1950s and 60s.

6   Ambika Majumdar: otherwise known as Ambica Charan Mazumdar (1850–1922), presided over the Indian National Congress' thirty-first session in 1916.

7   Shyama Prasad Mukherjee (1901–53): Indian politician, barrister and academician, who served as minister for industry and supply in Prime Minister Jawaharlal Nehru's first cabinet after India's Independence. After falling out with Nehru, Mukherjee quit the Indian National Congress and, in 1951, founded the right-wing Hindu nationalist Bharatiya Jana Sangh, which later evolved into India's ruling Bharatiya Janata Party or BJP.

8   Hindu Mahasabha: right-wing Hindu nationalist organization founded by Madan Mohan Malaviya in 1906 to 'protect the rights' of the Hindu community in British India, after the formation of the All India Muslim League in the same year.

9   Subhash Chandra Bose (1897–?1945): president of the Indian National Congress between 1937 and 1938, Bose had left the party, after differences with Mahatma Gandhi, to form his own party, Forward Bloc. For the Calcutta Municipal Corporation election in 1940, Bose allied himself with the All India Muslim League in order to break the monopoly of the Congress over the civic body.

10 Khaled Choudhury (1919–2014): legendary Bengali theatre personality, who worked for major directors of both Bengali and Hindi theatre in various capacities, as set decorator, costume designer and later as music director.

11 Jasimuddin (1903–76): also known as Jashimuddin, a Bengali poet, songwriter, folklore collector and radio personality; commonly known in Bangladesh as 'Polli Kobi' (the rural poet) for his faithful rendition of Bengali folklore in his works.

Interview, 2001

Q. At that particular point in time . . . when most of your friends were also slowly entering the world of cinema, what made you choose cinema? You were already in the throes of a certain political orientation, you had already embarked upon a political thought process—so what made you turn to cinema?

A. In a city like Calcutta, it is natural that everybody must have some sort of a political inclination. It is unavoidable. I, too, was very close to radical leftist politics, for obvious reasons. And this resulted in my being familiar with its presence in the different media . . . print, etc. And most importantly, in theatre. My interest in theatre grew rapidly as a consequence of my having watched the IPTA [Indian People's Theatre Association] plays. At that time, I had been unable to perceive that all this was short lived. That was just before the war.

Q. Actually the 1940s.

A. Yes, around 1940–41. At that time, I was deeply impressed by the IPTA's aesthetics. Their plays, their choreography. I could never conceive that a half-hour-long ballet could be created out of the subject—Gandhi and Jinnah meeting again [*Gandhi Jinnah Phir Miley*]. Could this be possible, I wondered. But when I watched it I was very impressed. It was emotionally very valid and politically, I think, very sound. Or at least that's what I thought at that time. I will not be able to assess the political aspect of it, but emotionally, it was very valid. Therefore, I think it has a place in art. I kept watching plays . . . and so my gradual involvement with show business . . .

Q. What about your direct participatory involvement in IPTA? Did it begin with *Shahider Dak*?[1]

A. I never had any.

Q. Never?

A. No, never. I was always on the fringe.

Q. But in *Shahider Dak*? Did you have any hand in the scriptwriting process?

A. No, but I was fascinated when I watched it. Then I wrote something like that. *Jamir Ladai* [lit. 'fight for the land'] or something like that. It was a cause very close to my heart.

Q. A sort of a script?

A. Yes I wrote a script. It was more a prelude to a play. Without knowing anything about cinema, I had unconsciously incorporated certain cinematic features. I had thought about things in terms of 'close shot', 'long shot', moving the source of light either closer or further away, trying to superimpose images. I had done all these things, which however weren't present in *Shahider Dak*. I would not say that it was executed with a great degree of professional acumen.

Q. Was this produced?

A. Yes, not by IPTA directly but by some other group. I was a part of it and Tapas [Sen (1924–2006), lighting designer] was involved too. Once, something very interesting happened. We went to Rampurhat [in Birbhum District, West Bengal]. Incidentally, therein lies entangled a matter of the heart. Geeta [Sen (1930–2017), actress, wife of Mrinal Sen], too, had gone there with her group. So there we were—Tapas and I in Rampurhat. There was a power failure. What would we do for lights? Tapas suggested, 'What about the light of a bicycle? That can surely serve as a source of light.' So I told Tapas, 'Well, if that's what you're going to do, we can use the varying speeds of the bicycle to monitor the amount of light. And if we can get hold of another bicycle . . . when one dims, the other can get brighter. We can use that very effectively for superimposition. One can fade out while the other fades in. It won't be possible for us to achieve this in any other way.' He was quite taken with the idea. And he did it, armed with his professional imagination and effort. So you see, with experiences like these I was growing . . . the horizon was expanding. I had no steady job then. This was also the time when I used to frequent the Imperial Library.[2] And I used to read everything. Just to give you an idea, and not to drop names . . . Fitzgerald's translation of Firdausi's *Shahnama* . . . I read up all the thirteen or fourteen volumes. I had no idea to what end I was going to use all that reading. Then, I read *Childe Harold*, Nietzsche's *Thus Spake Zarathustra*. I got very interested in Nietzsche although I had heard that he was regarded as the 'Father of Fascism'. Prior to this, I had read Havelock Ellis who wrote that Nietzsche's supposed support of Fascism was nothing but a grave misconception on the part of the world at large. It was wrong. This aspect of multiplicity within a human being is what fascinated me . . .[3] What if I believed that both notions were true? This attracted me greatly, although it bore no direct relation to cinema. That's when I also read a biography of Nietzsche, written by his sister.[4] She vigorously contests and challenges the rumour about Nietzsche being afflicted with syphilis. And certain things mentioned in that biography have actually been corroborated by Havelock Ellis. Sick and deranged, one day he suddenly sent off a telegram to [Richard] Wagner's wife, Cosima [daughter of Franz Liszt]. Nietzsche was one of Wagner's first admirers, and a close friend for several years.

I'm remembering all this now as I speak to you . . . it all comes back to me. It's strange how man suddenly remembers by association! All these memories had been lying buried until now. It's like what Freud has said—Like Pompeii, memories are never annihilated. He had used Pompeii as an example. If you excavate the destruction Vesuvius wrought, you will still find Pompeii underneath. Not in the same shape, though. It will be different but it will be there. Like memory. It is also there but in a different shape.

Sorry, I'm afraid I have digressed . . . Nietzsche's telegram read, 'Cosima, I love thee. Dionysius.' Dionysius is the protagonist in *Thus Spake Zarathustra*. All this seemed terribly interesting to me. Then again, he suddenly dashed off a telegram to King Emmanuel of Italy, 'I am arriving. I would like you to receive me at the station.' Needless to say, he did not know the King at all. So I was reading things like this, and, at the same time, also reading Abhedananda [(1866–1939), disciple of Ramakrishna Paramahansa].[5] I was reading Ramakrishna's . . .

Q. *Kathamrita*?[6]

A. No, no.

Q. Romain Rolland on Ramakrishna.[7]

A. Yes, and even Romain Rolland's *I Will Not Rest*.[8] My reading was completely undisciplined. I was never a card-holding member of the Communist Party. So I was not under any obligation. Free of all such responsibility. Therefore, I read everything that came my way. I never had the money to buy books. Once, Ram Halder [1929–99] of Kamalalaya[9] had lent me a book which had just arrived, Jean-Paul Sartre's *Intimacy*. I had taken it to 46 Dharmatala Street.[10] The third floor. It's a place where you had to deposit your brain for restructuring [*laughs*], for it to be remade anew by the political leaders. So there I was, with *Intimacy*, a collection of Sartre's short stories. The moment I was sighted with that book, everyone attacked me, not because I was reading a book titled *Intimacy*, but because I was reading a work by Sartre. I was charged with: Oh! Jean-Paul Sartre! You have traces of petty-bourgeois vices in you! Believe me, I read Buddhadeva Bose [(1908–74), author, poet, scholar][11] much later. I was not allowed to, then. They spoke of him in such a manner that I never read him.

Q. Since you were not a [Communist] Party member, why were you nevertheless subject to these pressures?

A. Though I was not a member, I was very close to the Party, its people and its activities. Even when the Party was banned and during its underground phase, I was treated as a member. I was even a go-between for all sorts of correspondence. When they did their posters . . . the dumping of those posters between the writing and the pasting was a very tricky job. The police could come and raid the place whenever they wished. So where could one dump them? That became my responsibility. We used to set off, under cover of darkness. Some were arrested. Some were even shot at, putting up those posters. The Party had some sort of a faith in me. Gopal Haldar [(1902–93), journalist and scholar of linguistics][12] had told me on innumerable occasions that the Party leaders—in those days, 'leadership' consisted of only two people: Bhabani Sen [1909–72][13] and . . . that other man . . . from Andhra Pradesh . . . of the undivided [Communist] Party . . . P. Sundarayya [1913–85] . . . Gopal-da used to tell me, 'They have asked you to become a member.' I refused, saying, 'I am sorry but I cannot. I don't understand all these things. Let me go my own way.'

One day, Ritwik [Ghatak (1925–76), filmmaker] brought along a play he'd written. It was absolutely horrific! We used to live in Park Circus then, and used to meet there regularly. Ritwik, Salil, Bhupati-da,[14] and a few others. So Ritwik read his play. The play had a Communist teacher in hiding in a militant village. A Master-da. With its association with Surya Sen [1894–1934], leader of the Chittagong armoury raid in 1930, and several young Communist activists who had gone out to the villages as teachers and agents of political conscientization, Master-da had come to stand for a Communist intellectual mobilizing the masses. This character, however, really was a 'master-da'—he was a schoolteacher on the run. He seeks shelter for one night in the house of a young couple. He leaves instructions with them: 'Wake me up before daybreak tomorrow.' 'All right,' they say, 'will you have some tea, then?' 'Yes, and I'll leave immediately after that.' So they wake him up early next morning and bring him a cup of tea. As he prepares to leave, they ask him, 'Where are you going?' He replies, 'I can't tell you that. If I ever come back, then perhaps I shall meet you. Tell you where I have been.' The young woman was one of his students. She says, 'Master-da, do you remember that poem you used to recite? It was so wonderful.'

It was one of Tagore's. I don't remember which one. Something about the 'shukno amlokir pata'—dried gooseberry leaves falling to the ground. Something like that. So she tells him, 'Please. Recite that one more time.' And he says, 'No, not now. The branches of the amloki will no longer sport dried leaves but the severed heads of the *jotedars* [landowners]. Kakdwip[15] is witnessing the birth of a new poetry.' As he read these lines, everybody broke out into applause saying that it was great and this was absolutely revolutionary theatre!

When we were leaving, I went up to speak to him. In those days, I addressed him formally as 'apni'. I said, 'Are you really drawn to this image? The horrific sight of those severed heads dangling from the branches of a tree? Do you really think it a pleasant image?' 'You are right,' he replied. 'I shall correct that.' I went on, 'Don't listen to these people. I am not a Party member.' 'Neither am I,' he responded. 'I have a feeling you might become one. But don't listen to them. This is not what you are aiming at. Don't do this.'

He was a prolific writer and came back the next day, with yet another play. This one was even more macabre, even more horrifying than the last one. I realized that this man was incorrigible! There was just nothing one could do. This particular attitude of Ritwik's persisted right till the end. I have always been critical of Ritwik. I admire him for many things in many ways but I also think this about him ... for example, he desperately wanted to do *Pather Panchali* but had he done so, he would have completely ruined it. In order to make a film out of *Pather Panchali*, which is deeply rooted in the rural soil, one needed a Satyajit Ray, a man possessed of an acutely urban consciousness. It sounds a bit peculiar when one speaks such a thought out loud. How could an urban sensibility do justice to a rural subject matter? I had my own resistance to the whole thing, too. How, after all, would Karuna Banerjee [(1919–2001), actress][16] act? How could she abandon her intrinsically urban personality? But I believe that Karuna Banerjee succeeded precisely because of that. Her city-self provided her with a tremendous amount of restraint. She knew exactly when to move, when to stop, how far to walk. A coconut drops to the ground. How does one surreptitiously hide it among one's clothes, away from the eyes of the neighbours? She did it absolutely extraordinarily. Nobody else would have been able to do that, quite in the same way. Which is why, in comparison, a professional actor like Kanu Banerjee [1905–82][17] fails completely. Even the other actresses, professionals all, couldn't deliver a performance remotely comparable to hers.

So . . . I can discern this lack of refinement in all of Ritwik's films. That day, after Ritwik's death, there was Manik-babu [Satyajit Ray], Bijan-da [Bijan Bhattacharya (1915–78), playwright, actor, director][18] and I . . . Manik-babu delivered an impassioned speech. He said of Ritwik, 'He was more Bengali than I may ever hope to be.' When we walked out, he turned to me and said, 'Mrinal, I think I overdid it a bit. Don't you think so?' I replied, 'Yes. By quite a bit. And you'll soon know by how much exactly. The bill will come later.' Worried, he asked, 'You think no one caught on to the fact that I had my tongue firmly in my cheek?' 'No,' I retorted. 'No one did. Not even I. You spoke that way because you're afraid . . .'

Q. To return to the topic of our discussion, you were recollecting the days when you used to visit the Imperial Library and were coming under various influences through your reading . . . various contradictions . . .

A. Yes. So there I was, completely undecided about the future. That's when I came across the writer Karel Capek [(1890–1938), Czech novelist and playwright]. I had absolutely no idea about him. I had requisitioned a book and was waiting in the catalogue room. He had written various belles-lettres, essays, novels, plays. A remarkable writer. I am very fond of him. So, while going through the cards in the catalogue room, I came across a playlet called *Mother* [1938]. It's a topic that's been written about extensively. In English, in Bengali, in Hindi. Numerous languages. It was a slim volume. I requisitioned it. I read it and was floored! I immediately made it a point to read everything the library had by Capek. They were all Chatto & Windus publications. The publishers confessed that none of his books paid back but they loved doing them, nonetheless. And so they had all his works translated. I read a posthumous novel called *The Cheat* [1938]. I read it there, and translated it as well. I didn't have the money to buy it from Allied Publishers who were the agents of Chatto & Windus. I was paid about seven dollars or so. That was my first publication. Capek was thus introduced to India through my translation. But I had no idea that the accent above the C transformed it into a 'ch' while pronouncing the name. So in Bengali, I erroneously used the letter denoting the sound 'k' instead of the one for 'ch'. He continued to be known thus until later translations in Bengali corrected this oversight.

Q. What did you call it, in Bengali?

A. I kept it as *Cheat*. An extraordinary work. I had frequently asked Sombhu-da [Sombhu Mitra (1915–97), actor-director, playwright][19] why he wasn't doing anything based on *R.U.R* or *Rossum's Universal Robots*.[20] 'Why don't you read this? Why don't you adapt it?' He had said,' There are various problems.' Well, problems would always be there.

R. U. R. is located in an Earth with only 300 human beings left on it. Ignorant of how to breed. Incapable of furthering their species. There is a factory where robots are being manufactured. The first scene opens with the Managing Director, a human being, writing a letter to the US government. About the millions of soldiers they have lost in the war against the English. He mentions how grieved he is about the loss and then gets down to matters of business. Writes about the billions of soldiers ordered and how much it will cost. And this is followed by him writing a similar letter to the British. This factory thus conducts a 'wholesale' business of sending robots to various places in the world.

A woman comes to this factory from Paris, from the Society for the Prevention of Cruelty to Robots. She wishes to speak to the robots. The Managing Director, also a human being like her, agrees to her proposal. So she begins to speak to a robot. She asks, 'Were you born here?' 'No. I was made here,' it replies.

If one thinks about it, what is the simplest definition of a worker? The answer is: [one who is] honest and hardworking. Someone who will not be slipshod about his work and who has the capacity for hard work. That is his/her job. The robots were built to fulfil these requirements. However, complaints start pouring in, suddenly. Something is terribly wrong. While working, they would occasionally get crushed within the machines. Or topple off from the tenth floor. Some sort of preventive measure would have to be thought of. So the engineer comes up with an idea. He tinkers around with their nervous systems and introduces the capacity to feel pain. This would automatically ensure that the robots would not allow themselves to be destroyed and henceforth, be inclined towards self-preservation. What happens is that, along with the feeling of pain, they are automatically also endowed with its corollary: the feeling of pleasure. Thus the robots soon begin to change. They feel tired after eight hours of work and want to continue no longer. The engineer is now faced with a new problem.

Then there is a Librarian who decides to unite the robots of the world, all of whom are suffering similarly. The mariners, who bring the raw material for the manufacture of robots at the factory, are robots too. Now, they refuse to supply their cargo. Instead, they bring with them a vast quantity of leaflets which proclaim, 'Robots of the World, Unite!'

The robots decide to rebel. The humans—the Managing Director and other board members—are suddenly confronted with a vast body of discontented robots. An immense and solid wall of anger. They attack the factory. As they approach, the humans frantically try to save themselves. They instruct the Engineer to burn the formula for creating these robots. It will never be possible to create such robots again and this seems like the only hope for this handful of humans who are staring death in the face.

The robots arrive, led by the Librarian. The dictatorship of the robots is established. No one is spared under this regime except the Engineer. 'He's not like a human being. He's not a parasite. He works.' He is allowed to live and is told by the robots, 'You may conduct as many experiments as you wish to. We give you permission to do anything you like.'

He begins his experiments. One day, he falls asleep in the middle of work. He wakes up suddenly to hear loud peals of laughter. He discovers that a male and female robot are laughing together. He is amazed at their 'creative' laughter. This happens a short while after the dictatorship of the robots has been established. As the engineer looks on, the female robot strolls over to the window and tells the robot, 'Look! The sun is setting.' And then she confides, in tones of wonder and amazement, 'You know . . . last night, when I was asleep . . . it was as though I had gone away . . . far away somewhere.' The robot says, 'I know what you mean. You had a dream. I, too, have such dreams. I have been told about dreams by the Librarian.'

The man is astounded. He tells them not to move an inch. He brings them a book. *The Science of Man.* And explains that he wishes to dissect them individually. The robots are not allowed to resist because the scientist has been granted free reign for the purpose of his research. The female robot quickly steps forward and asks the scientist to dissect her, but to spare the male. The male, too, steps forward and volunteers to be dissected, only if the Engineer will spare the other. He tries to reason with them. 'What is the relationship that you share? Who are you, to her? And you, to him?' Suddenly, the male robot rebels. Tells the Engineer, 'You can't dissect either of us. I won't let you. We don't care about the order. You can't lay a finger on either of us.' The Engineer merely stares at them, for a few moments. He says, 'Perhaps I am no longer required, Adam and Eve.' And walks away. That is the end of the play.

So these are the kinds of plays I read. At about that time, suddenly
. . . I must mention that I was not even a habitual filmgoer then . . .
except the odd movie once in a while . . . I came across a book. Called
Film. Now it's known as *The Art of Film*. Published in 1931. Written
by Rudolph Arnheim. When I read it, it was not as if I understood
everything, but I was terribly impressed nevertheless. 'Amazing!' I
thought to myself. 'Can all this truly be possible in cinema?' Thus it was
just by accident that I walked into cinema and this is the manner of my
initiation. Then I read another book from the Library. *Cinema as a
Graphic Art* by Vladimir Nilsen [(1905–38), Russian cinematographer
associated with Sergei Eisenstein], one of Eisenstein's brightest students.
Much later, when I met Jay Leyda [(1910–88), film scholar, authority
on Russian cinema][21]—he told me that Nilsen and he had studied
together. Nilsen was killed in Stalin's purges. I did not know of this then.
It was not mentioned in any of the books that I had read. Leyda told
me, 'Mrinal, you cannot even begin to imagine the manner of his death.'
He was one of the very first students. And along with him, that man
from the British Labour Party . . . Montagu?

Q. Ivor Montagu [(1904–84), founder member of the London Film
Society in 1926].[22]

A. Yes, Ivor Montagu and that man who translates Eisenstein's works?

Q. Herbert Marshall [(1912–91), author, filmmaker, theatrical director,
and scholar].[23]

A. Yes. So, I read Nilsen's *Cinema as a Graphic Art*. This one I could
understand even less, but whatever little I managed to grasp was all
about Eisenstein. I had not even heard of Eisenstein in those days. None
of us had. It was there, sitting in the Library, that I came across his name
for the first time. There were a number of interesting anecdotes about
him. Once, he told his students, 'If you were to prepare a script on
Pushkin's *The Bronze Horseman* [1833], how would you go about it?' I
was acquainted with this work of Pushkin myself: Evgeny is rendered
homeless when his home, on the banks of the Neva, is swept away by
the river in spate. Finally, he arrives at St Petersburg. Bereft of all his

belongings, and with no money whatsoever, he has turned mad. One night, he falls asleep at the foot of St Peter's statue, in St Petersburg. It begins to drizzle. The moon is occasionally covered by clouds. Suddenly, he wakes up. Looks about him. And imagines that the statue is about to leap upon him. As though St Peter is glaring at him fiercely. He stands up and, shaking his clenched fist at the statue, yells out, 'You worker of miracles, enough, enough of you!' I realized the full import of these words much later. When I had grown quite close to the Communist Party. Somewhere near Rome, six workers had been shot dead by the police. Then the leader of the Communist Party—the leader of European Communism...

Q. [Palmiro] Togliatti [(1893–1964), one of the founders of the Italian Communist Party (PCI) in 1921].[24]

A. Togliatti had made a speech after those killings where, speaking against the King, he had said, 'You, worker of miracles, enough, enough of you!' That's when I noticed the difference. How their political leaders could quote from Pushkin, after such an incident, and thereby establish a connection between life and literature. I was enjoying this entire process thoroughly. That of discerning these differences for myself.

To return to the story. The moment Evgeny utters these words, it seems to him that the statue comes alive and springs down from its pedestal. It chases Evgeny who begins to run. The horse-rider pursues the fleeing Evgeny all night. In the morning, Evgeny is found, lying face-down in the grass. And the statue is on its pedestal, as it has always been.

So Eisenstein tells his students to create a script out of this story. And the script that Nilsen had prepared was remarkable. His script, along with detailed sketches, was reproduced in *Cinema as a Graphic Art*. There was a sequence that Eisenstein had liked in particular; he had even mentioned it in his writings. Rain. Clouds obscuring the moon every now and then. Every time the moon reappears, it is reflected in Evgeny's eyes, which gleam in the darkness. When he screams aloud in a fit of insanity, the moonlight illuminates the statue's face. Evgeny is convinced that the statue is alive and about to attack. So he starts running. What he actually does is run around the fencing, all night. And Nilsen's camera moves in the opposite direction. The pedestal is not shown. And this creates the illusion that the statue is really chasing Evgeny. Evgeny is shown running, and the statue is shot in such a way that the head of St Peter seems to be in motion, in pursuit of the mad-man. He constructs the entire sequence in this manner. Remarkable! I was very impressed. That's how my interest in cinema deepened. Then I began to read every book on the topic that I could lay my hands on.

I'm sorry. To arrive at this point, I have waded through many digres-sions . . . I read Spottiswoode, *Romance of the Movies*, and many, many more. I read about the difference between two kinds of photography—socialist photography and bourgeois photography. These, too, were pointed out by Nilsen. Socialist photography consisted of light and shadows, contrasts, and the bourgeois sort used diffusers and 'dollish faces'. Nilsen was against the latter. I had no idea that these differences existed and learnt about them through my reading of such books. I read Eisenstein, I read Pudovkin. I remember, in one place, Eisenstein indulging in wishful thinking—if only he could convince Mayakovsky to become his editor; he had such a terrific sense of rhythm. If only Milton were a contemporary, Eisenstein continued, because he would have made an astonishing script-writer with his remarkable visualiza-tion. And that if he ever did anything in colour, then he would turn to Eliot who had used colour so very innovatively. This interaction between the various arts always fascinated me. I used to read novels too, and try and find some connection, some common thread between all of this. I began to write, too.

All these influences were working upon me simultaneously. The Spanish Civil War had just taken place. I had been reading all this ever since I came to Calcutta in 1940. I think the book, *The Spanish Civil War*, was also published roughly around this time. I read that and Auden's *Poems of Spain* [1937]. Also, Ralph Fox's [1900–37] *Novel and the People* [1945]. Fox was later killed in Spain. Another poet,

Christopher Caudwell [(1907–37), British Communist writer and intellectual],[25] also killed when he was in his thirties. He had written poetry. He had also written *Illusion and Reality* [1937]. It was a book on aesthetics.

Q. And there was *Studies in a Dying Culture* [1949]...

A. Yes, and *The Crisis in Physics* [1939]. So he had written on such diverse topics. I was deeply impressed by *Illusion and Reality* and equally fascinated by *Novel and the People*. After I read these ... that was in 1946 ... I began to watch films. The films, however, filled me with a deep distaste. This distaste for Indian films and my passion for the cinematic medium which was cultivated and sustained through my reading—these were two simultaneous intellectual developments. This is one reason why, even today, I can never be a historian of cinema. When the British Film Institute asked me to make a film about the history of Indian cinema, I resisted it initially. I told them that I had no flair for archival probing. I never liked Indian cinema, right from the start. I began to hate Pramathesh Barua [(1903–51), actor-director].[26] Incidentally, Manik-babu hated him as well. Ritwik was all praise for him, though. He wrote somewhere, 'We are not worth the dust off his feet.' So the next day, I asked Ritwik, 'Why this sudden adoration? We were just talking about him yesterday and you expressed nothing of the sort ...' He replied, 'Forget it. To put someone down, one has to push someone else up. *Dhyanga-ta ke namatey hobe.* ['The tall one (i.e. Satyajit Ray) has to be pulled down.'] So, if I must laud Rammohun, I must lambast Vidyasagar, and vice versa.'

I wrote a piece then. *Cinema and the People.* Greatly influenced by Fox's *Novel and the People*. And in that article, I critiqued Ritwik extensively. It was published in the *Indo-Soviet Journal* [organ of the Friends of the Soviet Union, published during the War years], edited by Hiren Mukherjee [(1907–2004), Communist leader and academic] and Snehangshu Acharya. It was a bi-monthly and most of the articles were from Russian sources. But I was most aggrieved when my article finally appeared because it was attributed to a 'Nirmal Sen'! 'Mrinal' had been somehow transformed to 'Nirmal'. I went to their office in Dharmatala Street and pointed out the error. They realized their mistake and put in an errata in their next issue. I therefore used to buy both issues whenever I wanted to give anyone a copy of that article! So that was my first piece of writing.

Q. The first, on cinema. What were the films that you were watching, at that time?

A. I was watching everything that was being made, then. And I disliked everything immensely. One of the few that I liked was *Dharti ke Lal*. And another was *Neecha Nagar*. Although the latter was quite flawed, I liked it nonetheless. I had spoken to the director—Chetan Anand—and asked him if he had read *The Bronze Horseman* script, for I spotted many elements that were directly inspired by it. The costumes, for example . . .

Q. But when you watched *Neecha Nagar* later, did you still like it?

A. No, not at all. That is also what makes me realize that the politics, the aesthetics of the IPTA too, were no longer valid. After the 'transfer of power', the IPTA . . .

Q. Their entire aesthetic became outmoded.

A. Looking back, I can see that they were too . . . for example, they believed that our only enemies were the English and their lackeys . . .

Q. Everything was perhaps too black and white . . .

A. Yes. It was all about standing up to the British and their lackeys . . . In one of Premchand's [(1880–1936), major Hindi–Urdu writer] last few works, written in 1935, called 'Mahajani Sabhyata',[27] he had commented, that though the British—the white *mahajans* [lit. 'usurers']—would soon be thrown out of India, they would be immediately substituted by black ones. And he warns his readers against this new class of black *mahajans*. He had written this in 1935. After the war, after Independence, it had become extremely difficult to discern the difference between an enemy and a friend. The whole issue became very complex. Politically complex. And, therefore, it is not only difficult but almost impossible to fit the old ideas into the new situation that was developing. Although this disjunct was never articulated it was nonetheless responsible for the problems encountered by people like Sombhu-da. Perhaps you [Samik Bandyopadhyay] will be better at understanding this. And I'm sure that, apart from this ideological difference, personal equations also played a part. But this was definitely one of the reasons for the break-up of the IPTA. There is a term for it, which the Russians used . . . it is also a feature of Russian cinema . . .

Q. . . . Socialist realism . . .

A. Yes, and the tendency to regard everything in clearly defined blacks and whites. Anyway, so this was when I entered into the world of cinema and was thinking seriously of making a film.

Q. At this time, when you were contemplating a film of your own, on the one hand, we have your recognition of the power and the significance of the Russian school, of Eisenstein and his collaborators. And on the other, your awareness of the inadequacy and the stupidity of Indian mainstream cinema. Armed with your recognition of these two parallel streams, you felt that you could make a film of your own. But the kind of films that you made initially . . .

A. Yes, that's what I was trying to explain . . .

Q. How did they happen? These thought processes were quite clear in you, then?

A. Well, I thought I, too, could make a film. Then Hiren-babu wrote to me, mentioning how he had read my piece and appreciated the connections I made between art, literature and cinema. I had written about Subhash Mukhopadhyay's [(1919–2003), Bengali poet][28] poem 'Micchiler Mukh' [lit. 'the face of the procession'], and elaborated upon the effect of the phrase, 'haather aranya' [lit. 'a forest of hands']. I had done the same with instances from Tagore's poetry too. These had lent themselves to certain visual designs in my mind. I had even decided to make a film in Kakdwip. Fortunately, that never happened, because around this time, Frederic Joliot-Curie [(1900–58), French physicist and Nobel Laureate][29] and J. D. Bernal [(1901–71), Irish scientist, one of the founders of molecular biology][30] visited India, to attend the Science Congress. They had smuggled in a bunch of documents from the British Communist Party which suggested that India was going the wrong way; this was not the way to achieve the desired goals. So the revolution came to an end.

All this while, Ritwik, Salil and I, without the slightest knowledge of cinema, had been planning to go to Kakdwip to make our film. We had managed to get hold of an ancient camera, and even decided on a place to process the 16 mm film. I prepared a script. *Jamir Ladai*. Ritwik was to be the cinematographer and Hrishi [Hrishikesh Mukherjee (1922–2006), film editor and director][31] was to edit. The whole thing was planned in utmost secrecy. Everything was fixed, when we were suddenly told that we could go on no longer. We were saved!

Although we couldn't go, all the equipment stayed with us. This was also the time when the police raided my house. I used to live in Park Circus at the time. I had stepped out to buy a cigarette and had just puffed at it a couple of times when the shopkeeper informed me that the police were planning a raid that night.

Q. He was an informer . . . ?

A. Yes, but he was very fond of us. I rushed home and burnt that script. It was replete with the influences of Eisenstein and Nilsen.

Ritwik used to claim that he understood photography really well. I had no idea about the veracity of this claim. He was, however, given this responsibility.

At one time, we were planning to raise money for a film. The problem with us was that we could never see such attempts through to the end. We could never persist in our requests until the final stage—when we would have to be answered with either a 'yes' or a 'no'. A 'no' would crush us completely, so we perpetually nursed hope, and hovered at the penultimate stages of these negotiations. We dwelt in fantasy. And thus indulged our own aspirations. This fantasy was our only source of sustenance. There was no other avenue of survival open to us.

A friend of ours came to us one day. He was willing to give us the money on the condition that the film be about Bhawal Sannyasi [(1883–1946), or Ramendra Narayan Roy].[32] We were shattered but Ritwik jumped at the idea. He said, 'Let's do it! We shall give the whole thing a Marxist interpretation!' He was always like that. The rest of us, however, refused to be convinced. And that film didn't happen.

Soon after, I managed to interest a producer. Ritwik found a producer as well. Some producer who had quarrelled with the director, Nirmal De, the one who made the film *Sadey Chuattor* [1953]. He had begun work on a film called *Bedeni* [1951] . . .

Q. That remained incomplete, didn't it?

A. Yes. So then Ritwik was given the responsibility.[33] In the process, he managed to create quite a chaotic situation. Many of the people hired by Nirmal were refusing to work. He was a good cameramen, though. Now, he began work with Ritwik. His film *Sadey Chuattor* was one of Suchitra Sen's early films and quite a hit with 'Mashima, malpoa khamu!'[34] and all that. The one he was working on with Ritwik also had Manoranjan-babu [Manoranjan Bhattacharya (1889–1954), actor].[35] Ritwik asked me to go along with them and watch what they were doing. I accompanied them to Ghatshila [in Purbi Singhbhum District, Jharkhand]. I never did anything except watch the entire process from the sidelines. A great deal of raw stock was exposed without any takes. But when we returned, the editor complained that all he had been given was a large amount of exposed film. It was all blank. I told Ritwik, 'He says there's nothing on it. It's all blank. Don't bother printing any of it.' Ritwik was adamant. 'No, no, I have to.' I tried to reason with him. 'But it's all blank. You can see for yourself. What's the point? There's not a single image to be seen.' He went ahead with the printing regardless of my attempts at dissuasion. I was with him when he had a look at the printed result. Predictably, it was all blank. That's when the producer abandoned ship and fled!

And that's the only reason why it happened. Various stories have been built up around this incident but this is the only reason.

Then I went off, working as a medical representative. Without knowing anything of medicine.

Q. Approximately when was this?

A. This was in the 1950s.

Q. So *Bedeni* was abandoned . . .

A. And in the mean time, I had already worked as an assistant with numerous people although I hadn't enjoyed those experiences in the slightest. I wrote a story called 'Dudhara'. I was the assistant director, and watched a long line of directors come and go. It never came to anything, ultimately. I waited patiently, watching all this unfold. And continued assisting every director who assumed the job. Geeta had a role in that film. That's when I got to know her.

I remember, when we were young, we used to visit the railway station nearby. There would always be some wagons parked there, with goods being loaded on to or off them. I would clamber into one of them and then scribble my name in some obscure corner. Where no one would be able to spot it. I would then memorize the number of that particular wagon, and for months afterward, keep looking out for it. When it would return, after having travelled far and wide, I would run to it eagerly . . .

Q. . . . . Searching for your name.

A. Yes, and oh how thrilled I would be to find my name exactly in the same place! I used to feel as though it was I who had journeyed through the world and returned once again.

There was a book on the French Communist Party by Maurice Thorez [(1900–64), French politician]. That was the kind of stuff I was reading. I used to enjoy such books primarily for the kind of approach they presented. I read very little about and by the Communist Party of India—I enjoyed these others much more. Another book I hugely enjoyed was by the Sanskrit professor—sorry, the professor of mathematics . . .

Q. D. D. Kosambi.

A. Yes, and that's how far I got. My reading never progressed beyond that point. They were difficult books, very difficult. But I used to read them nevertheless.

Q. Before we come to *Ratbhor* [1956], let me just ask you something. What about contemporary writing in Bengali? You were in contact with the literary group of *Parichay*; they were prominent by the 1950s. And this was also the time of *Natun Sahitya*.[36]

A. Yes, that too had arrived by then. We began to write in *Natun Sahitya* too.

Q. How did you react to contemporary Bengali novelists and play-wrights? So far, all the books that you have mentioned are those written by foreign authors. For example, Samaresh [Basu (1924–88), Bengali novelist][37] was writing then . . .

Q. I enjoyed Samaresh's work. And those of Nani Bhowmik [(1921–96), Bengali novelist, short-story writer],[38] which had greatly impressed me at that time of reading. I also enjoyed reading Ramesh Sen [Rameshchandra Sen (1894–1962), physician in traditional Indian medicine and major Bengali writer of short stories]. Although I must shamefully confess that I first read Tagore's *Shesher Kabita* [1929] in English translation.

A. *Farewell, My Friend.*

Q. Yes. Translated by . . .

A. Krishna Kripalani.

Q. Yes. It was an awful translation and I hated it. It was so terribly literal! Then I read the original. The translation had appeared in the *Hindustan Standard*. I was not very impressed with the original either. Later, one of the ashramites, Somen Bandyopadhyay, had confided, 'Don't quote me on this, but I believe that the entire novel is merely a preface to the poem at the end. That poem is the only portion that may be regarded as literature.'

I read Manik Bandyopadhyay [(1908–56), Bengali novelist and short-story writer][39] too. I loved his *Padmanadir Majhi*. The space cleaved out for dialect is truly astonishing, and comparable to only one other work, *Dhonrai Charit Manas*, by . . .

Q. Satinath Bhaduri [(1906–65), Bengali author, scholar].[40]

A. He was the only other author who afforded such space to dialect. So, one day, I asked Gopal-da—Gopal Haldar—'I can't quite fathom this character. Who is this Hussain-miyan [in *Padmanadir Majhi*]? I don't understand him at all. Don't recognize him. And is he a fascist? Or a social reformer?' Gopal-da grasped my hand warmly and said, 'I am so very glad that you have had the courage to voice this thought. I, too, have felt the same way. To me, that is the book's one weak spot.'

Many, many years later, just a few days ago, I met Banaphool's [(1899–1979), Bengali novelist and short-story writer][41] younger brother. Aurobindo Mukhopadhyay. He is a film director. He was reminiscing of the days when he was a student at the Patha Bhavan, Santiniketan: 'Sometimes, Gurudev [Tagore] would come by and teach for a while. Rarely. About one or two days a year. So we asked him, "How did you like *Pather Panchali*? And *Aparajito*?" "Besh bhaalo. Kintu boro khai-khai!" ' ['Quite fine but too much hankering for food.'] And when he was asked, 'How did you like Manik Bandyopadhyay's *Padmanadir Majhi*?' he replied, 'Tell me, who is this Hussain-miyan? I'm afraid I don't seem to know him.' I was so pleased to hear him say so. So I explained to Aurobindo, 'When you make the film, ensure that Hussain-miyan is left deliberately uncharacterized. I had spoken to Gautam [Ghose (b. 1950), filmmaker] too. 'Please don't try to lend him a flesh-and-blood personality. Keep him as ambiguous as possible.' I was told, 'We've put in everything possible.' I despaired. 'Then you have ruined him utterly.' A similar misinterpretation had ruined *Putul Naacher Itikatha*.[42] Botuk-da [Jyotirindra Moitra (1911–1977), singer-lyricist, composer][43], who worked on it, had said, 'From start to finish, I've put in all I could think of!' I had told him that at the very minimum, the same story would yield material for three separate films.

Q. But why *Ratbhor*?

A. Someone came to me with a story. She was an actress, and she said, 'Mrinal-da, I've grown very fond of you. I'd like you to make this film.' But I had no idea that I was capable of such abysmal work. While I was making it, I would often think to myself, 'What on earth am I doing?' There were far too many borrowed elements which crept in. I seemed to have become temporarily devoid of all intelligence whatsoever. It was so humiliating for me to watch the film, finally. I refused to leave home and meet people. And for the next two years, I didn't do anything. I had made this film after quitting the medical representative job. I was living in extremely straitened circumstances.

Two years later, Hemanta Mukherjee [(1920–89), popular singer and composer][44] produced *Nil Akasher Niche*, which was greatly appreciated. Nehru, when we met, said, 'You have done a great service to the nation.' Then, Subimal Dutta, [India's then] foreign secretary, said to me, 'Are you Mrinal Sen?' 'Yes,' I replied. 'Are you the director?' 'Yes,' I replied again. (This was at the President's house.) 'Do you live in a rented house, in Calcutta?' I nodded. 'And how much do you pay each month?' 'Hardly anything, really.' I answered. 'Aapnar boyosh koto?' ['How old are you?'] He pronounced it 'bo-yosh' which revealed his Chittagong origins. And then suddenly, 'Don't you think the film has a tendency to go Left?' I explained to him that I had made the film about a certain period in history. About a Chinese hawker. A salesman. Selling his merchandise, his wares. Who roams the streets and, one day, is swept up into the heart of a rebellion. A revolution. Led by the [Indian National] Congress, and anti-British in intent. 'And if the revolution goes Left, I'm afraid that I can't help it!' I concluded. 'That's a clever way of talking,' he retorted and strode out of the room. Obviously, he wasn't too happy about it.

The president, Rajendra Prasad [1884–1963], sat cross-legged on the floor and watched the film . . . the president was not wholly unacquainted with Bengali, so he could follow what was going on . . . Indira Gandhi, then president of the Congress Party, was also familiar with Bengali. The minister of information, Gopala Reddy, had studied at

Santiniketan and so the language posed no problems for him. [Jawaharlal] Nehru was, in fact, the only one who didn't possess even a working knowledge of Bengali.

I sat a little away from Nehru. Anxiously following his reactions. At one point, Acharya Kripalani's wife, Sucheta Kripalani, leant towards me and asked, 'What's that? I didn't quite get it. What's that over there?' We were at the 1937 portion of the film by then. The girl had been freed from jail. The Chinese hawker, too, was returning home. There had been a worldwide appeal to all his countrymen, to return to their homeland and lend their might to the revolution. What she was pointing out to was actually a tattered poster—part of a very badly prepared set. I could not afford anything better at the time. The set recreated a narrow alley. I told her, 'That's a poster.' 'I can see that,' she replied, 'But what is written on it?' 'Well, it's torn.' 'I can see it's torn,' she persisted. 'But what does it say?' I have never seen anyone here display the same amount of interest and curiosity about something so insignificant as that poster. I read it for her, it says "The Andaman Repatriation Movement". That too had taken place in 1937. Rabindranath had written to the political prisoners in Andaman and assured them that the country had not forgotten them; that they should carry on with their struggle. The moment I told her what the poster said, she exclaimed, 'Say that!' I was amazed at how involved she was with the whole thing and how seriously she was treating every aspect of what she watched on screen.

Hemanta-babu, his wife [Bela Mukherjee] and I. When it was all over, Nehru patted me on the back and said, 'You have done a great service to the nation.' Immediately Hemanta-babu put in a request. Holding out a piece of paper, he asked, 'Thoda likh dijiye, na.' ['Please write it down.'] Nehru merely said, 'Usme kya hai, bhai? Usme kya hai?' ['How does that matter, my friend?']

This is when times were rather grim, for Nehru. That was the very day when his secretary John Mathai had resigned. And Nikhil-da [Nikhil Chakraborty (1913–98)][45] had run an exclusive on the story. Everyone had assumed that Nehru wouldn't turn up, or even if he did, there was no way that he would stay till the end. However, that's precisely what he did, and also, constantly made probing enquiries about various aspects of the film. A week or so later, at a meeting of the Congress Working Committee [executive committee of the Congress Party], Nehru mentioned that he had recently watched a film about a Chinese hawker that contained references to one of Mahadevi Verma's stories ['Chini Feriwala']. And he requested them to watch it at the earliest available opportunity.

I, of course, was motivated by the political philosophy of the whole thing. And by the fact that our country's struggle for Independence is inextricably linked to the struggle of the liberal world against fascism. Both these elements have been fused in the film, and I agree completely with the idea. But the film is incredibly and unnecessarily sentimental. The acting, in most cases, is of very poor quality. It is replete with bad situations although a few are quite all right. And finally, cinematically, I find it extremely clumsy.

This film nevertheless afforded me some space. It lent me a certain standing. Then I made my third film [*Baishey Sravan*]. On my own terms. Perhaps I had been weak earlier. Which is why my first film had been such an outright disaster. I simply cannot understand how I could have possibly made something like that. It is beyond me.

I didn't mind Ritwik's *Nagarik* [made in 1952, released in 1977]. Even that was better than my first attempt. Although his use of the violin strings snapping was ... [*Laughs*]

But I kept growing. And I am very fond of my third film, very proud of it too. Although made many years ago, I still think it's a really good film. It was shown in Venice. In London. After the Venice screening, I was asked by India House to show it in London. In Venice, a full-page spread of Madhabi [Mukhopadhyay][46] appeared for the first time.

It was in 1960. They told me, 'We have seen the film. And now it's on its way to Venice [Film Festival]. But the sequence of a man, eating ... (They were obviously discussing Gyanesh [Mukherjee]) licking his fingers and smacking his lips. We found the whole thing quite nauseating and the foreign audience is bound to find it even more so. It's best if you got rid of that all together.' 'You surely can't expect me to do that,' I replied. I never have any food sequences in my films but this one was imperative to the entire narrative. This man is looking at food after three days. Which is why, hunger-stricken and greedy, he doesn't even bother about whether his wife gets her share or not. He's stuffing his mouth with food as fast as he can, constantly looking from one side to another, in case someone arrives to claim a portion. His wife sits before him. Staring at him unblinkingly, her eyes full of hatred, and refilling his plate. Watches him gorge. It is not just that she is doing so out of a sense of wifely duty—because a wife must serve her husband first and eat only after he's finished his meal. No, there is something else, here. A deep loathing. An overwhelming revulsion. And I had explained all this to Madhabi, who brought it all out excellently. So I refused the idea of the film going abroad without that very sequence. 'You can't expect me to put a fork and a spoon in his hands, can you? I'm afraid it stays and it goes that way,' I insisted. They opted out; said that they could then be of no help to me. So I sent it to the organizers of the London Film Festival directly. I have the right to do so as an Indian citizen, and so that's exactly what I did. The film went to a couple of other places too. So that's how I made my beginning. Although I still made a few more bad films. You could say that all my life I have made either good, bad or indifferent films.

Q. I'd like to ask you something at this point. Satyajit [Ray] had appeared on the scene by that time. Just before your *Baishey Sravan*, he had made his *Pather Panchali* [1955] and *Aparajito* [1956]. What impact did those films have on you?

A. Their impact was tremendous! I watched the first night show of *Aparajito*. The very next day I paid him a visit. I met Subrata Banerjee and Karuna Banerjee there. I remember it all very clearly. They left in a short while and I too got up to leave. Satyajit-babu said, 'No, no Mrinal, please stay. I'll just finish dinner and then join you.' He would always have his dinner at seven in the evening. His mother [Suprabha Ray], too, asked me to stay for a little longer. 'I want to hear what you have to say,' she said to me. He returned shortly after and they both sat down to hear my views on the film. I told them, 'The film won't do well at all. The Indian audience in particular will be hard-pressed to accept it, much less appreciate it. You've wounded their sentiments and values. But I won't be surprised at all if it wins a major international award. I'll rate this one very high. And the relationship between the mother and her son—an extremely complicated relationship, almost like that between lovers—I would say that is partly autobiographical. I do hope that you'll accept this opinion in the right spirit.' Apu's mother is supposed to wake him up so that he may go to the station to leave for the city, but she doesn't. Suddenly, something startles him awake. 'Why didn't you wake me?' He is enraged and leaves without even speaking to her properly. Flings on his clothes and leaves for the station in a huff. Arrives to see that there's still some time for the train. He sits down. Waits patiently. The train arrives. And leaves soon after. He comes back home. 'What's this? You haven't left?' He is silent; bending down, intent upon cleaning the mud off his shoes. 'No . . . I missed the train.' And then taking off his shoes, he leaps into the pond. What an absolutely remarkable moment. Remarkable! So I told him, 'These are the very things that the people will not like; perhaps not understand. These human characters have been shown by you to be so much deeper into reality. I am not interested in what Freudian interpretations they may lend themselves to. But this relationship is so clear and so lucidly expressed.' Another one: when Apu tells a friend in the city, 'I've "managed" Ma. Sent her two bucks.' Simple things like this. When he watches his friend Pulu pull out a pack of cigarettes and light up. Or when Pulu rubs the monkey nuts between his palms to loosen the skins and then pops them into his mouth. And Apu watches him, agape, amazed. A tremendous admiration. That chap becomes his hero. 'Want some?' And immediately Apu withdraws. Retreats. I had spoken of all this to Ray, that evening.

I remember that Bishnu-babu [Bishnu Dey (1909–82), modern Bengali poet][47] had expressed his dislike of the bit about Apu 'managing' his mother. And later, he spoke about Apu slapping his brother-in-law who brings him the news of his wife's death. This was in *Apur Sansar* [1959]. When I met Manik-babu after that, he asked me, 'Were you there? Did people laugh at that?' 'Yes,' I replied. 'And they will continue to do so. Time and again.' 'But why?' he demanded. 'Will you give me a patient hearing?' You see, despite the awful quality of my own films, I was nevertheless possessed of certain sensibilities. And I think those sensibilities are absolutely necessary. Perhaps it is even possible for a man to make a good film, once he has acquired them. But I, however, was unable to do so, at that time. So I explained to him. The entire situation had been developed in a certain way. The man in the office who shows him the milk bottle. The letter Apu keeps reading in bits and pieces. Glancing over his shoulder constantly as though all of Calcutta is reading it through a 100 mm lens. He comes home. Climbs up the stairs to his room on the terrace. There's a woman sitting on the stairway, sewing. He instinctively hides it from her too. So there's this tremendous situation that's been building up for so long. Finally, he's there, on the empty terrace. The whole thing's been shot in the light of the falling sun. Everything is dull, gloomy. And his brother-in-law tells him that Aparna is dead. Impotent rage. Apu lashes out, and slaps him. The very next shot is of the brother-in-law, stunned. Standing there clutching his cheek. Mumbling, 'Oh baba!' That's exactly when the audience falls apart. They start laughing and the moment is destroyed. I told Manik-babu, 'That's been your greatest mistake. You've completely forgotten about your editing there. There is no room for that shot in that sequence. You should have made Apu slap him and then turn around and rush back into the room. His tremendous agony would have been conveyed thus. And not a man would have laughed.' Manik-babu's wife interrupted, disagreeing, but he stopped her. 'No. Mrinal is right. That one shot has set it all awry.' 'Yes,' I carried on. 'And I was furious. I wasn't angry with those who were laughing but with you. That man is insignificant in that sequence. There was absolutely no need to focus on him at all.' Apu is a man who is suffering and is therefore incapable of any control over his own actions.

Q. Yes, he has no idea what he is doing.

A. Everything is beyond him. He cannot think. All his reactions are instinctive. Time is out of joint. That boy had no place there. Perhaps, if the sequence had been longer, he too would have started laughing in confusion. Or if he had been the angry sort, he would have slapped Apu back. Anyway, I still stand by my opinion that *Aparajito* is Ray's best film. Except for one moment. One scene. I have read many of Bibhuti-babu's [Bibhutibhushan Bandyopadhyay (1894–1950), Bengali novelist][48] stories after that. He never brings in death directly. Never makes the reader confront death. Never brings death into the forefront. For example, in *Anubartan*. When Naran-babu the schoolmaster is about to die. It's an urban tale. Published at about the same time as Rabindranath's essay 'Sabhyatar Sankat' [A Crisis of Civilization, 1941]. Both of these enabled me to get a comprehensive idea of the history of the times. The history of the War years. They were instrumental in my stepping out into the greater world. And ensured that I became a citizen of the world. That was a tremendous opportunity granted to me by these two works.

In *Anubartan*, Naran-babu lives alone in a small room. He cooks his own meals. He maintains a notebook, within which he makes meticulous entries. For example, one entry consists of the name 'Progyaborto Dutta' with the information that this student is encountering problems with the use of the definitive article—'the'—in class, and thus needs to be taken aside and given special attention. This is the kind of dedication he brought to his job. As he lay dying, sometimes he would send for Progyaborto. Progyaborto never came to him, though. The day he finally does visit, the schoolteacher is in a state of delirium. Murmuring to himself, 'That village . . . the akondo flowers . . . the orchards where we stole fruit off . . .' And at one place the delirious rambling peters out into an ellipsis. A space. And the next sentence is something about Jadu-babu who is asking for his meal. That's it. Nothing more. So you see, he never takes it beyond that point. There are no deaths in *Anubartan* that are put down in so many words. Perhaps because of its awesome nature, it cannot be made credible. And the focus is not the death. It is the events and the situations developing around and after the death.

In *Aparajito*, when Harihar lies dying, Sarbojaya sends young Apu to fetch some water. On the way back, he notices a man. Almost a pre-historic man, seen in the light of dawn, grunting with the effort of his exercises. A solitary wrestler, swinging his club. At that moment, that strange sight is more exciting to Apu who momentarily forgets his errand and the water for his dying father. That was such an incredible scene. And only Satyajit, with his completely urban consciousness could have achieved that. When Apu returns, water is given to his dying father. That is absolutely awful and totally unnecessary. The saving grace is the shot of the birds erupting into flight, immediately after. I had told him about this too. That it had really struck me as a flaw. A blot.

Ray resigned from the Calcutta Film Society at one point. In their journal, *Indian Film Culture*, Chidananda [Chidananda Das Gupta, (1921–2011)][49] wrote about Ray's film: 'It is only a picture postcard, nothing else.' I was sent to Ray, to persuade him to reconsider his decision. 'I have read what you have written. Why don't you write it in *Indian Film Culture* then?' he asked me, when I was trying to reason with him. I had written a short piece on the film in the *Statesman*, to which he now referred. 'I can but it will only stir up more trouble. But you mustn't leave.' Finally, he did come around and stayed with the film society.

The same thing happened when I made *Kharij* [1982]. Chidananda was scathing. He used to work in Delhi then. And the piece came out in *India Today*. I met him, at the film festival, and asked him, 'I am not presumptuous enough to believe that this film is comparable to *Aparajito*, but you will regret your words. You have to regret them. I think you've made a mistake. Perhaps you shouldn't have condemned it in such haste.' 'I fear you are angry with me,' Chidananda responded. 'Not in the least. In fact, I have learnt quite a lot from your article. Certain American words which were hitherto unknown to me. "Surfing" and so on. Words which they don't use themselves though. "Brainstorming". What a terribly violent concept. Why don't you use something more positive? For example, "brainwarming". It's much better than both "brainstorming" and "brainwashing". You see, I've picked up all this from you.'

Chidananda used to frequent Hawaii. Once, I was invited to Hawaii too. To be a part of a [film-festival] jury. I asked the people inviting me about who the others were and they mentioned a few familiar names. They sent me an economy-class ticket. I told them that it was not as if I didn't travel by economy class. When I paid for my own ticket, that's how I chose to travel. But when I was being invited to be a part of a jury, I must have first class. Both my wife and I. And my wife too must be invited. For that's how these things were always done. They responded by saying they had a paucity of funds. So I asked them, 'You've told me that Mifune [Toshiro Mifune (1920–97), renowned Japanese actor] has been invited. Pauline Kael too. Will they also be travelling economy class?' They had nothing to say. I refused to go. I would not tolerate Indians being taken for granted. Soon after, they sent me a first-class ticket. I told them that I had no time to spare and that I would be unable to make it. They screened *Kharij* outside the competition. They also sent me a plethora of papers, perhaps to impress me enough to accept their invitation a second time. One of the papers contained an article by Chidananda who had praised *Kharij* to great heights. So much so that I was distinctly embarrassed.

I was relieved. After making *Baishey Sravan*, I had been restless. I would often ask myself: Why can't I, too, make a good film? Now I felt that I had achieved that aim to some degree.

I went to Manik-babu again. He spent a great deal of time discussing things with me, calmly and patiently. The last thing he said to me was: 'Nothing came of it, you know. Your effort has gone to waste.' I told him that I disagreed with him totally. 'This is not a great film but it is a very important film. It gives me a place from where I can walk further and faster. Because of it, I have learnt to walk.'

So we met often, and interacted often. Shared ideas and opinions, although we didn't always agree about everything.

Q. With *Baishey Sravan*, you first emerge as a filmmaker in your own right. With your own style. And you choose what we would aesthetically term as realism. That is what you pursue for some time.

A. I'd like to add something here. Perhaps it will help you to make a connection later. After watching the film, Naren Mitra [Narendranath Mitra (1917–75), Bengali short-story writer],[50] one of our most important writers, someone who has explored middle-class life very closely . . .

Q. . . . One of the greatest realist writers of our time . . .

A. . . . He asked me, 'Why didn't you bring in a third young man who is loveable, and with whom the young girl could have perhaps had an affair? A relationship?' 'That's not why I made the film,' I explained to him. 'I tried to fathom the depths of this particular relationship.' So you see, therein lies my difference. And my disinterest in such contrived elements of storytelling was cultivated through my reading of Aldous Huxley. Although the whole thing has nothing to do with him really. I used to read him a lot at one point in time, and admired him greatly. I liked his cynical attitude . . .

Q. . . . A certain sophistication, a certain critical perspective . . .

A. Yes. He could make his narratives implode in a startling way. All this perhaps acted upon me. One cannot always link everything into a coherent stream. I was very particular about the 'core' story. I believe this is what I have been trying to do in an unconscious way. While preparing the script for my latest film, I was very conscious of the fact that I was trying to build moments. By now, it has become a deliberate act on my part. These are the moments which give rise to situations. I always de-emphasize the plot structure. This was an element that had already made its presence felt in some Hindi literature. The English translations I read had revealed this. I feel that I have been following this trend for a long time now. I am not aware, however, if a more conscious implementation of this would have bettered my films or not.

Q. This tendency remains, but from *Baishey Sravan* onwards, till you come to *Akash Kusum* [1965], which I think again is a watershed. One phase comes to an end and another begins, and in that respect, *Akash Kusum* is a major break from the structure.

A. I think so too, yes.

Q. With realism, too, there have been instances of going against its grain. The concept of a total plot, with a beginning, a middle and an end, a neat narrative structure—these are the demands of realism. And even more so in the case of socialist realism which wished to take this further, to a futuristic utopian visionary dimension. Or at least very definitely point in that direction. It's the furthest extension of the logic of bourgeois narrative, the classical or plot narrative. You've always resisted that idea, and been apprehensive about it from the start. This instinct was being sharpened over the years.

Q. My problem is that I am not an erudite person. All these things were very deeply embedded in my mind, in my consciousness. I was perhaps unable to articulate them in terms of aesthetics and 'isms'.

A. So, in *Akash Kusum*, I think you are confronting this tendency openly and boldly. The broad category or framework of traditional realism—bourgeois or whatever one may wish to term it as—that persists up to *Akash Kusum*, with which there is a conscious break. What causes it? As far as I can recall, when I had spoken to you then, you were greatly encouraged by developments in international cinema. And your exposure and response to international cinema, too, was perhaps responsible for this? You were using the films of the West not to borrow directly from, but rather as a point of reference. Other directors do this too, but are perhaps not as candid as you are about the debt. You assert that point intellectually too.

Q. I never 'lift' directly.

A. Yes, that's what I just said. You're reacting to it. Taking it as a point of reference. Not necessarily *taking* it. This space opens up for you slowly—after *Baishey Sravan* and by the time you begin *Akash Kusum*, you make a conscious and complete break. Why don't you tell us about your exposure and responses to world cinema at that time?

Q. I was always influenced by international cinema, but could not harness the impact those films were having upon me in a way that they would then directly influence my own filmmaking process. I was very conscious of the realization that we were progressing toward a hybrid culture. Through our ideas and opinions and through technological developments as well. I disapproved of the concept of 'national cinema' right from the start. Within a few years from now, talking about national cinema will be an exercise in futility for the simple reason that a film is 'national' to the extent that it captures the national scene, the national characters and their characteristics.

Q. All the physicalities. Because cinema is physical.

A. And that can be cinema's greatest undoing—cinema becoming much too physical. The physiognomy is national, the food is national, the speech is national. If you do away with these elements, there is hardly anything 'national' left in it. When we see Indir Thakrun [in *Pather Panchali*] telling a tale about a rakshasa and you see a shadow lurking behind her on the wall, or when you have Maxim Gorky listening with rapt attention to a tale by his grandmother and she, too, has a frightening shadow on the wall behind her, am I to believe that Ray lifted this from Gorky? Absolutely not! It was created in their terms, worked out in their logic, in a specific ambience. And here the ambience is Indian. I will cite another instance: when the young Apu [in *Aparajito*] watches, mesmerized, the performing monkey in Benaras, I can identify the character of Apu with the little boy in Flaherty's [Robert J. Flaherty (1884–1951), US pioneer documentary filmmaker and explorer] *Louisiana Story* [1948]: The men come to buy the marshy land. They clinch the deal with his father. They get on to the motor boat and leave. The dog starts barking at them. The boat speeds off and the waves in its wake seem to be lapping against the edge of the shore. The dog is unnerved. He has never seen this before and continues barking. It appears stranger than the unknown men who have just left. They go out on an alligator hunt. The drilling starts later. The men call out to him, and ask him to sit down beside them. The little boy is hesitant; afraid that the machinery will crush him. He sits down, finally, and some sort of understanding is established. Again, later, he watches everything from a distance. And what superb editing! The whole thing moves beyond reality then. We see the nerve centre of the machine, with its metal teeth, its spikes. All other sound fades.

Q. The machine starts vibrating.

A. The boy takes out a toad from his pocket. Places it on the palm of his hand. That is his reality. That is what he must counter this startling mechanical reality outside with. That is what he must look at to make sense of things. And watches its Adam's apple bobbing up and down. That life source upon his palm and the mechanically alive machine before him. Somewhere he reaches a point of understanding, of reconciliation. I find so many parallels with Apu here.

So, I am contesting the concept of 'national cinema', both in terms of subject matter and in terms of form. The form is in a state of continuous evolution. And there is no reason for the existence of an 'Indian' form in particular. I've heard people comment on the 'slowness' of *Pather Panchali*. I've heard many people justify the 'slowness' of a film's development by saying it is thus because of the Indian ethos. Well then, what about Bresson? A young girl stands outside a man's house, staring at the doorbell, wondering whether she will ring it or not. There's so much thought going into that decision. And she knows that the moment she rings it, the door will open, and the young man will come out. And then, what of her dignity? It will mean that she has submitted to him. When I watch this moment of hesitation, of indecision, I am gripping the arms of my chair, waiting in suspense to see what she does ultimately. As much suspense as if I had been watching a Texan film. I cannot accept the fact that because a film is a slow one it must therefore be labelled Indian. Indian life, and therefore Indian films too, can be very fast in terms of movement.

And we Indians are also bound by the examples set by our predecessors. We are not trying to break away and create styles and forms of our own. I believe that Indian cinema and its language have been oversaturated. In painting, in theatre, in music, everywhere language is changing. In literature too. Everywhere except in cinema. This is what defeats me. Strikes me as impossible. Why should it be so? There have been a few attempts but they are just that, too few to mention.

Q. After *Baishey Sravan* and up to *Akash Kusum*, you made two films which I personally consider very significant, *Punashcha* [1961] and *Pratinidhi* [1964]. What were you trying to explore at that particular point of time? In *Baishey Sravan*—a historical situation: the famine and the experience of the famine and how it completely shakes up the foundations of human relationships. It doesn't remain a mere historical fact but gets socialized somehow.

A. Without showing the physicality of famine.

Q. All this you bring into *Baishey Sravan*. Then you move to the space of the middle-class family—family relationships, the individual, new values coming in and getting resisted—something that Bengali films had avoided for some time. These are the issues that one can pursue up to *Punashcha* and *Pratinidhi*. What were you trying to do?

A. Nothing beyond that. I was merely trying to shake up the prevalent and somewhat stagnant middle-class values. We seem to have fallen asleep over these values. They have become static. I wanted to shake them up out of their torpor. Startle. Surprise. Contest them, if necessary. This is what I have tried to do, in my own small way in both these films. I haven't done anything more, I believe.

Q. In a way, *Akash Kusum*—apart from the technical and stylistic elements which at that time had a certain shock effect—was thus resisted by many people. I personally welcomed it for being gimmicky, why not! This is one aspect of it. On the other hand, the trappings of realism in the film—the story, the relationships that unfold and develop, even clash against each other—break away from the structures of realism and move towards more of an abstraction in terms of film language. There is a desire: a dream of success in life and career, and success in love— the two are almost linked to weave a fantasy, and then, trying to live that fantasy. The plot, predominant in realism, with its psychological relationships, slow developments, breakages, cleavages—you break away from all of this and move daringly towards a level of abstraction in your film. This aspect appeared to me to be much more striking than the technical . . . call it gimmickry or whatever you like . . .

A. It is not that I got it from Truffaut, although his films did help me a lot. In *Pratinidhi*, the uncle from an earlier marriage, Anup, rushes up the stairs. He has missed the lift but cannot afford to wait for it so he runs up all the way. I had deliberately made that dramatic, but perhaps I needn't have. Anyway, he reaches the door and stands there gasping for breath. Soumitra opens the door and asks him, 'When?' That's the only word he speaks. Doesn't ask, 'What about her? Is she still alive?' Nothing but that one word. And Anup replies, 'About an hour and a half ago.' And the little boy, the child from the girl's first marriage, who had just begun to establish some sort of bond with Soumitra, stands there, clutching a curtain. I wanted to end it right there. With the silence. But I couldn't get the mental space to do so. I thought it would be best if I could increase the length of that shot, by making multiple prints of it. That would actually result in a freeze, which at that point I was unaware of. So I made 100 frames of that. There are 24 frames to a second, so you can imagine what happened. I increased it by 150 frames and then did a slow fade-out. Later, I realized that it had resulted in a 'freeze'. I first saw this 'freeze' in 1928, in a film by a German director. Then later in an American commercial film . . . *Steps to Heaven* or *Stairway to Heaven* . . . something like that. So, wanting to lengthen the shot, I accidentally stumbled upon this technique.

Then, I saw it next in *400 Blows* [1959]. And in my infantile enthusiasm, I brought in a truckload of freezes into my film—something I shouldn't have done. Perhaps I wouldn't have gone quite so overboard today. But that is true for all my films, when I look at them in retrospect. Even if the film has been talked of very highly, I still wish that I could do it all over again. When I look at my films now, I wish those attempts could be treated as dress rehearsals and that I could simply make the film from scratch, all over again. I think that perhaps everyone thinks this way. Nothing is, after all, the last word.

Q. Even Ray, in fact, had tremendous reservations about *Charulata* [1964]. Every time he saw it later . . . I remember being effusive with praise about it, and he would invariably contradict by saying, 'Oh no! There are lots of errors.' [*Laughs*]

A. Yes, and that's a fact. I, too, can point out plenty of flaws in *Charulata*. Anyway, no matter. [*Laughs*] There are certain elements and aspects of the film which are very much unlike Manik-babu. He is the one we have learnt from. He is the one who had the courage to do everything first. Sorry, you were making a point about the content of *Akash Kusum*.

Q. I was saying that in *Akash Kusum*, it appeared to me that you were consciously breaking away from reality and going towards abstraction— a desire, a dream, a fantasy.

A. Yes, but there are moments that I absolutely loathe. When at the end, the character looks, stares, waves . . . oof! Unbearable! Uncalled for. An unnecessary attempt at establishing a certain wholeness, a rounding off.

Q. It was uncalled for, considering the heights to which the film had reached.

A. There was absolutely no need to be sentimental about it. I have realized this now. In my latest film . . . I ensure that when the characters arrive at a moment of truth, they have to live with their own logic. There is a married couple. They have three children. The woman had an earlier marriage which lasted for only a few months after which they were divorced. The talaaq was not their fault; it was caused by others. They were not asked for any explanations. Nonetheless, that short-lived marriage left them with some secrets. Secrets which they themselves preserved. Now, in her present, those secrets sometimes cast shadows. She loves her second husband dearly. But even he has no idea of the secrets. Despite their differences, complaints, shortcomings, their hide-and-seek games with the debtors, the couple still choose to live together, with their own sense of dignity and respect. With their own logic. This moment of truth arrives unexpectedly. Suddenly. That turns out to be pure cinema. I cannot write down, and so I haven't. She meets the ex-husband one day. But realizes that they cannot meet. They stay apart. This meeting is quite a ruthless occurrence. I have been able to reach this point only at my age. It takes time to learn all these things. This is the most important point I have arrived at, but it has been a very difficult journey.

It reminds me of Antonioni's *La Notte* [1961]. I watched it alone in Finland, at an archive, on a Steenbeck, in 1965. In the last scene, when the couple come out . . . They lived as husband and wife. They lived under the same roof for ten years and though they realized that each was lying to the other, they never articulated it. One night, they go to a party and then the deception comes to light. After the party, they walk home together. In the middle of a field, in the early hours of dawn, the woman takes out a letter from her purse and starts reading it: 'I suddenly woke up, and turned to see you sleeping beside me. And I saw a hair, fallen across your lips. I moved it away slowly. So as not to wake you. Then I pressed my lips upon yours, very gently.' She reads this and the man is staring at her intently. Trying to fathom who the writer of the letter might be and the woman to whom it was written. 'Who has written it?' he asks. 'You had,' she replies, 'long ago. Soon after we were married.' She puts the letter away. She can read it no longer because she has a lump in her throat. Suddenly one of them says, 'Can't we go back to those days? To those days?' 'It's all over. We can't.' 'But we must.' And then, they have sex. That's where the movie ends. Hrishi saw the film first. He told me, 'The end is absolute pornography!' When I watched it, alone in a room, I felt a lump in my throat. I watched it again and again until I broke into tears. When I returned to Calcutta, I told Hrishi, 'How could you have dismissed it as pornography? You only saw the physicality of it? You didn't see it intellectually?' Long ago, Rabindranath spoke of observation with the entire consciousness, not merely 'seeing' it with the eye. And that is what Eisenstein speaks of repeatedly when he distinguishes between physical perceptions and intellectual perceptions. One must intellectually perceive the whole thing. It is as simple as that. And as difficult as that.

I read Antonioni's script after that. Hrishi would not agree with me. 'Mrinal, you are indulging in too much intellectual banter,' he said. 'But it must be intellectual,' I replied, 'don't you see that too?' I asked. The script was incredible. It ended with the lines . . . 'It leads to sexual intercourse. In remembrance of what once was and what will never be.' I realized that I had reacted and responded correctly. This is the kind of thing that I have tried to arrive at here. It's been done already, and in bits and pieces in my earlier films. Here I have tried to do it as clearly as possible. Like Antonioni's *L'Eclisse* [1962]. I had asked Bansi [Chandragupta (1924–81), virtuoso art director],[51] 'Can you script the last scene?' He had replied, 'Impossible!' So there are some things like that. So completely visual that one can never hope to put them down on paper. Just the juxtaposition of certain shots.

I have achieved certain levels which are very ruthless but also very human. I have been fighting to do this all my life. But I have also been growing, realizing and moving towards new places like this. I am very happy thus, even at this age. In *Ekdin Achanak* [1989], therefore, which you didn't like, it is said that the greatest tragedy of man's life is that you live only once.

Q. Why don't you tell us a little about the unpleasant adventure called *Genesis* [1986]? With those talents, those actors . . . what went wrong?

A. Smita [Patil] knew she wanted the part. And Shabana [Azmi] knew she wanted it too. They knew that I was working on this film. They were then acting together in [Shyam Benegal's] *Mandi* [1983]. Shabana was the landlady. Smita was the prostitute. And Sreela [Majumdar] was in it too. Both Smita and Shabana called me up and said that they wanted to act in my new film. And Sreela too, following their example, pitched in with her request. I told her to calm down. 'You are practically family. Stop worrying.' I sat down and wrote to both Shabana and Smita. 'You are definitely acting in my next film. But unlike Shyam [Benegal], I cannot move about with a harem, like a Mughal emperor. He can take plenty of women at a time but I can't take more than one woman at a time. I start with you. After you, I'll take on another actress. You are a

Uttara Baokar, Arjun Chakrabarty, Manohar Singh and Shabana Azmi in *Ekdin Achanak* (1989).

great actress. So is the other one.' I wrote 'Dear Shabana' on one and 'Dear Smita' on the other. I deliberately interchanged the envelopes and sent them off. I got to hear of the result much later, from Shyam [Benegal]. They were at the dinner table. It was during the filming of *Aarohan* [(1982), produced by West Bengal Film Development Corporation] (They had exposed 10,000 feet in order to shoot some lightning. I was told by the best laboratory of Western Europe that they had never seen lightning shot this way before. I had borrowed some of that for *Genesis*.) Shabana came to dinner, wearing a long face. And told Smita, 'This is a letter for you.' And Smita too, pulling out a letter from her wallet, said, 'Here, this one's yours.' [*Laughs*] They confessed that they'd had a big laugh about it.

Shabana could really put one on the spot. One couldn't say no. One never had a chance to do so. I was visiting Shabana once at her father's place in Juhu. As I got up to leave, she gave me a rose. We exchanged kisses and left. This was before *Khandahar* [1983]. The moment I stepped out, I met Smita who had come to collect her parents. They were on the way to Prithvi Theatre to watch a play. There I was, outside Shabana's house, clutching a rose to my breast. Like a Mughal emperor on his way to war! 'Mrinal-da, I've caught you at it!' she exclaimed and hugged me. I didn't know what to say. 'I'm sorry. Do forgive me.' 'No. I've caught you this time. There is only one way you can atone for your sins. Tomorrow you must watch my film *Umbartha* [(1982), Marathi film directed by Jabbar Patel].' 'But my plane leaves at noon tomorrow.' She was not to be swayed and fixed it up so that I could watch it at the laboratory itself. Somewhere near the Film City. It took for ever to get hold of a print and by the time we began watching it, it was almost 10.30. The film was a long one, and Smita's parents were there too. I sent off a young man who was with me, to the airport, to check in. The moment the film ended, I ran to the car. 'I cannot speak with you now. I must be off or I'll miss my flight. Well done.' I patted her on the back and set off. 'Next time I come, I'll have *puran poli*s with you,' I told her parents, her mother in particular. She used to make them especially for me and send them over. Smita's mother used to tell me about how she had spent a lot of time travelling with her husband, on political work for the Congress Party. She said to me, 'I would like to be with your team when you work. I can cook. I have heard so much from Smita. All of you become like one big family. I would like to be a part of it.' I promised Smita that I would call her when I reached home. But she called me first. 'How did you like it?' 'I thought you did very well, although I have my reservations about the film as a whole,' I said. 'I forgive you then, since you did make time to watch the film,' she replied.

After that, when I completed *Khandahar*, I received a long fax from Cannes. In those days my faxes would come to the Grand Hotel [now the Oberoi Grand, Calcutta]. They had written that although they had seen *Khandahar*, they could not accept two films from the same country. They had heard of Ray's *Ghare Bairey*. And were convinced that

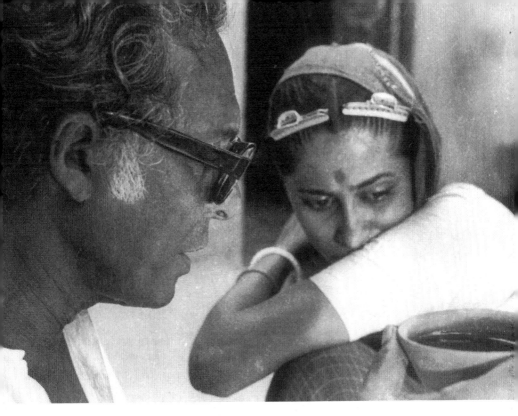

Mrinal Sen (ABOVE) with Smita Patil during the shooting of *Akaler Sandhane* (1980); (BELOW) with Shabana Azmi during the shooting of *Khandahar* (1983).

this was his last film because he had fallen sick while filming. They had started this festival with *Pather Panchali*. Let the festival end with *Ghare Bairey*, they requested. No one had seen his film yet. And everyone was worried—if my film won an award and his didn't, then that itself would perhaps kill him off. They said they would extend every support to me and my film but that I must concede to this one request. They screened it, but out of the competitive section. I had nothing to say.

The people at Venice were enraged. 'Why didn't you give it to us?' Anyway, then it went to Montreal. Where it got the Second Prize. And to Chicago where it got the Best Film Award. Then, it was also included in the *Film Guide*—where the five best films from all over the world are chosen every year.

Gilles Jacob, director of the Cannes Film Festival, was present at the Montreal Festival. It is a French-speaking region and Smita was part of the jury too. Gilles called me up one morning: 'Mrinal, though I'm leaving this morning, and a friend of mine from India is also leaving, can we meet over breakfast? We perhaps have no time for lunch.' I agreed. I also knew that the friend she wanted to bring for lunch would be none other than Smita. She congratulated me warmly, and said, 'Mrinal-da, I simply have to tell you this. I have never seen Shabana look so beautiful before.' It was such a compliment and such an honest confession. Although there were undercurrents of tension between those two leading ladies. Just before that, referring to Smita, Shabana had told me, 'Mrinal-da, this woman is sick in the head.' That was the difference between the two. Geeta was very fond of Smita.

Gilles Jacob said, 'You've taken her for one film which won an award at Berlin. I want you to make another film with her, which you must give to me. To my festival.' I agreed. Smita quickly picked up a paper napkin and wrote down this decision, and I signed it, putting down the place and the date. Gilles signed it too and so did Smita. And I remember absolutely clearly, how lovingly and gently she folded it and put it away in her handbag. Three months later she was dead. I was getting hourly updates on her condition. The moment I heard about her death, I sent off a fax to Jacob. And he called me back immediately. 'Whom can I call up, to pay my condolences?' I gave her Smita's husband's number. It was very sad.

Q. It was so unexpected, so unnecessary . . .

A. Yes, absolutely. One of the city's most famous doctors had confided to me—a gynaecologist—'One of us is responsible for her death. I visit Bombay frequently and have heard about it. She died because of gross negligence.'

Q. To take up *Genesis* again . . . you had problems between Om [Puri] and Naseer [Naseeruddin Shah], with Shabana taking another position. Why don't you tell us something about that?

A. That was actually very interesting. In my script, we see that she has conceived, and that is proven beyond doubt when she suddenly feels dizzy while carrying the corn and sits down, in the front yard. Om was fetching water and Naseer was also carrying corn alongside her. They

Om Puri, Shabana Azmi and Naseeruddin Shah in *Genesis* (1986).

Mrinal Sen and Shabana Azmi on the set of *Genesis* (1986).

both ask her, 'What is the matter?' And she replies, 'Mai pet se.'['I am pregnant.'] Both the men then start wondering which of them is the father of the child. My script, however, did not have the furious verbal altercation that ensues between them. But all three of them felt that it was absolutely necessary, at this point. So Naseer goes to her room and asks, 'Whose child is it?' Om yells out, 'What is it to you? Why do you need to know?' So Raina [M. K. Raina (b. 1948), renowned theatre actor, member of the cast of *Genesis*] wrote it down. It was a very well-written piece. Only the place where Shabana says, 'I don't know. It's mine, that's all. Your enemy is within you. All I know is that this child is mine'—only that was already there in my script. The verbal battle was the part that Raina wrote down. It made the whole situation much clearer. When I look back, I think if only I had more money then, I could have done so much more—introduce an air of grandeur to the whole thing. Anyway, that would perhaps have diminished the credibility factor.

Before this additional scene was incorporated, one day Naseer came to me (Om is the quiet sort) asking, 'Tell me Mrinal-da, who is the real hero?' 'Well, the very locale is the hero. The actor.' I answered. 'And who is the heroine?' he asked. 'There's only one. And she's what this is all about,' I replied. 'What?' he was aghast. 'And we are nothing, I suppose? What about us? Who will win at last?' he asked. 'Nobody will,' I said, 'it's a tragedy we're depicting. A tragedy of immense proportions. And with it the hope of a new civilization. Here, all of you are the victims of history. All three of you.' 'No, no. I'm not interested in any of that'—Naseer was unrelenting. 'Who is the real hero? Man or woman?' Of course, he had a case. Now, both men—Om was there too—were turning upon the actress and she, with her back to the wall, had to come up with some sort of answer. So I told Naseer, 'Let's see what happens.' 'Oh well, the same old answer. But I'm a professional. And so I must keep working.' Naseer had been beside himself with anger that day.

And then Shabana! She came into my room at midnight. 'Mrinal, what are we going to do? What's going to happen?' I calmed her down. Explained that I was just projecting a certain social milieu.

Q. Let's come back to the films—to the sequence we were following. We came up to *Akash Kusum*. Two things happened after that: one being *Bhuvan Shome* [1969]—which can be called part of the 'Indian' New Wave or New Indian Cinema. This was a major landmark of New Indian Cinema, especially in terms of its sense of humour. What we had been seeing, and still are, is a sense of humour that is conveyed mainly through the acting. We've had great clowns (if we may say so) in the tradition of Indian cinema, who have done remarkable work even in indifferent films. But the humour—the wit, particularly—that goes into the making of the film, into the style of the film—that was evident for the first time in *Bhuvan Shome* and something that has remained a kind of an exception in your entire work in cinema. How did it happen? With *Bhuvan Shome* you discovered for Indian cinema such a remarkable perspective in filmmaking, using humour, wit—an element of social satire, but not overtly I would say, almost Brechtian, quite controlled—

opening up a whole new possibility of a style. Why have you not come back to it again?

A. I wanted to bring in Chaplin. Jacques Tati [(1908–82), French actor, pantomimist, visual humourist, author, film producer],[52] who is more inclined to Max Linder than to Chaplin, had used the phrase 'inspired nonsense' about him when he commented that Chaplin had lost this very trait after his films acquired sound. I disagree. I think that Chaplin's verbal humour was very much present and continued the tradition of his 'inspired nonsense'. I succeeded in bringing this in towards the end of my film. It's there throughout in snatches, but in the latter half I've deliberately tried to force events towards an impossible conclusion. Since the man works for the Indian Railways, in one instance when he laughed, I deliberately added the sound-effect of a hiss of steam emitting from the engine. Sadhu [Meher, fellow actor] was aghast. 'Mrinal-da, what on earth are you doing?' I reassured him. 'Just wait and watch.' He was both actor and my assistant in those days. It was all thought of in Chaplinesque terms and interpreted by those very same terms too.

He was imprisoned within those four walls. And we deliberately created that effect. Not by superimposition though. Then when he wanted to be an ornithologist, we showed him with birds circling his head! Vijay Raghav Rao, the music director, said, 'Everyone, start laughing very loudly.' He recorded our laughter at very slow speed. When we played it back, at normal speed, it sounded just like the chirping of a passing flight of birds! I believe there should be a release of madness on the Indian screen. And it was really a mad, mad, mad time that we had while making this film. We went completely berserk. Did every crazy thing that crossed our minds. We needed this. Especially because we were imprisoned within the suffocating walls of a very rigid tradition.

Q. It was historically necessary...

A. Yes, it was historically necessary There was a profusion of madness in the film. Let me narrate an incident. I told Utpal [Dutt (1929–93), revered actor of stage and screen; lead actor in *Bhuvan Shome*]: Let me tell you a story. It was about the time when I used to be a medical representative. Without knowing anything about medicine. I had decided to make a film. Irrespective of the fact that I would perhaps make an absolute fool of myself, in the trying. I had travelled to Jhansi, from Kanpur. I was visiting the doctors in Jhansi; riding here and there on a bicycle, supplying medicines. One day, there I was, riding down a deserted track. Nothing but green fields of paddy on either side of me. For miles around. As far as the eye could see. Suddenly, a girl in a red *ghagra* stood up amid the rows of green paddy. Oh! What an extraordinary moment! What a sight! I was alone there. I got off my cycle, propped it up against something and began yelling to no one in particular, 'You son-of-a-bitch you! Oh my God, I haven't spoken Bengali in three days. I can't stand it any longer!' There was a little boy staring at me, giggling. I tucked a ten- or twenty-rupee note into his hand. He was dumbfounded, and sped off, clutching the money in his fist. I got back on my cycle and returned to where I was staying. I felt tremendously relieved. Back at the hotel, in my room, I began to take off my clothes. Peeled off every layer, and stood before the mirror stark naked. That was in 1951. I screamed at my reflection, 'Bloody hell, Mrinal Sen! Weren't you the one who wanted to be a director? And make a film? And this is what you've become? A peddler? Bloody ass.' And then I broke down. So I explained to Utpal: 'Do you understand me now? You are a prisoner within this office. You cannot leave. But within these walls, do whatever the hell you want to do.' 'Mrinal, may I? Are you absolutely sure? What if I mess things up?' he asked. 'Don't worry. That's where I come in. I'll fix the mess.' And so we improvised to a great degree. For example, he would be shooting imaginary birds with his ruler. I made sure that when he actually shot one, the action coincided with the sound of a gunshot. I put in a sudden shot of a line of birds scattering at the sound of gunfire. Or perhaps, suddenly, just a group of village women disappearing into the distance. That's how I punctuated the shots.

I allowed him to indulge in this kind of burlesque. I consciously wanted the inspired nonsense to show through. There, too, Hrishi said,

'You have made this fellow out to be a mad man,' the same way that he had dismissed that last scene of *La Notte* as 'pure pornography'. I was at a loss to explain the tremendous agony below the surface and that this madness was the only way of release.

Q. When you give this kind of freedom to an actor—like you did here with Utpal Dutt, by sharing that story with him and letting him make of it what he would—you would need an Utpal Dutt to respond to it. You can't try it out every time.

A. Yes, absolutely. I could not have done it without him.

Q. You need an Utpal Dutt, with his level of culture and sophistication to respond to your story at that level and then to take off from it.

A. That's true. I had no idea how he would actually respond to it. Although I was sure that he would understand my point. He had understood me. Recognized what I was all about. And he always claimed that that role had been his best. I would not have been able to achieve the same effect with Sekhar [Chatterjee (1924–90), film and theatre actor].[53] He would have totally overdone things. Utpal had a tremendous sense of proportion. A profound sense. He would thereby deliver great performances even in the worst of films. He was a master at traversing the entire gamut, from the sublime to the ridiculous.

So I think this film should be regarded in isolation. Completely separate from anything else. It was a new venture for so many people. Mahajan [K. K. Mahajan (1944–2007), Sen's cinematographer] was fresh from the film institute. He had made documentaries but never a feature, so this was a first for him. Utpal was new to Hindi cinema. So was I.

Q. And also Suhasini [Mulay (b. 1950), actress in Marathi and Hindi films].

A. Yes, Suhasini too. Absolutely new. She had never acted, either on stage or in a film. I reassured her that that was not her problem, not for her to worry about. Vijay Raghav Rao had so far worked only on documentaries for the Films Division [a production house owned by the Ministry of Information and Broadcasting, Government of India]. He said to me, 'Dada-saheb, how about if we do our sound recordings at someone's house?' He took me to a Mr Dutta, a chemical engineer by profession. He welcomed us, and from the style of his greeting it was evident that he hailed from Comilla [city in eastern Bangladesh]. We set up our various recorders. The owner had only one request. 'I know this man,' he said, pointing at Vijay. 'He will bring on the percussion at the first available opportunity. But please make sure he does it before bedtime. Or else I'm afraid the neighbours may begin to complain.' Despite our best efforts, one morning I was told, 'There's been a complaint. You've got to bail us out.' So we did our sound effects and recording in that house. And tried out all sorts of crazy experiments. Various things. Altering speeds. Trying it faster and then slower, just waiting to get the right effect. To transfer it from 14 inch to 35, we took it to the famous recordist Minu Katrak of Bombay Laboratories. He asked us, 'Is it a documentary or a feature film?' 'A feature,' we replied. 'A feature on 35!' he exclaimed, clearly surprised.

Just the other day, I read somewhere that the sound director of *Ben Hur* [1959] had said that he wished he had a Nagra to work with, when he worked on that film. An entire house could be picked up from one place and set down elsewhere. I am not so sure what more could have been done to that movie.

Anyway, so I made that film with people who were completely new to this kind of work. All of us used to sleep on the floor together. Mahajan, I, Sadhu, Narinder Singh the sound recordist, Deshmukh. All of us would live in the house I was staying in then. And Mahajan would invariably appropriate my pillow. He would be so sozzled that he would forget what he had done with it. One morning, I visited Khwaja Ahmed Abbas [(1914–87), journalist, columnist, scriptwriter and filmmaker],[54] who lived next door. 'Abbas-saheb,' I said. 'I'm making a film.' 'Yes, I've heard.' 'And everyone in it is new. If I go to the Films Division, I know I will get plenty of people—Pratap Sharma and the like—whose voices I can use. But I don't want to. We are all such old friends. I want a new voice. Since everyone else is new, I would like this person to be an unknown figure too.' There was a young man there, among many others. Tall. Thin. He said, 'Mrinal-da, aami bangla jaani. Aami kolkatay chhilo.' ['Mrinal-da, I can speak Bengali. I used to live in Calcutta.'] I told him, 'Your Bengali is lousy but your voice is great. And for your information, my film is a Hindi one. The name is Bengali and the protagonist is also Bengali, but it's a Hindi film. I need your voice for a few words a little after the movie begins and then a little bit again, towards the end. Are you willing?' I had to trade with his director. This young man was working in a movie called *Saat Hindustani* [1969], at that point. His director, Abbas, said the chap was being loaned to me on condition—that I would get him Utpal in return. I agreed. I took the young man to Jagadish Banerjee's house—he had done some work for the Films Division—who agreed to do the recording. We had a budget of only 150,000 rupees and so had to skimp at every turn. Oh, what a trial that was. The sound of fish being fried next door and then the smell of that same fish wafting past us. It was impossible. I said, 'What the hell! Let's spend some money anyway.' So off we went to Blaze, where we finished the recording in twenty minutes. There was a Hindi translation of the phrase "sonaar Bangla" [lit. 'golden Bengal']. The young man asked me, 'Mrinal-da, shall I say "sonaar Bangaal" [i.e. combination of Hindi and Bengali]?' I agreed. When I went to pay him, he refused. 'This is my very first work in films. I simply cannot accept money for it.' I reasoned with him. 'Look, all of us are accepting payment. You cannot insult us like this. Take it professionally. Is this your profession?' 'Yes,' he replied. 'Well then, make a start with this.' So those 300 rupees were his first earning in the world of films. When I asked him for his name, for the credit line, he simply said, 'Amitabh.' At that point he was still undecided about whether he would keep the Bachchan part of it. Amitabh Bachchan [(b. 1942), probably India's best-known film star] had spoken the commentary for *Bhuvan Shome*.

So this is the way in which I made that film. The whole process was carried out amid much laughter and enjoyment. And all of us went absolutely wild. And that was hence to be treated as a case in isolation.

No one was interested in buying the film. Especially when I came to Calcutta. No one knew anything about it. Then, when it finally clicked, two producers came down from Bombay. They waited patiently for me to return. Put up at the Grand Hotel, and waited for me, for I was out of the city then. When they finally met me, they insisted I do a film each for them, just like *Bhuvan Shome*. I refused, for that was simply not possible. And that was a terrible time for Calcutta: 1969–70.[55] I was arrested. There were killings and murders around every other corner. I could hardly step out of the house. It was the worst of times for the country and yet the best of times for me to carry out experiments like this. To make an attempt at establishing some sort of difference. That was also when I was watching a lot of Latin American films. After I made *Interview*, I had reached a point of no return. There was no looking back. Then I made *Calcutta 71* and *Chorus* [1974] followed soon after.

Q. And some of these experiments have worked and some haven't. You have continuously broken away from the paradigm and tried to build anew.

A. Yes, and the success rate of these experiments hasn't really affected the larger body of my work in general. Then I reached a point where I felt that it was time for me to do something else. Make something new. I could not get a producer, for the films weren't doing well. The last film had been *Chorus*. It may perhaps have done well had it been made at a different time. *Calcutta 71*, too, did not really prove a success because of cinematic excellence, but more because of the time in which it was made and released. It was released at Metro [erstwhile iconic film theatre in central Calcutta]. There were serpentine queues outside the theatre. In fact, many 'wanted' people were actually arrested from those queues. It was released in 1972. Two young and fresh-faced boys ran up to me and said, 'When? When did you shoot this film?' 'I started sometime in the September of 1971,' I replied. 'You lie!' one of them exploded, in front of all those people. 'What's the matter with him?' I asked the other chap. 'Has he lost his mind?' 'Lies! It's all lies. You're a liar!' he went on, 'Tell me the truth: When did you make this film?' I could make neither head nor tail of the situation. So I asked the other one, 'Tell me, have you seen one of your friends in it?' It was full of footage of processions, speeches, demonstrations. Perhaps they had seen a familiar face? 'Yes.' He replied to my question. 'Dead?' I asked again. 'Yes.' 'Shot by the police?' 'Yes.' So I called him aside and explained, 'Listen. I have been shooting all this from 1969. I had no idea then what I was going to use all this for. So forgive me for misunderstanding you. I did not realize why you were upset.' Young boys like this would keep coming back. Perhaps with their family and their friends. They would watch it over and over again, just for another glimpse of their friend. I remember, once, I was standing in the theatre. Suddenly a lady let out a piercing scream. I immediately asked my assistant to rush to her aid. She had fainted. She had seen her son on the screen. Who had later been shot by the police. So you see, the times mattered a lot. If I had made *Calcutta 71* when I made *Chorus*, it may not have had the same impact. Yes, the quality of the film itself is an important factor, but equally important is the timing of the whole thing. The timing, therefore, contributed greatly to *Calcutta 71*.

I made *Matira Manisha* after *Akash Kusum*. I am still very fond of that film. I have to serve my own times. I have to serve the text. And I have to serve film as a medium. In attempting to serve my own times, I would have to invest the story with the contemporary sensibilities where it is my prerogative to be critical of the story. People had been enraged by this attitude and I was almost staring a libel suit in the face. They had gone to complain to Manik-babu. He had been vacationing in Puri then. They had asked him, 'Would you have been able to do this? With a story by Tagore?' One of the people who supported me wholeheartedly was Ramakanta Rath, now chairman of the Sahitya Akademi. At that time he was the chief secretary [state government's highest-ranking bureaucrat]. Then I made *Mrigaya* [1976]. I chose an Odia story for that. This was followed by *Oka Oorie Katha*.

Q. I have some questions regarding this stage. Although it was a flawed film in some respects, I found it very interesting and challenging when you took up Sudhendu Mukherjee's [(b. 1926), social scientist][56] report on pavement dwellers. That material, that document, excited you to such a degree that you took off from it immediately and thought of making a film, which resulted in *Parashuram* [1978]. So somewhere, there was a conscious critique of social reality as a document. And you made your movie beginning from that standpoint. That was also the kind of philosophy or attitude at work in a lot of Latin American cinema. Would you say this was in some way your response to Latin American cinema? Again, this is an exception, whatever be its cinematic quality.

A. I thought that was an extremely important document which the government finally didn't even bother to publish. I thought that it would be an interesting thing to attempt, punched with the tiger killing incident from [Lu Xun's] *The Story of Ah Q* [1921–22]. What I find very

Shooting *Parashuram* (1978).

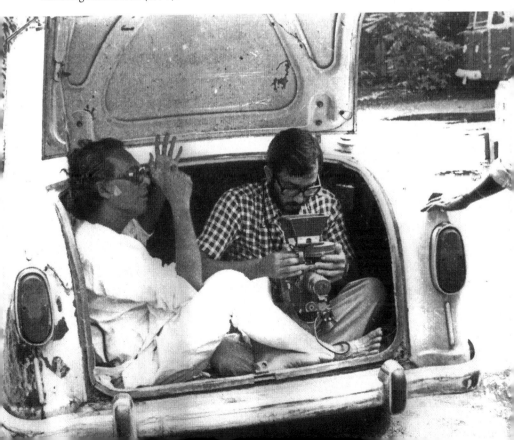

interesting is the character of the woman. She changes men three times. But she is possessed of no rage, no hatred, no ill will. And the audience also do not feel any of those emotions towards her. 'Have you stolen this?' 'Yes.' It is all so simple. So matter-of-fact. And this ease, this simplicity was all created. It has, however, flopped. It has failed. Especially as art. I have no regrets and I gained some interesting ideas from it. The shadow-fighting sequence in Wellington Square, for example. Fighting against darkness. Then, when the woman has run away with yet another man, the camera moves closer and closer. And suddenly, it seems the whole world has come to an end. Things are falling apart. Breaking down. Glass is shattering. He sees a tiny man. And a huge sandbag. The kind with which boxers practice. And there is the sound of tremendous explosions and devastation as he fights with the bag. And finally gets knocked out. Here, there is that strange element. Fighting in darkness. And fighting against darkness. Complete abstractionism. That particular sequence in itself fascinates me. Or even the beginning of the film. Miguel Littín [(b. 1942), Chilean filmmaker, screenwriter and novelist] had remarked, 'Mrinal! A fascinating visual!' So there were certain things that I succeeded in conveying or achieving and, therefore, have no regrets or grief about that film. The government incurred a loss. Ah well, so they incurred a loss.

Q. Another film that I find very interesting is *Padatik* [1973]. Where I think there is a development of a movement that becomes evident when one watches *Interview*, *Calcutta 71* and *Chorus*. Here, there is a more critical look at that movement. A more probing look. Earlier, there was a greater degree of admiration and reverence. The reverence is still there, especially the sequence with Bijan-da towards the end.[57] But there is also the criticism that comes out in *Padatik*. But again, even in *Padatik*, we find a very different kind of filmmaking, when we compare it with your other films.

A. Yes, there would be an element of a meaty story. I realized that it was time to make that sort of a film. And it yielded certain results too. Soon after I made this film, I got a telephone call. 'We need to meet you for

Mrinal Sen directs Simi Garewal in *Padatik* (1973).

an important matter.' I could make out that it was the voice of a young man. I told him that I was a bit busy then, and that it would have to wait. 'No, no. We must meet you immediately.' I realized what they were up to and said, 'All right. Why don't you come over and meet me?' 'We can't come. You'll have to come to us.' 'I am afraid it is not possible for me to come to you.' They were insistent. I told them that I was going abroad and that they could get in touch with me after four weeks. They refused to be put off. I lost my temper. 'One cannot rush a revolution. I will speak to you later.' But I also realized that I had succeeded in provoking them to a great degree. And, therefor,e my film had obviously achieved some sort of effect.

I feel that this was necessary. Samar Sen [(1916–87), poet and journalist][58] called it a 'policeman's report' and wrote an editorial on it. I was quite disappointed in him, and have always considered him to have been overrated. I do not deny that the work that he has done is great but there have been incidents like this too. When I screened this film abroad, I have noticed ex-students of Presidency College [Calcutta], in Chicago, identifying with it completely, with Soumya [Soumya Chakraborty (b. 1950), physicist and musicologist, a friend of Mrinal Sen's son, Kunal] and so many of them saying to me, 'Mrinal-da, we are reliving those days.' There was a prevalence of demonstrations in those days. Chairs and tables would be broken by students who refused to sit for examinations, decrying the bourgeois education system. These used to be common occurrences. I remembered all that. Even earlier, in *Interview*, for example, the sequence of Ranjit Mullick's interview was shot in the office of a computer firm on Camac Street. Ranjit was supposed to be dressed in a dhoti and kurta. It was a conscious decision. I had no written script for that scene. I asked the people what they would do because I was depending totally on improvisation. They assured me,

During the making of *Chorus* (1974).

'This is what we do, every other day, don't worry.' I recreated a typical office with people of several nationalities, including a Bengali on the interview board who was supposed to ask: 'Have you read *Bibar* by Samaresh Basu?'[59] to which Ranjit would reply: 'Of course!' While shooting, I asked them to conduct the interview just as they would on any other day.

The first question: 'What are the headlines today, in the newspaper? Which one do you read?' 'I read the *Statesman*.'

He cannot answer satisfactorily about the headlines though. Then Nemai [Nemai Ghosh, (b. 1934), photographer][60] told me, 'Oh! Last week there was a terrific sequence shot for *Pratidwandi* [(1970), directed by Satyajit Ray]. It was absolutely fabulous! The interviewee was asked about the greatest event of the decade. And he answered, "The war in Vietnam." ' Hearing that, I said to myself that the fellow should have been hired then and there because he would have been an excellent worker. Here was a lad who had perhaps been in the Students'

During the making of *Chorus* (1974).

Federation of India [the student wing of the Communist Party of India (Marxist)] and had certain distinctive leadership qualities. Anyway, I made a pact with Nemai that he wouldn't disclose anything of this to Manik-babu. In the interview in my film, I put in the question, 'What is the biggest event of the day?' to which the interviewee replies, 'My interview' and gets up, chuckling heartily and taking leave with: 'See you soon!'

So that was the time when I thought that there was a need to pull in all these diverse strands into one larger pattern. I wanted to consider the past. Look back in retrospect and try to fathom where we had reached. One thing we were very careful about while making the film [*Padatik*] . . . when he says, 'Joley kumir, dangaaey baagh' ['The waters are infested with crocodiles; the shores, with tigers']. These words had haunted me for a very long time. Niranjan Sen [(1915–93), Communist theatre activist] was then general secretary of the IPTA. He was being pursued by the police. This was the period when the Communist Party had been banned and all Party members had gone underground. I was asked to smuggle a letter. Niranjan was hiding at my place. A man, similar to the cigarette-shop owner, told me one day, 'Saheb, today a man will come to you.' So we waited—my father, mother and I. A man came and asked Niranjan to follow him. We took Niranjan to Pijush Dasgupta's house on Congress Exhibition Road for the night. The next day we took him to the house of an Assamese zamindar. He was a wonderful man, a successful businessman who had worked with Bimal Roy in the films. He had a house on Southern Avenue, with an outhouse. He stayed there in hiding for a few days. We told him that Niranjan was a very dear friend of ours, who taught mathematics in Delhi. New to Calcutta, he had no place to stay. I would visit him every day and we would talk. One day he was calling out to me and I told him to come upstairs and chat with the rest of us. Ritwik, Salil, Nirmal and some others were there with me. He was frantic, 'No, no, don't tell them that I'm here!' They were all Party members whereas I was not. He asked me for some money. 'I haven't eaten in three days.' I was amazed. I hadn't been able to visit for a couple of days and when I had finally done so, he had not mentioned a word of this to me. I borrowed some money from my mother and handed it over to him. Then he left. That night, a man who was known in Party circles as Master-da came to me. He said he wished to speak to me, and took me near the No. 4 Bridge in Park Circus. 'We are very fond of you, and so are the Party leaders. But how can you befriend a man like this?' I knew this is what I would be told. For I was the one who had smuggled the letter to him. A letter full of accusations from the Party which also informed him that he had been suspended. After reading the letter Niranjan-da had told me, 'Mrinal, aamar joley kumir, dangaey baagh. Kothay darabo bol?' [his way of saying: 'On the one hand the police are after me, and on the other, the Party which refuses any protection. Where am I supposed to go?', using the same Bengali expression later employed in *Padatik*]. I lived through such events, at that time, and have been unable to forget them. So this Master-da who spoke to me told me, 'We would rather you didn't befriend him.' 'I'm afraid I can't do as you say,' I replied. 'You may avoid him or disown him. But I am not prepared to obey the Party mandate. I have no connection with the Party or its decisions. I will continue to act as I like. Go where I please and do what I please.' Niranjan-da, however, wasn't arrested. He left soon after, and then went to Bihar. Now, of course, he is dead. All these things therefore crept into the film. When Dhritiman speaks to Simi, I made him say those very words of Niranjan-da's. And she tells him, 'Why don't you stay at my house?' And he refuses. 'But the Party doesn't want you.' 'The Party is not anyone's personal property. I will fight from within and from without.' Then his contact man tells him, 'Your mother is very sick. If you wish to visit her, you may go now.' He thinks for a while. Is this a trap to get him out? Will they kill him? What if his mother really is sick! Finally, he decides to go. And she is really sick. He meets his father who tells him, 'Be brave! I have not signed.' We had a special screening at Priya [popular film theatre in South Calcutta]. Bijan-da, and many others—they had all come. Bijan-da was very happy with it and congratulated me warmly.

Sushobhan Sarkar [(1900–82), eminent scholar and historian][61] too was very impressed with it. 'You've done a very good job. But it would been more historically correct if you had shown that the man went out and was shot dead by the police.' 'Let me tell you something,' I said, 'I never made this film for anyone or any Party. I merely wanted to arrive at a certain conclusion, if I may call it that. An understanding between the father and the son. That was my priority. And everything else took second place.' That the father finally understood. Told his son to be brave. And said that he hadn't signed. There was something else working in that scene too. When he tells his son, 'I haven't told your mother anything. So that she may die in peace.'

That's where something of Ritwik's film *Meghey Dhaka Tara* [1960] was working in my mind: the sequence in which Anil [Chatterjee] who plays Shankar, the elder brother, visits Neeta in the sanatorium. 'How's everyone at home?' she asks. And as he recounts, he starts speaking of their little nephew and his antics. He says, 'He is the apple of Father's eye.' And she breaks down and sobs, 'Dada, I'd love to live. To live. Tell me, dada, for once, that I'll live . . . I'll live . . . I'll live . . .' Now, can any well-bred human being who has the slightest bit of sympathy or concern for her ever say those words in front of her? I couldn't accept this at all. Ashish Rajadhyaksha had retorted, 'So what do you think he should have said?' 'He should have lied!' I had replied. He argued, 'No. In every epic, there comes a situation where it progresses beyond logic.' Somehow I haven't been able to accept that. I happened to remember that. So in my film *Padatik* when I create a situation where the father tells his son that the mother knows nothing, has been told nothing—no one will be able to connect the two—only I am conscious of the agony which inspires that sequence.

So, if you add up all the pieces and see it in a wider perspective, you too may feel that I have succeeded in arriving at a certain point. Am I clear? How am I to forget these events? How can I deny history? Not a single one of man's experiences ever goes waste. In *Baishey Sravan*, my encounter with the old woman who lived in that house, when she says (about her invalid husband), 'Only I can understand what he is trying to say.' Even those words do not go waste. I have used them in *Akaler Sandhane*. When I was shooting for *Baishey Sravan*, I saw one of the residents of that house frantically rushing about. When I asked him what the matter was, he said he was looking for a rickshaw. His wife had gone into labour. I asked him how far the hospital was from there. He replied, 'Eight miles.' Eight miles by rickshaw? And the woman was going to have a baby? She would probably deliver midway! I called Bijoy-babu immediately. He was our producer. 'We have two cars, don't we? Can't we spare one?' 'Yes, of course we can.' And we sent the gentleman off with his wife in that car. He came back in the evening with a huge basket of sweets to celebrate the birth of his son. This I used in *Akaler Sandhane*. I suddenly remembered these little incidents. I had had a strange dream, while on the shoot. I saw that old man, who asked me, 'Ke tumi, baba?' ['Who are you, child?'] The very next morning I decided to improvise. Smita was made to say, 'Jayanta-da, she is refusing to let go of the dead body. And won't do so until her daughter arrives.' 'But where is the daughter? Where does she live?' Someone says, 'It's quite far off, and there's only one bus that goes that way.' 'We have a car. We can send that for her. Do you have anyone to spare? Who knows the way?' This entire episode was taken from that memory. From my experience during the shooting of *Baishey Sravan*. Which is why I say that no experience ever goes waste. You have to store it all away and then use it at a proper time. It is only then that memory becomes valid. It is only then that history becomes valid.

Q. Mrinal-babu, to return to where we began this morning. You mentioned that when you began work, you adopted or were exposed to a radical Left position, and hence, that was your starting point. When in the 1980s, in the larger political sphere, in the international sphere, things begin to slowly give way until 1990, when we have the dissolution of the Soviet Union—how does this affect you? Because so far it has been very evident, even when we were talking about *Padatik*—that entire history with its contradictions—that you have never regarded your Left radical position with undue reverence and admiration. Your criticality has always been there. Despite that . . .

A. Yes. In *Padatik* I have tried to make this whole thing politically valid. I have used Mao Zedong's 1926 speech at Canton: 'The Analysis of Classes in Chinese Society'. I never mentioned the name or else the Censor Board would never have allowed it. But I made Sundar [Dhritiman Chatterjee] speak those very words: 'All our revolutions have come to naught, because we have not been able to distinguish our friends from our foes—something we must have done right at the beginning.' Thus, in a way I have tried to say something about it.

Q. You made a political statement.

A. I have tried to be vocal about the ideology of our times, tried to take a firm stand.

Q. But what happens after that?

A. Yes, I made a political statement. If you pick up any of Mao's books, be it a Chinese publication or an Indian one, this would be the very first item—that the biggest mistake has been in who exactly the enemy is and who is a friend—a problem faced even by the IPTA after Independence. This, I believe, was also one of the primary reasons for the IPTA breaking up. Each one reacted differently. Bijan-babu was an honest man but he was not articulate. Sombhu-da was articulate but possessed of other angularities. He went off with Humayun Kabir [(1906–69), politician, poet, editor][61] and started doing work for the Congress Party and so on.

Q. What I am trying to say is that though you have been aware of this, when, between the 1980s and the 90s it actually collapses, then can you still hold on to your agenda of examining history, social change and even relationships from a radical leftist position—a pattern that emerges consistently from your films so far? Or do you now seek something else?

A. I'd like to say something else first. I could see that there was something wrong somewhere. This was soon after the 1977 elections when the leftist forces won with an overwhelming majority.[62] That is when I realized that we were looking at imminent disaster. At a completely different level, I was making a film about the rural proletariat—about Ghishu and Madhab. And there's something even more interesting. Premchand wrote two stories. One, in 1923 or 1924, called 'Shatranj ke Khiladi' [made into a film in 1977 by Satyajit Ray], about two idlers in an affluent situation, where he brings in elements of social tension in one way. And another, 'Kafan' (I based my film *Oka Oorie Katha* on this) was an exploration of another extreme of society—two idlers in absolute poverty. I found that to be very interesting.

I received the news of this landslide victory while shooting this film. Calcutta was apparently ablaze with lights. And that's when I realized that despite all the promises made, they had actually failed to deliver the goods. That's also when I thought that instead of pointing my finger at the enemy outside, I should point my finger at the enemy inside me. That's when I began making films about my own community and that is when I started doing films like *Ek Din Pratidin* [1979]. I deliberately underscored the inherent flaws in our inherently flawed selves. And when people asked me why I was making films like this, I said that it had now become imperative for us to recognize ourselves. Identify the faults. Understand the lapses. If we could identify the enemy outside, perhaps the land-reform movement would have been even more successful.[63] Though there is no connection between the two. Except that if you are a better person, then automatically you have a better chance at making a movement a success. Otherwise, everything we attempt will be doomed to failure.

A lot of people have also said, 'Finally, did it need to end on such a despairing note?' Geeta lights the clay stove, and sits there quietly. 'Could you see nothing else in it?' I asked them in turn, 'Hidden behind this external despair, could you not see the inherent strength in this woman?' You see, the problem is, no one is prepared to read between the lines. A woman who tells her daughter as she stands undecided on the threshold—as the inquisitive neighbours throng the windows of their apartments and the lights come up one by one—'Come in now, and don't make a laughing stock of yourself,' and goes into the room with her youngest son. Her husband stands by the eldest daughter. The son says, 'Didi, come inside.' The mother sits, quietly. And the girl goes to the younger sister [played by Sreela Majumdar] and says, 'What if I had an accident? You wouldn't have had to worry about anything then. You would have had some excuse to offer. But aren't you going to ask me where I was? I may have something to say, after all.' And then the landlord rushes in, and so on. If I had made that film today, I would perhaps never have painted the landlord so black. That was my IPTA legacy, which neither Ritwik nor I had been able to forget or disown. I have tried my best to rid myself of it, but have not succeeded. Today, I would have made it differently. For example, today I think in that scene where the father enters his daughter's room and sees her sari flung on the bed, while she hastens to go to work, I should have made him lean over and very carefully fold that sari. Now I look back and rue my missing out on that touch. I could have given a more complete picture of that family crumbling to pieces. No one actually stopped to ask themselves, 'I wonder what will happen next.' As far as the structure of the film is concerned, if one pays attention to the opening narrative in voiceover about history from India's First War of Independence [the Revolt of 1857] to this landlord Dwarik Mullick, it becomes clear that these common people too are part of history—part of the larger continuance of events that make up history.

At one point in the film, when the family has given up all hope of her return, the dark girl says, 'One day I too will complete my education. And then I too shall leave, like Didi. I will go to another poorer home. And then, just like this, you too shall wait for me.' And she breaks into sobs. 'Didi, is this what you are going to leave us with? Is this what you want to do to us?' This is history that will be, compared to history that was. I have done this very consciously. And not one individual has mentioned it to me. I have tied my narrative to a history that is poised between that which was and that which will be. I think that the mother who was so reticent and quiet until now, steps out into the new day. An aeroplane flies across the sky. She enters the kitchen and lights the stove, shutting the door carefully behind her so that the smoke does not fill the house. An old habit. She knows that none of her neighbours have the guts to come to her and ask questions. And even if they do, she knows how to tackle them. And this courage, this metamorphosis occurs because she faces reality. And she survives. She possesses that inner strength. She stays there, sitting where she was. A while ago she had been hiding away. But not any longer. So hidden behind this apparent despair, there is a great strength which keeps her moving, keeps her looking beyond, living, dreaming. And that is the only logic of one's existence.

I have tried to work with this idea in both *Kharij* and in *Khandahar*. While shooting for *Khandahar*, one day Geeta asked me, 'What is going to happen next?' So I told her, 'You tell me.' She said, 'For the next few days, not a word will be spoken. The daughter will carry on with her

Geeta Sen in *Ek Din Pratidin* (1979).

Shabana Azmi and Naseeruddin Shah in *Khandahar* (1983).

chores. She will take care of her mother and bathe her. Feed her, dress her and take care of her just as she was wont to do. Then on the sixth or seventh day, the mother will tell her daughter, "Jamini, bring some paper and pen. Write to your sister and tell her that we are coming to her.'" I was completely overwhelmed. This is what humanity and human-ness was all about. When humans face reality. And they survive. And rethink their own ideals. I cannot tell you how much I liked this conclusion that was suggested by Geeta. Sudhendu had said, 'Why don't you do it this way?' I didn't want to. I wanted to keep it open-ended. Wanted each person to think it out for themselves.

So, such things have been present in my films. One must believe in oneself. I am trying to look forward. And yet I know at the same time that it will in all probability come to nought. And yes, as you say, after it all collapsed, I was greatly saddened. I had nothing to hold on to. I

Anjan Dutt, Mamata Shankar and others in *Kharij* (1982).

had made a grave mistake and I remember you had criticized both Manik-babu and me. I needed to look at history from a certain distance. One can never view history with the proper objective until one is distanced from that history. I am speaking of *Mahaprithivi* [1991]. I should never have made it at that time. Certain things which I found particularly unpleasant, I voiced through Anjan [Dutt]. And his father. It was necessary to say those things at that point. And there was that girl who was sick in the head. These things I found to be very important. Although they do not offer me any excuse to make comments on history. I should have taken some more time. When I watched East European films, later... when I watched the film by [István] Szabó [(b. 1938), Hungarian screenwriter and director of films and operas] about two girls who come to Warsaw. Looking for work. Both of them teach Russian and have lost their jobs. They find no work, and do not speak

English. One of them becomes a prostitute. And another one probably kills herself. When I watched it I realized what a terrible time they were going through. This was necessary. I made a mistake. I cultivated no distance between myself and the history I sought to portray.

However, once again I have no regrets because one learns through these mistakes. Even today, I can still make another film. I have never had a funding problem. But now that I am about to make a new film, I find that I have nothing to hold on to. What am I to make a film about? Where do I stand? I've trudged a long way in all these years. Where am I, now? I can see the sorry state the Left parties are in. And on the other hand, there is the frightening streak of Talibanism which I see in almost each and every one of us. It does not operate only on the level of religious compulsions. It operates on very many levels. There is plenty of Talibanism at the ideological level too.

Q. Scratch someone and there's a Taliban lurking underneath.

Soumitra Chatterjee in *Mahaprithivi* (1991).

A. How else do you explain the fuss made over *Taurus*?[64] Biman [Biman Bose (b. 1940), Communist leader, then chairman of the Left Front, the ruling coalition in West Bengal] called me and said, 'The students are going to give us hell tomorrow. It's already begun, today.' I had no idea. 'And what I want to know is, how can this take place where Mrinal-da is involved? So I've held them off a bit while I check with you,' he continued. 'Listen, I am not involved in any capacity whatsoever. No one has ever bothered to ask me anything. And I am not sure what my response would be, had they asked me in the first place. I am very happy about the director. And regard him with great affection. In the Moscow Film Festival, in 1997, we watched one of his films. *Mother and Son.* Everyone was against it, except I. I was the only one rooting for him. Another person, who kept absolutely quiet throughout the proceedings, was [Oleg] Menshikov. He was an actor and had spent a year acting in England. Finally, after forty-five minutes of arguing, I managed to win them around to my point of view. And ensured that he won the Best Director award. I am sure he will never have interpreted things the way you suggest. It is possible that someone may be anti-Lenin, but this man is incapable of showing things in the manner you are accusing him of. And how can you make such accusations? Just like fascists? Don't do this. Fascists do this—burning books and such like. Do not let fascism in.'

I have begun a new film now. In these days of wanton killing and devastation, if I can say something about human compassion, then that perhaps is the only way to combat the horrors we are being forced to live through and live with. This is the only way in which we can fight terrorism. I go back to the past, to the confrontation at Kargil on the Kashmir border [May–July 1999], a mini-war between the two recently nuclearized neighbours, India and Pakistan. One evening, during one of my brief trips to Delhi, I was watching television all alone in my room. Rajdeep Sardesai, the NDTV correspondent, was on the screen, moving about in Islamabad, interviewing politicians, bureaucrats and people, known and unknown. His camera caught a vegetable vendor on the pavement. He asked the man to say a few words about the 'war'. The man, most possibly unlettered, looked back, looked up, over the shoulder, and said a word, just one word: 'Nooksan' ['loss/damage']—and turned back to the job at hand. That was all, nothing more.

All alone in the room, I was shaken. Who was he? An unknown man of whom history would take no note, one who, in turn cared nothing for history, an ordinary vegetable seller speaking his mind. I was shaken, and I immediately felt that his double on the other side of the border, irrespective of caste, creed and nationality, would surely have said the same thing, meaning a lot more than the word literally meant.

It meant a lot to me. Loss. Loss of life, of values, of human decency, of all that make the family and the society delightful, people living, loving, desiring. Now is the time when we need to chant a mantra that evil is not man's natural state.

I have taken one of Afsar Ahmed's [(b. 5 April 1959), contemporary novelist and short-story writer][65] stories and worked on it. When I was writing to the producer in Bombay, I wrote, 'It doesn't have any specific story-line as such. It concerns three major characters, Muslims, in a rural set-up.' Later, I felt quite shocked at what I had said. I should have just mentioned the names of the characters. There was no need to specify their religion. Just their names would have sufficed.

So I questioned myself. Why did I have to specify that the three major characters were Muslims? The producer told me, 'Given the state of affairs with Muslims being seen only as terrorists, why don't you come up with a better story?' 'I would have been happier had you asked me for a "safer" story,' I replied.

I decided to go to someone else. I was determined to make this film. Sundar was passing through, one day. I told him a bit about the story. The estranged couple would go their separate ways and then marry other people. As I've said earlier, I build moments which give rise to situations. And I constantly seek to de-emphasize the plot. I would like to arrive at a moment of truth. And also arrive at the ultimate truth about human compassion.

The agony never ends, though. That is evident in the film—it shows forth cinematically. It remains even after the film is over.

So this is the film I am making now. And I hope to reach a new point, a new place with it. I have made many errors, many mistakes, but I am still trying. I have no idea where it will all lead to. But I am still trying.

[*Interviewed by Samik Bandyopadhyay at the Seagull Arts and Media Resource Centre, Calcutta, 7 November 2001. Transcribed and translated from the Bengali by Sunandini Banerjee.*]

Notes

1 *Shahider Dak*: shadow play narrating the history of India's Independence movement and the Hindu–Muslim riots around the Partition of India; produced by the IPTA, Bengal Squad.

2 Now the National Library, Calcutta.

3 *Die Geburt der Tragödie* (1872; English translation: *The Birth of Tragedy*, 1909), with its celebrated comparison between Dionysian and Apollonian values, was dedicated to his friend, Richard Wagner.

4 Nietzsche completed his autobiography in 1888, but it was withheld by his sister and not published until 1908, eight years after his death.

5 Abhedananda: scholar, religious teacher and sannyasi of the Ramakrishna Mission.

6 *Kathamrita*, or *Sri Sri Ramakrishna Kathamrita* is a record of about 50 interviews/sessions of Hindu religious leader Ramakrishna Paramahansa with disciples and visitors during the last four years of his life (1882–86), maintained in the form of a diary by one of his leading disciples, Mahendranath Gupta (1854–1932), better known as Sri M (pronounced 'sri-maw'). This remains one of the most authoritative accounts of the master's teachings.

7 Rolland's *Life of Ramakrishna*, published originally in French as *La vie de Ramakrishna* on 2 December 1929. First translation in English published in 1930 by Advaita Ashrama, Calcutta.

8 English translation of Rolland's *Quinez ans de combat* [Fifteen Years of Combat], translated from English to Bengali as *Shilpir Nabajanma* [The Rebirth of the Artist] by Sarojkumar Datta, later ideologue and leader of the radical Naxalite movement, assassinated by the police.

9 Ram Halder: one of the founders of Cine Club of Calcutta, Calcutta's second film society, founded in 1960. Kamalalaya Stores was the first departmental store in Calcutta started by a Bengali entrepreneur; it housed a popular bookstore.

10 The office of the Progressive Writers and Artists Association, and later of the IPTA, and site of readings of new works by major leftwing writers and exchanges with visiting writers and artistes from the rest of India and abroad, including scientists Frederic-Joliot Curie, Joseph Needham, N. W. Pirie, J. B. S. Haldane, J. D. Bernal, writers Louis MacNeice, Clive Branson, Faiz Ahmed Faiz, Ali Sardar Jafri, Kaifi Azmi, film personalities V. I. Pudovkin and Nikolai Cherkasov.

11 Buddhadeva Bose: known as leading figure of modern Bengali poetry as well as for novels such as *Tithidore* (1949) and *Raat Bhore Brishti* (1967), and as editor of the highly influential poetry periodical *Kavita*. He had ideologically adopted an anti-Communist position and came to be associated with the Congress for Cultural Freedom.

12 Gopal Haldar: imprisoned during India's Independence movement, he came to write the first major political novel in Bengali before joining the Communist Party in 1941. Emerged as a major critic of Bengali literature from a Marxist perspective and remained a Communist activist.

13 Bhabani Sen: instrumental in consolidating the peasants' movement (1940–42), leading the Tebhaga movement (1946–47); member of the central politburo of the Communist Party of India. In 1964, the party split and Communist Party of India (Marxist) came into being.

14 Ritwik Ghatak is known for his films *Ajantrik* (1957–58), *Meghey Dhaka Tara* (1960), *Subarnarekha* (1962) and *Jukti Takko aar Gappo* (1974), and is often considered one of the most radical and significant Indian filmmakers; Salil Chowdhury (1922–95), music composer, lyricist, actively involved in the cultural wing of the Communist Party of India, later a major music director in films; Bhupati Nandy (1920–86), singer and composer, associated with IPTA.

15 Kakdwip: in southern West Bengal, site of one of the most militant battles between peasants, fighting for their rights and economic demands under the leadership of the Communist Party of India, and a brutally repressive police (1948–49).

16 Karuna Banerjee: best known for her memorable performance as Sarbojaya, the mother of Apu and Durga in *Pather Panchali* (1955) and *Aparajito* (1956)—the first two parts of Satyajit Ray's *Apu Trilogy*. Late in life she appeared in *Interview* directed by Mrinal Sen.

17 Kanu Banerjee: actor, played Apu's father Harihar in Satyajit Ray's *Pather Panchali* and *Aparajito*.

18 Bijan Bhattacharya: wrote and co-directed *Nabanna* for IPTA, starting off the new theatre movement in Bengal and continued to lead groups like Calcutta Theatre and Kabachkundal, with plays such as *Mara Chand, Debigarjan* and *Garbhabati Janani*, all of which he wrote and directed; acted in films directed by Ritwik Ghatak and Mrinal Sen.

19 Sombhu Mitra: led the theatre group Bohurupee till the early 1970s; best known for his productions of *Putulkhela, Dashachakra* (adaptations of Ibsen's *A Doll's House* and *An Enemy of the People* respectively), Tagore's *Raktakarabi* and *Raja, Oidipous, Pagla Ghora*.

20 *R. U. R.* or *Rossum's Universal Robots* (1920; English translation, 1923), an internationally acclaimed play by Karel Capek, about a dehumanized post-industrial society. It led the way for a new kind of science fiction as well as introducing the word 'robot'—from the Czech *robota* meaning drudgery—to the English language.

21 Jay Leyda: author of *Kino* (1960) and *Eisenstein at Work* (1982), and translator/editor of Eisenstein's first works in English, *The Film Sense, Film Form*, and *Film Essays*.

22 Ivor Montagu: accompanied Eisenstein on his visits to France and Britain in 1929–30 and to Hollywood in 1930, first translator of Vsevolod Pudovkin and producer of three of Alfred Hitchcock's British films.

23 Herbert Marshall: studied with Eisenstein at the Moscow film school, State Technical School for Cinematography (GTK, later GIK), graduating in 1935; translated and edited several works by Eisenstein including *Immoral Memories* (1983); was Professor Emeritus (Performing Arts), Southern Illinois University.

24 Palmiro Togliatti: part of the Comintern Secretariat in charge of Communists fighting in the Spanish Civil War. Returned to Italy (1944) and played a key part as Party secretary in presiding over the PCI's development from a relatively small group of militants to the largest Communist organization in the West.

25 Christopher Caudwell: best known as author of *Illusion and Reality* (1937), *Studies in a Dying Culture* (1938) and *Crisis in Physics* (1939)— all published posthumously; killed in the Spanish Civil war as a member of the International Brigade on his first day of battle.

26 Pramathesh Barua: known for his Hindi films *Devdas* (1935), *Grihadaha* (1936) and *Zindagi* (1940), and Bengali film *Mukti* (1937), among many others.

27 Premchand's 'Mahajani Sabhyata': described as 'his literary will and testament', published in the last issue (September 1936) of *Hans*, edited by Premchand who died on 8 October 1936.

28 Subhash Mukhopadhyay: began as a Communist Party activist and journalist in the 1940s and developed a poetic idiom that draws on the rich suggestiveness of the everyday colloquial—an idiom that goes to the making of his equally remarkable prose.

29 Frederic Joliot-Curie: member of the French Communist Party and president of the World Peace Council; died from cancer caused by lifelong exposure to radioactivity, like his wife and co-awardee of the Nobel Prize, Irène Joliot-Curie and his mother-in-law, Marie Curie.

30 John Desmond Bernal: member of the British Communist Party, and historian of science from a Marxist perspective.

31 Hrishikesh Mukherjee: a close friend of Sen and Ghatak in his Calcutta days, moved to Bombay as editor of films, including the early films of Bimal Roy, emerging as a director with his own distinctive style, with films such as *Musafir* (1957), with story written in collaboration with Ghatak, *Anuradha* (1960), *Guddi* (1971), *Abhiman* (1973), *Mili* (1975) and *Khubsoorat* (1980).

32 Bhawal Sannyasi: Eleven years after Ramendra Narayan Roy, the 'mejokumar' or 'middle prince' of the wealthy Bhawal estate in Dhaka, now in Bangladesh, was reported dead in 1909, a sannyasi (or Hindu mendicant) appeared in Bhawal who was soon widely acclaimed to be none other than Ramendra. Finally, in 1921, he confessed to being the

mejokumar. His identity was affirmed by family members and the people of the estate, but the British government declared him an impostor. The case went to court in 1930, and hearings were held from 1933 to 1936 at the Dhaka District Court, which ruled that he was who he claimed to be. The government appealed in the High Court, which upheld the judgement in 1940. Finally, the case was heard by the Privy Council in London, which ruled in 1946 that he was indeed the rightful owner of the estate. He died a week later.

33 'The film, *Bedeni*, was initially started in 1950 with Nirmal De as director, who left it unfinished. The producer, Sunil Roy, sold his shop and mortgaged his house two years later, to raise money to finish it, with Ritwik-da, who was at one time Nirmal-da's assistant. As director, Ritwik-da rewrote the screenplay and renamed the film *Arupkatha*.' (Ketaki Dutta, in Ritwik Ghatak, *Rows and Rows of Fences*, Calcutta: Seagull Books, 2000).

34 A celebrated one-liner spoken inimitably by the comic actor Bhanu Bandyopadhyay (1920–83) in *Sadey Chuattor* (1953), also one of the first films to feature prominent Bengali actress Suchitra Sen (1931–2014).

35 Manoranjan Bhattacharya: actively involved in armed resistance against British colonial rule while still a student, subsequently becoming an actor in 1910; popularly known as 'Maharshi' after his appearance as Maharshi Valmiki in Sisir Bhaduri's play *Seeta*; founder of theatre group Bohurupee with Gangapada Basu and Sombhu Mitra.

36 *Parichay* from the 1940s and *Natun Sahitya* from the 1950s: left-wing literary monthlies.

37 Samaresh Basu: his story 'Uratiya', included in the collection *Pasharini* (1955), is the basis of both Mrinal Sen's *Genesis* (1986) and Buddhadev Dasgupta's film *Uttara* (2000). 'Esmalgar', also by Basu, included in another collection, *Akashbrishti* (1953), was filmed by Sen as part of *Calcutta 71*.

38 Nani Bhowmick: spent a large part of his life in Moscow as translator from Russian to Bengali; best known for his novel *Dhankana*.

39 Manik Bandyopadhyay: best known for *Padmanadir Majhi* (1936), made into a film by Goutam Ghose, and *Putul Naacher Itikatha* (1936).

His short story 'Atmahatyer Adhikar' (1933) was filmed by Sen for the first part of *Calcutta 71*, titled '1933'.

40 Satinath Bhaduri: gave up his position as advocate to join the Indian National Congress during the Independence movement; first recipient of the Ananda Puraskar for his novel *Jagori* (1945); best known for his *Dhonrai Charit Manas* (1949–51).

41 Banaphool: pseudonym adopted by Balaichand Mukhopadhay, one of Bengal's most celebrated literary figures. A physician with a busy medical practice, he still succeeded in turning out an impressively large number of literary works, including novels, short stories, plays, poetry, essays and autobiographical writings.

42 *Putul Naacher Itikatha* (1949), directed by Asit Bandyopadhyay with music and lyrics by Jyotirindra Maitra.

43 Jyotirindra Moitra: associated with IPTA; directed music for Ray's documentary *Rabindranath Tagore* (1961) and Ghatak's *Amar Lenin* (1970)?

44 Hemanta Mukherjee: legendary singer, composer, music director in Hindi and Bengali films; also associated with IPTA.

45 Nikhil Chakraborty: Communist Party activist, who later came to edit the journal *Mainstream* and was appointed chairman of Prasar Bharati, India's national broadcasting authority.

46 Madhabi Mukhopadhyay: Bengali actress, best remembered for her roles in *Charulata* (1964) and *Mahanagar* (1963) by Satyajit Ray, and in *Subarnarekha* (1962) by Ritwik Ghatak.

47 Bishnu Dey: eminent Bengali poet, critic and translator, one of the pioneers of modernism in Bengali poetry, committed to Marxism.

48 Bibhutibhushan Bandyopadhyay: published short stories in the literary journal *Prabashi* from the early 1920s; best known for his *Pather Panchali*, first serialized in 1928–29 and immediately recognized as a landmark in Bengali fiction, and its sequel, *Aparajito*, the two works that provided the text for Ray's *Apu Trilogy*; he also wrote *Aranyak* (1937–39) and *Anubartan* (1939).

49 Chidananda Das Gupta: with a professional background in public relations, was a founder member of the Calcutta Film Society in 1947, and was a leading film critic with several books and newspaper reviews to his

credit. Has edited *Span*, the journal of the erstwhile United States Information Service in India, and directed documentaries and feature films including *Bilatpherat* (1972) and *Amodini* (1994).

50 Narendranath Mitra: eminent Bengali novelist and short-story writer, a journalist with *Anandabazar Patrika*, the popular Bengali daily. One of his best known stories, 'Abatarnika', was made into the film *Mahanagar* by Satyajit Ray.

51 Bansi Chandragupta: part of Satyajit Ray's team of young talented artistes for *Pather Panchali*, continued to collaborate with Ray in *Aparajito*, *Jalsaghar* (1957), *Kanchanjungha* (1961), *Charulata*, *Mahanagar*, *Nayak* (1966) and *Shatranj ke Khilari* (1977), among others; also worked with Mrinal Sen in films such as *Baishey Sravan*, *Akash Kusum* and *Calcutta 71*.

52 Pseudonym of Jacques Tatischeff: began his career in the music hall; best known for portrayal of the lugubrious, pipe-smoking Monsieur Hulot, forever beset by physical mishaps and confrontations with modern technology in films such as *Les Vacances de Monsieur Hulot* (1951) and *Mon Oncle* (1958).

53 Sekhar Chatterjee: remembered for his adaptations/productions of Bertolt Brecht's plays in Bengali, his performance in the stage play *Kallol* (1965), directed by Utpal Dutt, and films such as Sen's *Icchapuran*.

54 Khwaja Ahmed Abbas: best known for films such as *Dharti ke Lal* (1946), *Anhonee* (1952), *Rahi* (1952), *Munna* (1954), *Shehr aur Swapna* (1963) and *Pardesi* (1971), an Indo-Russian co-production with V. I. Pronin as co-director.

55 This period refers to the turbulent aftermath of the armed peasant revolt known as the Naxalbari Uprising (1967), mainly led by local tribal and Communist leaders. The event became an inspiration for the so-called militant ultra-leftist Naxalite movement, carried out under the 'ideological leadership' of Mao Zedong, which spread rapidly across West Bengal and to other parts of India. Around 1969–70, the Naxalites gained a strong presence among the radical sections of the student movement in Calcutta, leading to rampant bombings and assassinations. Eventually, the West Bengal government instituted strong counter-measures that included wholesale torture and widespread extra-judicial killings.

56 Sudhendu Mukherjee: urban sociologist with the Calcutta Metropolitan Planning Organization, followed by a long spell as deputy director of the Calcutta Metropolitan Development Authority; known for his book *Under the Shadows of the Metropolis: They Are Citizens Too*, a detailed account of the pavement dwellers of Calcutta.

57 In this memorable sequence, the Naxalite protagonist, played by Dhritiman Chatterjee, already getting disillusioned with the Naxalite movement, and yet on the run from the police, learns of his mother's death, and visits his father only to be trapped and arrested by the police. But before that, his apolitical father, played with exemplary dignity and pride by Bijan Bhattacharya tells him that he had refused to sign a loyalty bond at his workplace and asks him to 'be brave'.

58 Samar Sen: associated with the All India Radio and *Hindustan Standard*, had a long spell in Moscow as translator from Russian to Bengali, and edited *Now* and *Frontier* on his return to India—both with a strong radical leftist slant.

59 *Bibar* (1965): novel by Samaresh Basu that was banned on publication by the government on charges of obscenity.

60 Nemai Ghosh: best known for his photographs of Satyajit Ray and stills for Ray's films and theatre photographs, collected in albums like *Satyajit Ray at 70* (1991), *Dramatic Moments* (2000) and *Manik-da* (2001).

61 Sushobhan Sarkar: professor at Presidency College, Calcutta, and Jadavpur University; author of *Notes on the Bengal Renaissance* (1979), a Marxist analysis of nineteenth-century Bengali culture; an influential teacher of several generations of students, many of whom were initiated to Marxist thought by Sarkar.

61 Humayun Kabir: educated in Calcutta and Oxford, taught philosophy for a number of years, before emerging as a leader of the Congress Party, and serving as minister in charge of several departments of the Indian government. Known also as poet and editor.

62 In a major turn of events, the Congress Party, which has been ruling India since Indpendence, lost the general election of 1977. In the simultaneous election to the state legislature in West Bengal, the Left Front led by the Communist Party of India (Marxist) won a landslide victory. The Left Front would continue to be in power in West Bengal for 34 years that followed, till it was voted out in 2011.

63 Land-reform movement: efforts to reform the ownership and regulation of land in rural India. After being elected to power in West Bengal in 1977, the Left Front government initiated gradual land reforms, such as Operation Barga (1978–c.85), resulting in the enumeration of and a more equitable distribution of land among landless farmers. Although controversial, Operation Barga has been considered one of the more successful attempts at land reform in the country.

64 *Taurus*: Alexander Sokurov's film on V. I. Lenin, became a point of controversy at the Calcutta Film Festival, November 2001.

65 Afsar Ahmed: major stories include 'Jalasrot, Janasrot', 'Gunaah', Jinnat Begum-er Biroho Milan'. Sen's last film *Aamar Bhuvan* [2002] is based on Ahmed's novel *Dhaan Jyotsna*.

Paradise Cafe

[I first wrote this piece a couple of days after Ritwik Ghatak's death in 1976. It has remained the same. Perhaps I have changed a word here or there, or put down something new.]

We had our little group, then. I write of a time twenty-seven years ago. Except for one of us, we were all unemployed. Relatively unencumbered, each of us busy avoiding the responsibilities we were supposed to shoulder, back home. First thing in the morning, we would get away. Crowd into a small café near the crossing at Hazra. It was a tiny room, about eight feet by twelve. A tea shop crammed with bare tables and broken chairs. Called Paradise Café. In our group, Ritwik was the tallest, the thinnest, and obviously the most daring.

Ritwik, Salil Chowdhury, Tapas Sen, Hrishikesh Mukherjee, Bansi Chandragupta, Nripen Gangopadhyay [(b. 1927), filmmaker, active member of the film society movement] and I—this was our group. Undying initiates in the thoughts and ideas of the time. Sometimes,

Bijan Bhattacharya would join us and at times, Kali Bandyopadhyay [(1920–1993), actor, involved in IPTA and Bengali theatre; played the lead role in Sen's *Nil Akasher Niche*] too. Our sessions would start at about eight and continue uninterrupted till one in the afternoon. We used to be forced out on the streets because it would be time for the shopkeeper to pull down the shutters. We would be back again, just before sunset. We would gulp innumerable cups of tea, and pooling in the resources from each other's pockets, pay off our bills. And if the times were bad, then we would just let the dues add up. And talk, talk, and lecture. A veritable fount of reasoning, arguments and conversation. Ritwik was at the core of all this activity.

What was it that we talked so much of? Day after day? That we never tired of?

What didn't we talk of? Everything under the sun was discussed across those tables. At every moment, we were completely engrossed in our debates and dissections. But despite our wide range of interests, the one question, the one argument, the one topic that we came back to, time after time, was cinema. Cinema, cinema and armed revolution. That is the time when we learned and realized how to live with our notions of cinema inexorably entangled with our notions of revolution. That is also the time when, having placed our firm trust in the Communist Party, we began to cultivate a fierce loathing towards our vapid indigenous films. Although we were not completely rational in that attitude. In that tiny room of the Paradise Café stuffed with an assortment of broken furniture, we were only too ready to build a new front. A front which would consist of cinema and revolution walking hand in hand. The one whose voice was raised the highest during those lively discussions was of course, Ritwik. The name that is on most people's lips is 'Coffee House'. How many know about Paradise Cafe! Nor could they be expected to. Perhaps because it was the haunt of outcasts and commoners. None of us had yet made a name for ourselves.

Ritwik was the most reckless amongst us. He didn't give a damn about anything. And he never had the patience to weigh the pros and cons of his actions. We were always borrowing money. Living in debt. We had to, since none of us ever had any money. We were always in debt over our tea and cigarettes. And we paid off those debts by becoming indebted elsewhere. Ritwik drank a lot of tea, but he never smoked cigarettes. He smoked bidis. In those days, bidis were three or four to a paise. Invariably, even those he couldn't pay for. Once, he owed a bidi shop eighty rupees for just his bidis! This is a prime example of his devil-may-care attitude. This is the very attitude that audiences have later perceived in *Ajantrik, Meghey Dhaka Tara, Subarnarekha*. In what he spoke of. And in what he wrote about.

When it seemed almost impossible for us to enter the realm of cinema, we decided to set up an active trade union comprising those studio workers and technicians who were not financially well off. Thus, began our expedition. We would visit the studios and the homes of the workers. Speak to them, explain to them. Try to infuse them with a sense of pride and confidence in their own strengths and powers. And all this came together, one day, when on the floors of the studio, we raised our voices collectively. And none other than the tall and thin Ritwik led that noisy procession.

One day, almost overnight, the studios were witness to a tremendous commotion. The studio owners rose up in arms against Ritwik, because the evening before, Ritwik had announced at a meeting of the studio workers, that alcohol would not be permitted within the studio premises. According to him, drinking in the studios amounted to nothing more than a despicable display of vulgarity, and it was imperative that a resolute and united protest be recorded against this practice. The owners were enraged; they claimed they had no control over the personal inclinations of people and moreover, this blanket accusation by Ritwik was unfounded and obscene. The rest of us by then were all preoccupied with Ritwik; how on earth were we supposed to tackle him! We seesawed between Ritwik and the owners. If the former saw reason the latter still saw red, and vice versa. Finally it took an incredible amount of effort to get the situation under control. But Ritwik's disgust of alcohol increasingly intensified. Although, in later years, it is this very alcohol that led to his ruin and this very alcohol that was his chief weapon of self-destruction.

That was when West Bengal and Telengana, in South India, were rocked by the turbulent forces of peoples' rebellion. On the one hand, there was the unrelenting battle fought by the rebellious masses, the farmers–labourers–middle class. And on the other, there were the oppressors with their sticks and guns and various other methods of repression and control. This was the same time when the 'Red Area' was formed at Kakdwip. And this was also the time when Ahalya, a farmer's pregnant wife, was murdered most brutally by the police. And Salil composed a poem called 'Shapath' [Pledge] in tribute to her memory and to the common's man revolutionary spirit.

All of us, within our little group, decided to run away to Kakdwip. We pledged to make a movie. A silent movie, shot on 16 mm film. We even discussed which laboratory we would use in Calcutta to secretly develop and edit it. And then, we planned to have screenings in various villages, on the sly. I wrote the screenplay. Salil named it *Jamir Ladai*. Ritwik managed to unearth a broken camera. Coincidentally, that was also the time when the European regional office of the international Communist revolution smuggled its papers into India. They were brought in with the help of two scientists of international repute who had come to attend a session of the Indian Science Congress. So they got to have their cake and eat it too. Those papers revealed that the Indian Communist revolution was heading in the wrong direction. So, along with other things, Kakdwip too was closed off. Our escape to Kakdwip thus became a redundant move. But Ritwik took the opportunity to tinker around with that camera and learned quite a bit about handling it, despite the fact that it was an ancient and rundown model. And I had my first try at writing screenplays.

We have quarrelled a lot, amongst ourselves. Then, and in later years. We have argued; there have been differences in opinion. And sometimes these differences have taken on terrifying proportions. And yet, time and circumstances have rendered us good friends again, just like we used to be.

We have behaved childishly; Ritwik, I, all of us. And I, too, have indulged this silliness to a certain extent. And been responsible for causing a distasteful incident or two. It is only later that I have realized this, and tried to return to the ease of our earlier relationship.

On 6 February, at five minutes past eleven at night, Ritwik died. We knew he would. He knew it too. On 24 December, he was released from the hospital or, rather, he forcibly discharged himself. He came to our home and I noticed that he was gasping for air. Gasping, and talking, laughing. He ate a lot. He said, 'I won't drink any more.' He also said, 'I won't live for very long now. I didn't cop it this time. Let's see.'

On that terrible night of 6 February, Ritwik didn't see me. But I was beside him as he lay there, dying. Comatose Ritwik, larger-than-life Ritwik, reckless Ritwik, heartless Ritwik, indisciplined Ritwik. Ritwik died.

Who knows, perhaps death is what ultimately saved him. The last few years of his life were like one big unfortunate accident.

Today, while watching his films, I get glimpses of certain blurred experiences which, in the days of Paradise Cafe, had become clear through Ritwik's actions. In thought, in idea—he remained always the same larger-than-life Ritwik, reckless Ritwik, heartless Ritwik, indisciplined Ritwik.

['*Ritwik o Aamra*' (*1976*). *Translated by Sunandini Banerjee.*]

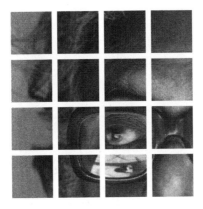

A Terrible Dearth of Dreams and Dreamers

Fourteenth of August 1947. Midnight. Jawaharlal Nehru spoke to the people of his country: 'Long years ago we made a tryst with destiny, and now the time comes when we shall redeem our pledge, not wholly and in full measure, but very substantially. At the stroke of the midnight hour, when the world sleeps, India will wake to life and freedom.'

That was the moment when a new era in history unfolded.

Nineteen sixty-three. We were nearing the sixteenth anniversary of the country's Partition and Independence, when Debesh Ray [(b. 1936), novelist, best known for *Teesta Paarer Brittanta*, an epic novel set in the foothills of the Eastern Himalayas] penned a modern young man of Calcutta as a character in one of his novels. At first sight, the young man appears to be insolent—obstinate, argumentative and obviously very intelligent. In conversation with an internationally acclaimed film director—also one of his father's friends—he commented, 'All of you are too obsessed with history. Riots, famines, the Partition, things like that. Although looking at you, it's hardly obvious.'

With an air that acquiesced the thrust and yet resisted defeat, and perhaps partly in self-defence, the gentleman replied that he had witnessed these events firsthand.

'That may be so. In fact, it must be so. But even if you hadn't seen all this, you would have still remained the same.'

'Are you trying to say that having seen all this for ourselves, we still haven't changed in the slightest?'

'Have you? The stories you tell—of war, of violence, of famine—should have scorched your faces with the flames from the funeral pyres, should have covered your very bodies with layers of ash from the burning ghats. But, look at you! Every one of you so smug and settled. So happy. Fulfilled. Your lives are complete. You live in nice houses, eat good food and your walls are hung with snapshots of your various successes. You seem to have made quite a killing out of this history you are so fond of. But we have not even that history—no wars though there are deaths, no riots though there are killings, no Partition though there are refugees, no famine though there are people dying of hunger. The events you witnessed have all found shelter under the protective folds of a particular history. But the events that we must witness daily—the deaths, the dying, the killing—on the pavements of this city or its streets or splashed across the pages of the newspapers, these have no history in which to seek refuge.'

That is, they were abandoned, unprotected, shelterless.

Sometime in August 1996, a rough draft of a story by Amalendu Chakraborty [(b. 1934), novelist and short story writer, contributed the text for Sen's *Ek Din Pratidin* and *Akaler Sandhane*] happened to come my way. This was therefore just at the beginning of the country's fiftieth year of independence. A schoolteacher, in his early thirties. Living in a village somewhere in Barddhaman. Cycling to work one morning he suddenly notices an expensive red car on the road. He moves towards it. He has no difficulty in recognizing the man who steps out of the car. It is the same film director who came to this village sixteen years ago in order to make a movie—on famine, on the search for famine. The famine of 1943 which reduced the rural areas of Bengal into nothing more than fields of corpses. That director had now come back—suddenly. The young man who had then been a teenager was now a schoolteacher, into his thirties. In these sixteen years, he has seen a lot happening around him, gone through many experiences. He starts talking to the director, now middle-aged and wiser, and takes him back to his little home. They keep talking and the conversation flows along easily. At one point, although not in a tone of complaint, he says, 'Sixteen years ago you had set out amidst undivided Bengal in search of famine and that quest had brought you to this village. What have you come for, today? Will you notice only the clothes and the food we so desperately lack? And not the dignity, the decency, the honesty?'

The man's voice throbbed with emotion; not despair but a terrible agony. Because every day was a battle for survival against an all-consuming problem for him and others like him.

He continued, in a somewhat saddened tone, 'You know, our grandfathers had Gandhi, our fathers had socialism . . . and we? What do we have?'

Although sixteen years ago, the day that the entire film crew had arrived at this village—the word had already been spread that the cinema 'babus' were coming—September 1980—I remember how an aged farmer, his body nothing more than a bundle of bones, had suddenly spoken up, almost in jest: 'The babus have come looking for famine. But here we are the famine; it is present in every pore of our beings.'

And he had burst out laughing. Guileless laughter. Therefore, these people—these half-fed hunger stricken people—had learnt to survive by virtue of their own peculiar logic. They had not the slightest iota of interest or enthusiasm in how these cinema 'babus' were trying to capture their condition so as to be able to hold it up for the rest of the world to see nor in the change this might cause in their lives, in the future. There was no reason for them to feel any different.

The history that Debesh Ray's insolent-obstinate-intelligent young man had spoken of had not yet been created when I came to Calcutta, in 1940.

I knew that the war had started in Europe in 1939 and about the Japanese attack on China. News about the Spanish Civil War had reached us too and we were aware that in that war, famous personalities—artists, authors, poets—had lent their names and support to the faction that demanded democracy. Together they had formed the 'international brigade' whose motto was 'no pasaran' ('they shall not pass'). I was familiar with snatches of these world events even before I came to the city. But my perceptions were, so long, clouded in amazement; it was only in Calcutta that the despair and terror that these happenings now invoked engulfed me. This was between 1940 and 1942. And it was in 1942 that the Quit India Movement began.

I was in Calcutta during the famine of 1943. Ever so slowly, the entire city was teeming with glimpses of Bengal whose countryside had been reduced to nothing more than vast burning grounds for the dead. And day after day, every day, I witnessed visions from hell that littered the city' s pavements. Like those around me, I was at once severely distressed and yet possessed of some inhuman strength that kept me alive. And in this way, countless people died and with them, even the figures denoting their existence were lost without a trace. And to couch it in the parlance of the young man—the obstinate and argumentative young man created by Debesh Ray—all that remained secure in history was that 'famine'. That is the 'famine' that one day found expression through the works of novelists and poets, on the canvases and in the colours of the artists, the voices of our singers and in the play *Nabanna* by the Gana Natya Sangha.

The wizened old farmer comes to mind—how he had laughed at the sight of the 'cinema babus'. How he had flaunted the famine that was in 'every pore' of their beings. A cruel taunt and a heartless jest but

I cannot deny that it was the play *Nabanna* that tempted me to take that first step in the direction of cinema. And it was not just *Nabanna* but many other influences at work as well.

Once this historically 'successful' famine was over, the political arena was in the throes of a struggle for power and a series of riots and violence broke out that would have rocked the very foundations of hell. And the next year, after the entire nation had been thrown into turmoil, Delhi witnessed the partition of the country and its freedom at midnight to the accompaniment of dazzling fanfare and celebrations. And in that festive atmosphere, the prime minister of the newly independent country spoke to his countrymen, 'At the stroke of the midnight hour . . . India will awake to life and freedom.' Only one man remained aloof from that historical moment, that moment of tremendous excitement, and spent it almost in self-willed exile. Mahatma Gandhi.

But, it must be acknowledged that the leaders of the independent nation possessed no magic wands that would wave away the problems of the people in a jiffy. So, after the festivities were over, we realized that nothing had really been solved in the mean time. In fact, new problems arose at every level of society and added to the already existing ones. Then there were the refugees from East Bengal who crossed over to this side and crowded our streets and roadways. And before our very eyes, the hustle-bustle of the city was replaced by poverty and deprivation, processions and protest marches, unrest and anger. Debates raged about whether the famine was on the decline or not—both among the common people and in the Planning Commission [an erstwhile institution of the Government of India, responsible for formulating 'Five-Year Plans']. Alongside, there were the leaders who expressed sympathy and voiced reassurances to the public and in private, thought of nothing beyond accumulating power and position. And the minute the collective patience snapped, there were incidents of random bombings and callous shootouts. In fact, at one point, Emergency had to be declared.

This was followed by an era of rapid change. Science and technology arrived in a big way. In came the globalization and the open market

—partially in some places and completely in others. Many people came into money but the famine continued in other places. It was not just the shortage of food and clothing. Like Amalendu Chakraborty's story and the thirty-something schoolteacher, there was also the deplorable absence of dignity and decency, of honesty and of tolerance, of the promise of future generations, of generosity, of intelligence. And most of all, a terrible dearth of dreams and dreamers. And amidst this all-consuming famine of men and their minds, Debesh Ray's bright-eyed young man seems to be bewildered and at a loss somehow, without any history in which to seek refuge. How am I to believe that at such a god-forsaken moment in time, the litterateurs, the artists and the performing artistes are feeling any different? That they are still steadfastly holding on to their original convictions of principle and belief?

['*Itihasher Ashray-e*'. Translated by Sunandini Banerjee.]

To Say Something New

I read Banaphool's *Bhuvan Shome* in 1959. At that time, I was busy with *Baishey Sravan*. The story impressed me. Banaphool was then at Bhagalpur. I wrote to him, explaining how, if I succeeded in procuring the finances, I would like to make a film based on his story and would therefore need to acquire the film rights. He assured me that there were no contenders for the rights and even expressed surprise over the fact that I wanted to make a film out of this particular story. He enquired about my age and then requested that I share some of my thoughts about the film. I wrote back, answering his question, and also provided him with my ideas. He wished to meet me and sent an invitation expressing the same. The visit never worked out, then. Several years later, in 1968, I finally met him just before the shooting of *Bhuvan Shome*. In the mean time, I kept on writing to him, enquiring whether the film rights of the story were still available.

After reading a story, I try to forget the sequence of events . . .
I keep in mind the elements of the story that attract me. I preserve only that part in my thoughts and then proceed slowly.

No one was willing to produce this film . . .
One person agreed, on the condition that I make Shome-saheb younger, so that some kind of relationship with the girl was possible.

Later, at the insistence of one of my friends, I submitted a draft script of seven or eight pages to the Film Finance Corporation. I made the film in Hindi with 100,000 rupees only. In those days, a film star in Bombay was paid ten times the entire cost of *Bhuvan Shome* for just acting. When *Bhuvan Shome* became popular, producers from Bombay would come to me with blank cheques. I used to stay in a rented two-room flat. I was not seduced. Calcutta, at that time, was in turmoil. Anger and unrest dominated the political scene. I started work on my next film—*Interview*.

Bhuvan Shome is a person confined within four walls . . .
Heaps of files come to him and he clears them. The telephone rings. He is either answering calls or making them. He follows all the rules and regulations to the letter. He sacked his own son because the fellow went off to see his guruji in Kashi, leaving his work undone. He is against bribery. Very reserved. What happens when this person is placed in an alien world, outside those four walls? Does he change or does he remain the same? These are some of the questions I intended to explore.

Let us see how he behaves. First, he encounters the cart driver, then the girls carrying water. Then, he encounters Suhasini Mulay. Her husband is the ticket-checker who takes a bribe. Again, there is the encounter with the birds. All these experiences steer Shome-saheb towards a situation where, instead of sacking Suhasini's husband, he transfers the man to a railway station where there are more opportunities for bribes.

In the process, Bhuvan Shome comes to understand himself, tries to fathom where he stands. Somewhere, amid the various layers of the

film, there is humour. Embedded deep within it there is an effort to discover one's self. We all know very little about ourselves; we are alien to
ourselves. After being acquainted with Suhasini, Shome-saheb learns that
her husband is Sadhu Meher. It is from that juncture, that moment of
knowledge, that his crisis begins. This is a recurrent theme in my films.

In Banaphool's story, the humour was tongue in cheek...
I deliberately created humorous and flippant situations. I made fun of
all those things that we usually consider 'improper'. At the beginning
of the film, I tried to create some imagery which would succeed in
projecting the idea of 'sonaar Bangla' ['golden Bengal']. I showed
Vivekananda, Rabindranath Tagore, Satyajit Ray; the procession of
cinema workers where Basu Chatterjee [(b. 1930), Indian filmmaker,
associated with Indian 'Middle Cinema'] and Bansi Chandragupta
participated; political processions, slogan-chanting, lathi charges,
bombs; a poster of a charter of demand pasted over a hoarding of
An Evening in Paris [1967] showing a partially clad Sharmila Tagore.
Satyajit-babu once told me, 'I thought I would use you in one of my
films.' I replied, 'You have missed the chance. You could have shown me
in the ghost-dance sequence of *Gu-Ga-Ba-Ba*' [i.e. *Goopy Gyne Bagha
Byne* (1969), a comic film by Satyajit Ray].

While I was making Bhuvan Shome, *I felt the need to break the conformist
narrative pattern...*
I realized the time had come to say something new, in a new style. The
political environment had been changing since 1967. Cinema, at that
time, in respect of structure, seemed over-saturated. So I tried to search
for a new form. *Bhuvan Shome* had an element of fun which I believe
was an extra advantage. Within its theme, a kind of social order emerged
where nothing was changeable. There were all kinds of characters and
possibilities, anything could happen. But ultimately nothing did. Thus,
with staccato movements or cuts, I designed the film in terms of attitude, in terms of situations, in terms of shot divisions and in terms of
editing. Moreover, there was the sheer delight of playing with the media.

This was not meant to be a gimmick. This was a sort of deconstruction of forms. Rammohan, of Bombay, was an expert in animation and I enlisted his advice.

Bhuvan Shome was an ornithologist. To emphasize this aspect, animated birds were shown flying around his head. Further, the opening and closing of files, swinging of doors, telephone calls, were also animated. This use of animation was an experiment yet to be tried at that time. I used mask shots to express the thoughts of Bhuvan Shome. I did not feel any difficulty transcending from this film to *Interview* though there was a major difference between the subjects. My efforts and objectives in these two films were similar. Who and what I am today is merely an extension of who and what I used to be. In fact, time is my most exacting mentor. I am always chased by my own time. I cannot escape it.

I believe in ambiguity . . .

Either this or that could have happened. Life itself is uncertain and inconclusive. Then why should I make a creation conclusive? Thus, all my films are open-ended. Even when I was making *Bhuvan Shome,* I was not sure of what would ultimately happen to Bhuvan Shome.

It was never my intention to tame a bureaucrat . . .

On the contrary, I wanted to punish him by paying him back in his own coin. I never tried to make Shome-saheb a bureaucrat in totality nor 'correct' at any point of time. I tried to outwit him, bring him to a crisis.

The film was popular and most of the spectators were sympathetic to Shome-saheb. The audience generally possesses a few stock responses because it is habituated to the structure of popular cinema. The viewers are convinced that circumstances within the film will ultimately transform a 'bad' person into a 'good' one. This is merely a kind of wish fulfilment. There is no difficulty in maintaining this status quo, however, nor in thinking that everything should be left just the way it is.

European audiences considered Bhuvan Shome *my most erotic film . . .*

There were some erotic undertones in the film, but those were not my primary objective. There was a complexity in Bhuvan Shome's character and temperament and I tried to foreground that element. He was a widower and a moralist; he stared at women and yet, almost immediately, averted his gaze. In his office, he aims his gun at a target but his attention is diverted instead by the women with their pots of water. Again, in the bird-hunting scene, when Suhasini puts her hand gently on Shomesaheb's shoulder, he shivers and steals a glance at her. While we were shooting, Suhasini enquired about the relationship being just a father–daughter one. Was there perhaps more to it than that? I would like to say that this element was only superficial and had no bearing on the real issues which I tried to address in the film.

When Shome arrived in an alien world, I arrived there with him . . .
We were shooting the film at Saurashtra, a location about sixty kilometres away from Bhabnagar. We were sitting on the sands. There were a group of girls, a little distance away. Earthen pots balanced on their heads, they were fetching water, singing as they went about their work. We were so enthralled by them that we asked the locals accompanying us to ask them if we could record their song. They began by refusing our request and finally, agreed only halfheartedly and sang in chorus for us, moving away quickly the moment they were through. But when we played back the recording, they listened, almost hypnotized. They had never experienced anything like this. They were hearing their own voices from a machine. Their expressions prompted the realization that perhaps this was the first time that they were being recognized as individual entities.

The brother of the Raja of Bhabnagar, an ornithologist and a member of the Swatantra Party [a libertarian political party that existed from 1959 to 1974], helped us a lot. He told us about the flamingos and how, between twelve and twelve-thirty in the afternoon, they would come to feed at a spot approximately ten kilometres from Bhabnagar and then fly to a lake four kilometres away. We went to shoot this sight. There were so many of them that Mahajan, his eyes fixed on the lens, exclaimed, 'I cannot see anything'. I told him to shoot whatever was possible. It was an unbelievably beautiful scene. You must have seen it in the film. We were passing the sand dunes in order to follow the flight of the birds with our camera when Utpal pointed out a dilapidated house with a staircase going up to the first floor. A small house with a verandah. Beautiful. The sea, where the birds landed, was nearby. The Raja of Bhabnagar used to come here with his queen in the summer. The chowkidar said that the king no longer visited, and so, he received no pay. The house was now referred to as a 'bhoot-bungalow'. A haunted house. I went up the stairs alone. The chowkidar pointed to a large window. He spoke of a swing which, once, hung before it and on which the king and the queen would sit together. The king would narrate the stories of tigers-lions-ghosts, and after some time, the queen would fall asleep. This was exactly how I arranged the shots with Utpal and Suhasini. When Suhasini showed Utpal the house, he exclaimed, 'Fantastic!'

There was a shot where Suhasini was describing the story of the queen. Suddenly she exclaimed, 'Mrinal-da, look!' It was an unbelievable sight. Flocks of birds were descending over the sea. Mahajan said, 'The shot is ruined.' 'Nothing has happened,' I explained. 'She spoke while moving her face away.' I kept that shot aside. While dubbing, I made her say, 'Dekho! Dekho!' ['Look! Look!']. You have seen this in the film too.

One day, Suhasini's elder sister was singing at the breakfast table . . . 'Ghutacha . . . Ghutacha . . . '—a wedding song about the relationship between the bride and her sister-in-law. I used the song in the film, when Shome-saheb came back to Suhasini to return the bird. I usually improvised in this fashion. Not only did I do this in *Bhuvan Shome*, but in my other films also.

[*As told to Siladitya Sen. Originally appeared as 'Blank Cheques from Bombay Couldn't Seduce Me' in the* Asian Age, *23 December 1995.*]

An Old Letter

Who can escape a feeling of emptiness? A sense of void, so to speak? I, for one, cannot.

I do pass through harsh times, harsh and dry, when my brain refuses to work reasonably and I begin to lose the faculty of thought. A time of crisis which I encounter periodically between one film and the next, between completing one and looking for another, when I realize that finding a subject or a theme to work on is much more difficult than organizing financial backing. Failing to be inspired by anything in and around me, I seek a temporary escape from this state and switch on the television—CBI [Central Bureau of Investigation] throwing further light on the security scam, on Bofors, more on the Ayodhya construction[1] and a lot more from Parliament. Not of much consequence to me, when, to pull myself out of this irrepressible ennui, I look for something else, something which, even if for the time being, will keep my eyes glued to the screen—Wimbledon or, say, the French Open or a football tournament, but never ever a ring with boxers locked in savage fury or a wrestlers' bout or, for that matter, a group of riotous rugby players chasing opponents. Nothing, nothing of that kind. And then I discover I am sitting motionless before the screen, thinking of nothing, conscious of no inclination, all because of the dreary emptiness overpowering me. I move away to my writing desk, I sit in the chair, type out a couple of letters, not all that important or obligatory, put them aside, look around, ransack old files, pull out old papers and old ideas, all clumsily put together, some rejected, some as reserves or once written for publication. Or, who knows, even to record my instant reactions to things which, in the past, might have shaken me in small or large measure. And then, having journeyed into the past rather dispassionately, I come away to a bookshelf, stand before the books, leaf through a few, not out of any necessity though, and finally choose one, randomly. I just lie down on the bed, read a page or, at the most, a chapter, without applying my mind to the text, and then, all of a sudden, rush to the corner where my press clippings are carelessly dumped. They lie in a heap, in a state of incredible confusion, and I look for one, then another, and another, and so on and on until, as my eyes grow weary, I begin to fear there is no way out, no way . . .

Once, not so long ago, in a desperate bid to shake off this terrifying emptiness, I got out of bed in the middle of the night, walked over to my reading room, switched on the light and began to pace up and down. Then, getting more desperate, I pulled out a suitcase, ancient and battered, hidden, as it were, under a cot. I uncovered all sorts of rejected material and ransacked heaps of papers, periodicals, letters thrust into the corners, letters from a host of known and unknown people, not all of them worthy of preservation. In the process, I came across an old letter, in my own handwriting, written long ago to my wife. Written, as I see now, with care, but never posted or delivered through messenger, for reasons I cannot recall.

It was written from Somrabazar, a village, roughly three hours drive from Calcutta. There, in September–October 1980, my unit and I had based ourselves in an old feudal mansion while shooting my film *Akaler Sandhane*.

The letter brought me back to sanity.

Akaler Sandhane is a film within a film. On 7 September 1980, a film unit invades a village to make a feature film about the Bengal Famine of 1943 which, during the Second World War, killed millions of people in undivided Bengal. Those millions simply starved to death. The unit, in the film, consisting of technicians, workers and actors, stays in an old feudal mansion—almost a ruin—inhabited by an aged impoverished couple. The husband, a descendant of the feudal family, now ailing and, in fact, paralysed, and his charming wife. The film focuses on the continuous interaction between an epoch that is now part of history and the present that the film unit and the villagers live in. It was to be made up of all this—the Famine of 1943, the hunger, the starvation and the history of that famine effortlessly coexisting with our lives today.

My wife was also the creator of one of the most important characters in the film. The letter is, naturally, filled with talk of acting, weather conditions, the filmscript. Entangled with these details is another story. About the making of another one of my films—*Baishey Sravan*. Made twenty years before *Akaler Sandhane*. That film too was shot in a zamindar's house, dilapidated and derelict, about thirty kilometres from Barddhaman. In Mankor.

The letter, accidentally rescued from heaps of waste paper, in the middle of a dreary night, read thus:

September 24/1980
Camp: Somrabazar
11:30 p.m.

Dear Geeta:

Purgative, laxative and a deep annoyance at the bourgeoise: that was my week, wrote a famous French intellectual to a friend of his. That was a long time ago, sometime in the nineteenth century.

These words suddenly came to mind. And that is why today, while you prepare to go to bed and Babu and Nisha are perhaps already asleep, some new words come to mind quite easily. Heat, dust and a deep annoyance at the mosquitoes: that was our fortnight. That is what I write to you now.

Worked till 10.15 tonight. Started the day with the sunrise. The clouds were scattered and kept hindering our light. And this caused repeated interruptions in our work. What suffered most was our attempt at an uninterrupted shot for all of 4 minutes 45 seconds. Poltu was given the responsibility of wearing a pair of dark glasses and staring at the sun continuously. Everyone was ready, everything was set. Just waiting for me to begin. And I, in turn, was waiting for a green signal from Pontu. The minute he signalled to me, I yelled, 'Start!' and we were well into the shot. Almost thirty to forty seconds into it. Sometimes one and a half minutes or two, or once we had even managed to go up to four. And then, Poltu would suddenly let out a yell from his post. 'Cut!' Ruined! Almost out of nowhere, a tiny scrap of cloud would be courageously charging across the sparklingly clear sky with no other purpose in mind than to ruin our light. Eight takes were NGs out of which two were full takes. The producer's agent insisted that in view of frequent fluctuations of light, I should break up the shot. I asked him to make himself scarce. He did so, grudgingly. Finally, the shot was completed to some degree. The last take, take 10, was OK, perfect, the movement of the camera and of the characters were perfectly synchronized, well orchestrated, the performances of the actors excellent and the sun shone brightly. By then, all of us were exhausted, but happy. The only glum face belonged to the producer's assistant, primarily in charge of finances. I told him, 'Why don't you splash some water on your face and freshen up? Then come join us.'

Do you remember Mankor? And those unparalleled ruins of the zamindar's house? Last night I dreamt of that broken 'rajbari'. In my dream, I saw that old man—paralyzed and only half alive. It's with him at the back of my mind that I've been creating that 'husband' character

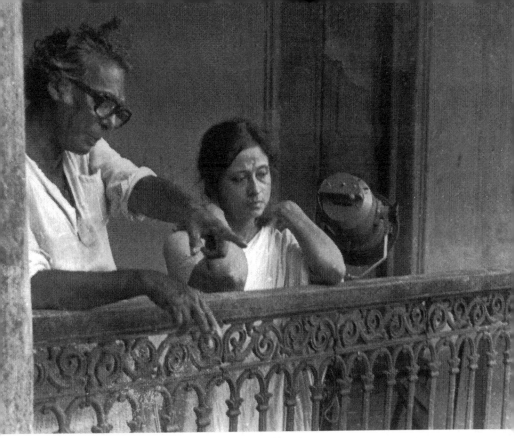

Mrinal Sen directs Geeta Sen in *Akaler Sandhane* (1980).

of yours. I saw him stand up. With an expression of absolute terror on his face. Staring at me. After a while, he asked me, '*Ke tumi, baba?*' ['Who are you, my child?'] And that's where the dream ended. And I woke up.

Strange! The old man, the entire ambience of that ruined house—after twenty years, it all came back to me so clearly. Perhaps . . . why perhaps . . . I am certain that the old man is no longer alive. Just thinking about it makes a shiver run down my spine!

I thought of a new sequence first thing in the morning, as soon as I woke up. In the way that I am wont to do, midway through the filming. All of a sudden. Thinking up something that is not there in the script. I am improvising a lot here. The sequence was something like this:

The old men of the village have all gathered before the zamindar's house. They have come for a last look at your paralytic 'husband' who has

Mrinal Sen directs Dhritiman Chatterjee in *Akaler Sandhane* (1980).

just died, the last descendant of a once-powerful feudal estate. There, they strike up a conversation with the film unit. Their talk is all about the last descendant of the zamindar, your dead 'husband'. They chat. Smita, 'the actress', suddenly appears. Ever since your 'husband' died last night, she has been spending all her time with you, 'the wife'. She walks up to the production manager and says, 'Jayanta-da, the lady's insistent. She's refusing to let go of her husband's body until her daughter comes home, from her in-laws'. She's crying a lot. Keeps saying, "Let her come and see her father just this one more time." What do you think we should do?'

The 'director' of the unit—Dhritiman—asks the villagers, 'Where is her in-laws' place?'

The villagers present say, 'It's quite a long way off. At least sixty or seventy miles.'

'Are the roads motorable?'

134

'Yes, yes. Although not as good as the city.'

The director steps forward and says, 'Give us one of your men, to show us the way. We can spare one of our cars. What do you think, Jayanta-da?'

'Yes, yes.'

The sequence, as improvised, was shot beautifully after breakfast. We made up the dialogues as we went along. And the movements. The whole affair went off rather well.

You know, last night's dream caused a miracle. I remembered Mankor, and a lot of things about *Baishey Sravan*, from twenty years ago. I remembered that day—an overcast morning. We were shooting in the front yard of the broken-down rajbari. Suddenly I noticed one of the owners of the house. Dulal Kabiraj. A man weighed down with the burden of impoverishment. Running about frantically. I went up to him and asked him, 'What's the matter?' Dulal-babu said, 'I need a cycle rickshaw.' 'What for?' he replied, 'To go to the hospital. My wife is in labour. She needs to be moved immediately to hospital'.

'How far is the hospital?' I asked.

'It's at Panagarh, fourteen kilometres away'.

'To Panagarh by cycle-rickshaw!' I exclaimed.

I asked him not to worry, had a word with my production manager and immediately packed off the pregnant lady along with her husband to hospital in one of our cars.

This incident that took place twenty years ago helped me to build the sequence shot this morning: the old lady (meaning you) begging for the girl to come, sparing a production car to fetch her et al. How spontaneous! How close to life! How compassionate! How easily experience metamorphosed into art. No end to surprises when you make your film! Autobiographical? Yes, it is, in bits. The whole thing will never cease to amaze me.

Now, as I write to you, I am struck by a thought. The day Smita comes to meet you, and walks into your room, and your half-dead paralytic husband is lying there on the bed, then if you say, 'You know, I am the only one who can understand what he is trying to say. No one else can, not even my daughter.' These words will do well as your lines, won't they? But believe me, these aren't my words. They have been borrowed. They were spoken by that lady, in Mankor. It was to me that she said them, when she took me to her husband. The man, lying there, half dead in a room where the light was half shadow. Those were the very words she spoke to me. 'You know *baba*, I am the only one who can understand what he is trying to say.'

Last night in my dream, that very husband spoke to me clearly and asked me, 'Who are you, *baba*?'

Some time next week, you'll have to come here. Your 'husband's' pallbearers will have returned after cremating his body. Then two widows from the village will take you to the ghats of the old 'rajbari'. There, they will bathe you, break your shankhas [conch bracelets worn by married women], wipe away your shindur [vermilion, also symbolic of married life]. A horrifying sight. Be prepared.

The scene of your husband's 'death', of course, will be shot in the studio, back in Calcutta. There was no difficulty in shooting it here. After all, when everything else happened here, and went off well, why not that too? It's possible yes, but I am a little uneasy with the idea. The few families still staying in that house, especially the elders, will have to see a death taking place, as it were, in one of their very own rooms. Even though it will all be make-believe, I am uncomfortable at the prospect. And what may be passing through the minds of the elders as they witness this. So, let such 'unholy practices' take place at Arora Studios. The man will die ten times over and ten times over shall you weep over his body. There will be nothing for anyone to say or think.

Keep well.

Yours ever,

Mrinal Sen.

Postscript: Once—and once only—I tried a mosquito net. I felt suffocated and threw it away and have since been applying ointment all over my body. When you come next week, bring a few more tubes.

[*Edited version of 'Somrajabajar Thekey Geeta Sen-ke' (translated by Sunandini Banerjee) and 'The Forgotten Letter', originally published in the* Statesman, Festival, *1992.*]

Note

1 '[T]the security scam, on Bofors, more on the Ayodhya construction': the contentious political issues in early 1990s India. In 1992, exploiting several loopholes in the banking system, a stockbroker named Harshad Mehta and his associates siphoned off billions of dollars from inter-bank transactions; when exposed, this came to be known as the security scam, for which Mehta was tried in courts for over nine years until he died. The Bofors scandal occurred during the 1980s and 90s, implicating the Indian prime minister, Rajiv Gandhi, and several other members of the Indian and Swedish governments who were accused of receiving kickbacks from Swedish arms-manufacturer Bofors AB for winning a bid to supply howitzers to the Indian armed forces. The Ayodhya dispute revolves around the construction of a Hindu temple at the site of a destroyed mosque, a site considered by many Hindus to be the birthplace of Lord Rama.

Interview, 1981

Q. Many people think that, given the social and political environment in India, it is impossible to make political films. In this regard, do you make political films or films about politics?

A. I make films which have something to do with the political situation and involve political characters, but I have also made films which do not have a direct political relevance. In all of them, however, I have always tried to maintain a social, political, and economic perspective. I am a social animal, and as such I react to the things around me—I can't escape their social and political implications. When I make a film on the relationship between a man and a woman, I try to understand the relationship in a larger context. [In] *Ek Din Pratidin* [...] although the camera seldom goes outside the home, the film has something to do with the social, political, and moral constraints which determine our social behaviour and condition our daily living.

I don't agree with people who say that you can't make a political film. It is true that censorship will not allow you to make subversive films but, then, all political films are not necessarily subversive. For a film to be termed political it is important to keep a sociopolitical perspective. The mere presentation of an MLA [Member or Legislative Assembly of a state in India] wearing a Gandhi cap and speaking funnily does not make a film political. It is the attitude which determines things.

Q. Some filmmakers argue that the nature of Indian cinema is such that you can only talk about political problems in allegory, that filmmakers can only go so far. Are you restrained from being political in your filmmaking by the environment, or by the limitations you impose upon yourself?

A. Sometimes it is difficult for me to do the right thing because of the official rules imposed on me. It is up to me, however, to find a way to either circumvent or work within the rules, which are often very stupid. I don't see why I should make films clandestinely, or show and discuss them clandestinely, as has happened in Latin American countries. Attending such clandestine screenings, however, involves a certain amount of risk. Only those who are already politically engaged can take this risk. A large number of people, with whom you also want to share your ideas, can't see your films. That's why it is important, at least in India, for films to be shown publicly.

Our role is twofold. On one hand, we have to fight the bureaucracy and the courts which restrain us, which inhibit us from doing things the way we should. On the other, we have to be pragmatic, to pretend to work within the existing framework for what we want to achieve.

A fine example of what I am talking about is the film *Aakrosh* [1980] by Govind Nihalani [(b. 1940), director and screenwriter well known for making socially relevant films]. On the surface, the film is about the tribal community and their paradoxical social role. Underneath, the film is an examination of the crisis of a middle-class intellectual and, perhaps more significantly, a searing attack on the Indian system of jurisprudence. After a point, you realize that the tribal community could very well be a plot device, because the film is a bitter criticism of how the Indian legal system operates. The film makes a very significant political point, and it does so by keeping within the framework of the stupid censorship rules.

Q. Nonetheless, many argue that we over-value the importance of film in the Indian context. They say that the establishment doesn't really care, and, furthermore, it knows that you can't be effective. Of course, the argument continues, if you can't affect the establishment and bring about change, why bother? Do you agree with this kind of thinking?

A. Film, like literature and other media, has a certain role in our society. It creates a certain climate. It may also provoke a certain kind of debate. My job is to provide information from a point of view which is clearly not neutral. In the process, I try to involve you as a spectator in something dynamic, something different.

I don't agree with Godard when he says that the cinema is a gun. That is too romantic an expression. You can't topple a government or a system by making one [*Battleship*] *Potemkin*. You can't do that with ten *Potemkin*s. All you can do is create an environment in which you can discuss a society that is growing undemocratic, fascistic.

Q. But effective filmmaking also requires an audience. Are the films reaching audiences?

A. We have been getting audiences but not in large enough numbers to satisfy the commercial industry types. What we have to do—and this is a prescription not just for us in India—is to make films at a very low cost. We have to show the monopolists who claim that filmmaking is a capital-intensive business and their monopoly, that filmmaking is everybody's business and nobody's monopoly. We have to think in terms of economics—getting the minority spectator who is interested in such films and then building a larger audience base.

Q. How about rural audiences? Has New Cinema reached rural areas?

A. No, and there is a strange duality at work in the rural areas, one that seeks political change but rejects political entertainment. In a particular area in Bengal dominated by poor, landless farmers, they voted a Communist candidate to Parliament. The margin was overwhelming. But in the same area, where most films never run for more than a week at a time, they thronged to see a film about a miracle man who triumphs over a scientist. The farmers in the film wanted rain but there was no technology to bring rain. So they went to a miracle man who not only helped bring rain but also everything else necessary for a good crop. The film ran for eight weeks in this area. This is a situation difficult to fight—an audience which votes for a man who will be fighting for change, for land reform, but at the same time will flock to a film which accents a mistrust in technology and faith in miracles. This is the kind of dichotomy we suffer from and have to fight.

Q. Talking of rural society, your latest film, *Akaler Sandhane*, is about filmmakers who go to a village to recreate the Bengal Famine of 1943. In the process, they totally disrupt the rural landscape. How much of this is a criticism of the rampant tendency amongst Indian filmmakers to make films about rural society, and how much is just self-examination?

A. The film tries to work on many levels. It tries to suggest that the Famine of 1943, which killed five million people in one year, continues. The conditions which contributed to that famine are just as valid today. But something else happens when the filmmaker walks into the village attempting to recreate the past. He is not prepared for the manner in which the past becomes the present. As long as the reality can be kept at a distance, for the purpose of filming, as a kind of museum piece, he is fine, he feels safe. But at the moment the past becomes the present, the contemporary reality, he tries to run away.

Q. Isn't there a tendency amongst many of the new filmmakers to go into the villages and shoot their images of rural society without any relationship to present reality?

A. Yes, but I don't want to make the mistake of walking into someone else's world and being misunderstood. So I take the burden upon myself to criticize myself—something I have tried to do all my life. Many of our directors have found a very favourable and fertile ground for their films in rural areas. They invade the villages with their cameras. Indeed, there are some very important directors who have made films on the Famine of 1943. So, my comments apply to them as well as to my own film on the famine, *Baishay Sravan*, which I made in 1960.

Q. When people talk about Indian cinema, they talk about three distinct influences: the traditional cinema; the cinema of Satyajit Ray; and the New Cinema of filmmakers such as yourself, filmmakers growing under Ray's shadow. Is the distinction accurate?

A. The largest body of cinema in India is still the traditional cinema, a cinema that has nothing to do with art or Indian reality. Then came Satyajit Ray as a great revolutionary figure. Not that there were no flashes before Ray, there were, but they weren't part of any whole, and were not strong enough to evolve into a movement. Ray was the logical extension of a certain awareness which was developing in various media.

Those of us who are part of the New Cinema have been categorized as people developing under the shadow of Satyajit Ray. But by now, Ray has become a demagogue, a sort of holy ghost, and, as you are aware, a ghost doesn't cast a shadow. Frankly, very few of us have grown under Ray's shadow. I, for one, was very much inspired by the fact that his films became successes all over the world, but I have my own view of reality which is quite different from Ray's. That's true for others, as well. We all have our own ideas, our own attitudes towards cinema and to the world.

Q. How do you and others in the New Cinema view film?

A. I have always felt that the cinema, unlike any other art form, is constantly evolving. The vocabulary is enlarging, multiplying at a more rapid pace than in any other art form. My business has been to see how I can keep pace with my own time, as well as catch up with the rest of the world. I started with traditional narratives but, as I came into contact with more cinema, I realized films could go beyond the traditional narrative form. Imagine, as far back as the 1930s, Eisenstein thought of making [Karl Marx's] *Capital* into a film.

In *Akaler Sandhane*, I tried to bring together all my feelings about film. At the same time, I have tried to get away from painting pretty pictures—pictures of poverty, pictures of rural life. It is very important for me to make things look un-pretty, to keep the rough edges. I don't want to remain a perfectionist or a traditionalist. That's not my intent. My intention is to communicate as effectively as I can, to provoke the audience. The filmmaker has to be an agent provocateur—one who disturbs the spectator and moves him to action.

More recently, however, I have been thinking of films which draw their strength from normal events, events which don't have any particularly exciting quality, but which are part of everyone's daily existence. That's what I have attempted to do in my latest film, *Chalchitra*. I feel that the more we try to find a dramatic cohesion of incidents in life, the more we realize that life is built of non-events. Why shouldn't we make a film about that?

Geeta Sen and Anjan Dutt in *Chalchitra* (1981).

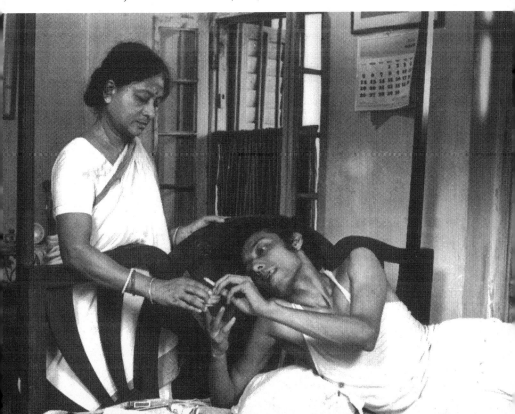

Q. But isn't this attitude the major problem with many filmmakers within the new cinema—making films that are personally interesting to the filmmaker, but of minimal concern to the filmgoer? Are you trying to find ways to bridge the gap between your own perceptions and those of the audience?

A. How do I know the expectations of a film audience unless I experiment? My method is one of trial and error. The Indian audience was once used to a certain kind of film, with songs, dances, and trite stories. Then Ray came along and proved his kind of film could also be popular. When I say that I am basing my film on non-events in a kind of non-dramatic structure, I am really only doing what the neorealists did. Indeed. Neorealism is to my mind a continuing phenomenon. So why not continue to use it? If you build incidents on inconsequential details—or those which appear to be inconsequential—and people feel enthused, if they acquire a sense of belonging and if they can define themselves with the details you provide, it's worth it. The best way to serve your audience is to serve your own conscience.

[*Interviewed by Udayan Gupta. Originally appeared as 'New Visions in Indian Cinema' in* Cineaste, *1981.*]

My Son and I

Many years ago, late one summer afternoon. My five-year old son and I were sitting in a public square in south Calcutta. It was a cloudy day; the sky overcast. A kalbaisakhi—a raging nor'wester in which the furious wind unsettles all that is calm and quiet until it blurs the horizon and subsides soon after—was imminent. Suddenly, the stormy wind was heralded by a terrifying flash of lightning. My son stared at the sky, amazed. So did I, frightened. It was tremendous in scale, stretching from one end of the northern horizon to the other. My five-year-old son turned to me and exclaimed, '70 mm screen!'

I was taken aback, yet hugely intrigued.

My grandfather, at the same age as my son, would have compared a similar streak of lightning to perhaps a huge mythical bird spreading its vast wings.

But now, with science and technology dominating the social and cultural scene, my son used an expression that came naturally to him and which belonged essentially to the technological world. Interestingly, he had been exposed to the 70 mm screen in a city theatre only a week ago. Which explains the immediate association arising out of that newly acquired experience—an expression which is no nation's exclusive possession. It was obviously a new addition to his vocabulary, and had no barrier—national, regional or linguistic. My son and I, both incorruptibly Indian, found it absolutely valid at the time, like anyone anywhere else in the world would. At the instant of my son's exclamation, I realized that the world had indeed come to our doorstep.

At the same time, I also felt that in my long career as a communicator, I had arrived at the crossroads. I will explain why . . .

Let us consider the case of a farmer boy in any village of India who has heard of cinema, has watched perhaps a few films, and obviously has no concept of the 70 mm screen. My son's spontaneous statement about the flash of lightning would carry absolutely no meaning for him. In other words, this particular expression, which defies all conceivable national, regional and linguistic barriers, cannot be accommodated in his vocabulary. It's the same for all those who, so far, have not been privileged with encounters of my son's kind. And the farmer boy's class throughout the country far outnumbers the privileged minority to which my son belongs.

So, I think I am right in saying that this vast majority living in rural India, when faced with a similar natural phenomenon, would either be amazed like my son or frightened like myself, but would, understandably, use an equally expressive word or phrase handed down to them by their predecessors. They could liken it to Jatayu or Garuda, both Hindu mythical birds, or Jibrail, Allah's messenger. And the picture must remain more or less the same even to this day. The mushrooming of video parlours in the villages and small towns must have introduced quite a few more words to the rural vocabulary. But '70 mm screen', I am afraid, is yet to find a place!

What I am trying to say here concerns neither the lightning, nor the 70 mm screen, nor, for that matter, the mushrooming growth of video parlours. I am trying to focus on the communication gap that exists and has been steadily widening between the urban and the rural clientele that my community—the communicators—addresses.

My question is a very vital one: whom do I, the communicator, address? The metropolitan variety or the rural masses? Which vocabulary, and going further, which wavelength, as a necessary adjunct, do I choose? Should I, therefore, try for the ideal middle path—both in terms of words and images, and in terms of attitudes? In other words, do I have no choice but to compromise?

All these are likely to raise diverse questions on the aesthetic front, none of which can be resolved easily. Can such a debate lead to any tangible conclusion? I wonder.

As a communicator, I need to and I must cultivate a wider communication area. But given the situation, how do I go about it?

Certainly not by taking the middle path. Not by compromising either. Does it, then, mean that I have no choice but to thrust a metropolitan culture onto the rural mind? Is that possible? Adopting a strictly moral world-view, do I have the right to be party to the ruthless business of eclipsing the sky and space and all that which offers life to the villagers?

I cannot. Which is why I say, as I move to an aesthetic position derived from the moral, the matter is a continuing debate assuring no easy solution.

In this context, I am tempted to quote a fascinating comment of Rabindranath Tagore's. How about, he had written musingly, sending a champion of the rural masses to invade a village with the sole intention of reading out to them a passage from Kalidas' *Meghadoot*? How long, Tagore doubts, will they suffer such torture? He suspects that it is quite possible that the listeners will treat this ordeal as a cognizable criminal offence. In his own language, with his inimitable sense of humour, he says, 'I don't know what category of poets Kalidas falls in, but as a poet he is praised by everyone. I ask you, if one gathers villagers together and subjects them to Kalidas, then can one not be charged under the Indian

(ABOVE) On location while shooting *Mrigaya* (1976); (BELOW) Mamata Shankar and Mithun Chakrabarty in *Mrigaya*.

Penal Code? If, in the time of Kalidas, the counsel of the masses over-threw Vikramaditya and forced Kalidas to produce assigned pieces, then would time have put up with that poetry?'

Allow me to digress in order to narrate an incident. It does not focus on the communication gap but relates directly to an issue that demands our immediate attention.

In the mid-1970s, I was filming a fictional work featuring tribals. This was something I had never done before. The village we selected was sparsely populated and surrounded by hills and forests. It had no electricity and was situated a kilometre away from a barrage.

My entire unit and I reached the location five days before the shoot. I thought it necessary for all of us to familiarize ourselves with the people and the place since we were planning to work there for at least a month. Everyone was left to themselves. My main actor, however, was assigned a very special task—to take lessons on archery from the young tribals. And before we began shooting, he assured me that he had been adequately trained and hence, I could proceed without any worries.

We started shooting on a certain day. The first shot was located near a bush, alongside a waterfall. The shot was that of my main character, a tribal and accomplished archer, aiming his arrow at an antelope hiding behind the bush. My actor adopted the perfect stance and remained intense before releasing the arrow. The moment I raised my finger—and that was the indication—the 'archer' released his arrow and I shouted 'Cut!' It was an excellent performance and an excellent shot. 'Great!' I said.

'No, it is not,' said a tribal who had been watching from a short distance away. 'It is all wrong,' he said in disgust. He turned to leave and I asked one of my unit members to bring him to me. He came to me, visibly agitated, and said, 'Your man should not have used his thumb to hold the end of the arrow.' When I asked why not, the man explained through gestures that the edge of the arrow should have been placed between the forefinger and the middle finger. 'Why not the thumb?' I asked. He almost shouted at me and said, 'Are we not the children of

Ekalavya?'[1] I was stunned. I realized then how strong and deep the roots of tradition were. How, through centuries, the ancient story of the dedicated Ekalavya and the cunning Dronacharya had been handed down to these unlettered Santhals, inhabitants of a village deep in the heart of Bihar. I was overwhelmed. But that which was most shocking and incredibly revealing about this entire episode struck me a year later.

I was in Paris at that time. At an informal get-together where I was doing most of the talking, I narrated the story of my days with the tribals and included the bit about the Mahabharata story involving Ekalavya and Dronacharya. When, at last, I told them about the connection made by an illiterate tribal in a backward village with an age-old myth, most of my listeners responded enthusiastically. But an acquaintance of mine, born of an African mother and a French father, came out with a shattering truth. He was somewhat of a professional archer as well and appeared to know absolutely everything about archery. From a position, which neither my friends nor I could contest, he said that my Ekalavya–Dronacharya story about the loss of the thumb was highly suspect. Archers all over the world including the African tribals and Australian aborigines, he asked me to note, would never use their thumbs. He added, 'Go anywhere, in any part of the world, even to the interiors of the inaccessible tribal belts, and you will see the archers placing the edge of the arrow between the index and middle fingers.' And it was from him that I learnt that anybody found using their thumb at archery could be safely treated as a pretender.

This was an eye-opener as far as I was concerned. To my utter surprise, I realized how a myth having no bearing on the basics of archery had become part of our culture through the Mahabharata. And nobody, neither our predecessors nor our contemporary academics, ever questioned it. Based on what I have just described, could I then arrive at a drastic conclusion that myths unrelated to life and reality must not be allowed to shape our history and tradition?

Here, again, I cite another example—another anecdote—which made me sit up. What baffled me and made me wonder was how a twenty-year-old tribal boy of the same village, unlettered and uninitiated, reacted splendidly to a provocative question by me.

It was a festive occasion and the day before the villagers began ploughing their fields. They offered services to their gods and sacrificed one pig, just one, by way of propitiation for they could not afford any more. They performed their rituals, drank aplenty and began to dance. With the first rains of the season, village women of all ages formed a circle in the middle of a sprawling courtyard and danced in celebration. It was a kind of gentle 'twist' consisting of graceful pelvic movements. Hypothetically, the land turned fertile with the first rains or, in other words, the land attained puberty. The movements of the dance were such that they also served as a kind of exercise ensuring easy childbirth. This, as an anthropologist friend pointed out to me later, indicated the existence of a fertility cult that has its roots in antiquity.

As the celebrating intensified, the men and women went wild. Having worked for a couple of hours with great difficulty, we decided to pack up for the day and watch the celebrations instead. My technicians and actors were left to themselves. I sat with a group of people and, at a certain point, asked them if they would be expecting a bountiful crop that year. The old man of the village, completely drunk by then, looked from me to the sky and then back to me. Shook his head and replied briefly, 'No.' I feigned innocence and asked, 'You cannot propitiate the gods by sacrificing just one pig, can you?' The old man agreed. Right at that moment, a young boy, hardly twenty, looked up at me and said sardonically, 'To propitiate the gods, we do not have to look upwards these days. All we need to do is to cross the hills and the barrage and meet the gods sitting immaculately dressed in the irrigation office and pray. If only they are pleased,' the boy gave a mischievous smile, 'grace will befall us and water and fertilizer will be released.'

I was shaken and amazed. So here, in a tribal village—primitive to a large extent—without even a primary school, NGOs or political parties invading the scene, a young boy with no education identified his gods as those seated not in heaven but at the irrigation office. Splendid!

I am not ashamed to confess that I am neither a research scholar nor an academic. It's a pity. Had I been professionally equipped, I would have rushed to that village immediately on my return from Paris. I would have located that particular boy, would have taken him into my confidence and asked him a straightforward question, 'If your society offers you a free choice, will you ever use your thumb to hold your arrow? Are you sure you will feel comfortable holding your arrow that way?' And then, going a step further, depending on the manner of his answer, I would have asked him to confide in me and tell me what he thought of the Ekalavya myth. I would have wished perhaps that he turned a heretic.

I wonder if I have left the story of my son and the flash of lightning far behind. Have I? I am not quite sure. But incidents like this—and indeed many more—have taught me a lot and made me more cautious, if not wiser.

Now, I move over to another of my encounters with my son. This is my favourite!

It happened in 1983. Shortly after Satyajit Ray suffered a near-fatal heart attack, a letter was delivered to our tiny Calcutta apartment. It had travelled a long way, from Chicago, where our only son was working while he prepared for his thesis in electronics and computer science. The letter was addressed to my wife but was meant for both of us.

My wife was busy cooking in the kitchen. She asked me to read it out. I pulled out a stool, sat on it and opened the envelope. I started reading it aloud.

Ma, do you remember? When I was a child, you had taken me to watch Satyajit Ray's *Aparajito*? You had watched it already. Even then, when it was showing at our neighbourhood Priya Cinema, the two of us went off. You had cried a lot while watching the film. Seeing you cry, I too had been close to tears. Back home, you had said to me, 'One day you, too, shall grow up and go away. And I? I shall be left behind, alone. Like

Sarbojaya. And then, one day you'll come back to find . . .'
I, Ma, hadn't let you say another word.

I had forgotten all of this. Suddenly, last night, it all came
back to me. Some of us friends, including Nisha, had gone to
the Chicago University Film Club, last evening. To watch the
very same *Aparajito* once again. This time, I cried quite a lot
through the film. Your words kept coming back to me. After
the show, we came back to our rooms. By then, all of us had
begun to heatedly argue various aspects of the film. Those
among my friends who had decided to stay on in America
didn't spare Sarbojaya. They said, 'The fault is Sarbojaya's. It is
because she was so selfish. Doesn't her son have a right to his
future? Will she keep him tied to her apron strings for ever?
It's not right. It's mean.' I was not on their side, however. I
argued with them fiercely. Ma, believe me, I won't stay here for
a day more than is needed to complete my work. I'll come back
home. I *will*.

Somewhere towards the end of this letter, I could read aloud no
longer. I had a lump in my throat. I looked up at my wife and saw her
crying silently. Glancing at the letter again, I noticed that he had written
it from the university laboratory—written in a hurry, in-between work
and deadlines, and dropped into some post box on his way home.

My wife washed her hands, wiped her tears, and came and took the
letter from me. I handed it over and went outside, onto the veranda. I
stood there for a while. Thinking things over. A modern young man. In
an extremely modern laboratory, studying in a university in Chicago.
He writes a letter to his mother. And his mother, busy in the kitchen of
an ordinary middle-class flat in Calcutta, reads it. And within an instant,
the vast geographical difference disappears and a beautiful emotional
bond links these two to each other. The basis of this bond is *Aparajito*,
which was composed in the 'old days' and whose events and characters
are all, literally, 'old fashioned'. Belonging to the 1920s. Though the film
was made in the mid-1950s, the filmmaker hadn't allowed a single

discrepancy to creep in while recreating the 'old-fashioned' times; neither in the set design nor in the costumes nor in the style in which his actors spoke or carried themselves. The temple, at Kashi, where one could observe the antics of the hanumans. The ghat, on the banks of the Ganges, where the *kathakthakur* [professional storyteller] reads aloud, every day. The throng of Bengali widows. The *palowaan* [muscleman] building his muscles by early morning light and the crows just beginning to caw. Those villages with skies yet uncrossed by high-tension wires. Villages unlike Calcutta, without neon-lit advertisements, without traffic lights at street corners. Villages without the city's trappings. All this—the rustic life and setting of rural Bengal as it seems to have remained through time immemorial—was recreated faithfully. The 'old-fashioned' air with which the modern young man was, in reality, completely unacquainted, was reproduced in minute detail.

But something happens while watching the film. A handful of young Bengali men in Chicago identify with it completely and at once. And, as if confronted with their own reflections in the mirror, each of them defends the character as if defending himself. The points of view in the heated discussion that ensues are coloured by each one's hopes and expectations of the future. Sarabojaya's behaviour, similarly, hurts their pride or causes discomfiture or simply, irritates. Some, on the other hand, shiver silently when confronted with her loneliness; in their imaginations, they run to her, comfort her.

Therefore, each of these young men is refracting the character of Apu—a man of the 1920s—through the lens of their own likes and dislikes, their experiences, their intellects. Therefore, each of these young men is able to recognize in Apu a young man, who has just crossed the threshold from his adolescent days and simple life and now stands, confronting an immense new world. Unknown and unending. Where fear, amazement and an intense fascination accompany every step. They can feel for themselves how the life he has left behind gradually loosens its grip upon his mind. And because of this new freedom, one day, at the Maidan, he can nonchalantly tell his city friends, 'I've *managed* Ma. I sent her two bucks.' They watch the mother, in Nischindapur, the eternal mother, Sarbojaya, still and stoic through the tortuous entanglements and upheavals of her emotional world. As I've said earlier, it is like looking into a mirror. Looking very closely and being alarmed, frightened, wracked with guilt or having a quite contrary reaction, which was evident in our son's letter. Reading which, for a few moments we are lulled into inactivity.

The ultimate success of an artistic creation is to dispel all differences of time and space and to create an intimate bond—a bond of the soul, as it were—with the viewer. A glowing example of such a creation is Ray's *Aparajito* which remains evergreen and eternal in my mind and in my thoughts and thus, also serves as an example of the modern mind and its creative processes. Ray's *Aparajito* scores as a mighty human document valid for all time.

My son, my wife and I keep in regular touch—over e-mail—he from Chicago, the same old Chicago, and we from Calcutta.

On 21 July 1999, I received one such e-mail in reply to mine. Here is what he had to say:

In a mail last week you mentioned some polls that you saw about cinema. You said: 'I am appalled by the colossal decline in audience taste—all over the world. Look at an opinion poll held last week in England among 60,000 people . . . In a list of 100 best films in the last 100 years the first place was that of *Star Wars*, the second was *Titanic* and in the list was *Gone with the Wind, Casablanca, It's a Wonderful Life, Godfather, Sound of Music, Schindler's List*, etc., etc. Nowhere in the list was Chaplin, nor Woody Allen. Orson Welles' *Citizen Kane* was towards the end, *Cinema Paradiso* was ninety-fifth.'

I think you are drawing the wrong conclusion from this. This is a popular vote, so why should the results be any different? Any time in our history, if we took a random opinion poll, you would have seen something very similar. It may be politically incorrect to say so, but art is an elitist entity—it always was and still is. [*I must point out that I do not agree with my son on this.*] If this was a poll of serious cinema enthusiasts, then you could have reason to be alarmed. Of course, it is possible that there is a general decline in audience taste, but this poll definitely doesn't prove that. All it proves is that *Star Wars* is a very popular film, just as Harold Robbins is more popular than Camus or Shaw.

The same thing can be said about your other observation: 'Recently, a television channel conducted an opinion poll on the world's best actor in the last 100 years: in the first place was Amitabh Bachchan. Chaplin was fourth or fifth in the list, Govinda was ninth or tenth.'

Why does it surprise you to see that Amitabh Bachchan is very popular? You already know that his films drew more crowds than anything else. If you poll the same people who crowded those theatres, then this is the expected result. There is nothing surprising or upsetting about it.

The bottom-line is that democracy has its limits. There are certain things where majority opinion is real but meaningless. If astronomical principles had to be decided democratically then we may still believe that the sun revolves around the Earth.

Unlike science, however, cultural preferences may be difficult to resolve in black and white. It is up to each communicator to choose his or her own shade of grey.

[*Originally appeared as 'Our Lives, Their Lives' in the* Little Magazine, *June 2000.*]

Note

1 In the ancient Indian epic Mahabharata, Ekalavya, a tribal boy, had mastered archery by himself in the deep forests, and regarded the great

sage-warrior Dronacharya, whom he worshipped from afar, as his guru. When the news of his talent reached Dronacharya, the tutor of royals was ashamed; he regarded Prince Arjuna to be his best student and had groomed him to take over his mantle. So he made a trip to the forest and asked Ekalavya for his *gurudakshina*, the tutor's traditional reward from a grateful student. He asked for Ekalavya's right thumb—this would maim the talented young archer and prevent him from ever rivalling the young prince as the best bowman of the land. Ekalavya, the tribal boy, complied.

Interview, 1982

Q. In the phase which began with *Ek Din Pratidin*, and has now come to *Kharij*, your latest, you have concentrated on the urban middle-class lifestyles, conventions and behaviour patterns evident particularly in Calcutta. The attitude is one of concern, anguish and suffering rather than satire and criticism. Is this a deliberate choice on your part, a resolution to probe this area of existence, or just an accident that you found these stories one after another, and found them interesting?

A. To be very frank, like any other art worker, I have been continually chased by my own times. My time pursues me at every moment of my existence. Time is perched on my shoulder, and time makes me work its way. Just as I am being shaped by my own time, I too continue reshaping time. This is a continuous process. I am not talking philosophy. I am talking my own experience. There has been a phase when I made several films on rural poverty, films that were good, bad or indifferent. I have made films on the city too. But my focus was primarily on rural poverty.

My last film in that sequence was about rural migrants in the city—
Parashuram. In the mean time, we had come to have a new government,
a Marxist government, giving us a new fund of hopes. We have just had
the same government back in power for a second spell. The new government has given me a lot of new ideas, and opportunities to work in
several directions. I can see the government involved in a valiant fight
against injustices. At the same time, it carries with it an irritating sense
of self-complacency which upsets me. This gave me the idea that now
is the time for me to seek a kind of silence, to go down within myself,
to ask myself certain questions, and seriously consider whether this kind
of self-complacency could lead us to disaster or not. What is true of the
situation in West Bengal, politically, is perhaps true in other countries
as well, as I have found out in conversation with people from other
countries. Last year, I had a long dialogue with a group of Cuban dele-
gates who had come to the International Film Festival in Delhi. When
I spoke to them about our problems, they told me, 'Don't think you

Mrinal Sen, on location, *Parashuram* (1978).

have a monopoly over these problems. They are our problems too.' So when my fire-eating friends complain that I am receding from the political scene, I feel that, on the contrary, I am very deep into the political scene, and it is a political urgency that has impelled me to make such films. It is almost like looking at myself. I stand before the mirror, I point a finger at myself, and say, 'I accuse you.' It is not to denigrate myself, not to run myself down. It is not a Christian confession. There are people who have asked me, 'Aren't you becoming masochistic?' I don't think so. It helps me to become a better man. It helps me to continue to fight, in the right sense of the term. That's where I start, and since I have the deepest love for myself, the world around me, and the time in which I grow, that's what I like to watch and study.

There's a sense of guilt at one level—guilt, because I'm not insensitive—and at another, a sense of love and attachment, and they are, after all, part of one larger complex feeling for my life and my time, and it is this that has gone into *Ek Din Pratidin*, *Akaler Sandhane*, *Chalchitra* which has been disliked by most people, and *Kharij*. It is the same theme that runs through all these films. A friend of mine, the other day, said to me that he considered my films to be variations on a single theme. I feel the same way about them. The theme interests me vastly because through it I can effectively gauge the contemporary sensibility. I don't know what point I'll reach eventually. But that's where I stand.

Q. Would you agree with me if I say that this process had begun in *Padatik*, which you have described as perhaps your only directly and immediately political film, dealing as it does with a political character and a political situation? In *Padatik*, there was an attempt to locate the roots of a political failure within a moral failure, within a failure to understand human relationships and human responses in human terms. The young man in *Padatik* shows the kind of arrogance you have just referred to. He thinks, 'I have gone through this. I know this. I'm doing a favour to this woman who shelters me, for that is the only way in which she can serve the cause, since she cannot serve it in the revolutionary manner in which I can.'

A. Also in his initial attitude to his father.

Q. True. Then, when he overhears the woman on the telephone, and comes to have a sudden understanding of her experience, and for the first time, the woman emerges as a human being, and he comes back to his father, to find he has taken a stand, he is at last able to relate to people.

A. You have got me.

Q. Statements by our Left Front [the ruling coalition of socialist and communist parties in West Bengal between 1977 and 2011] leaders reported in the press often carry an arrogance which is rooted in a total failure to understand the mind of the people. Given the over-balance of failure that goes with the undoubted successes of the Left Front government, would you say that you found it necessary to probe these common attitudes and relationships as a partial explanation of some of the political failures?

A. Absolutely. For that's how, by way of comment, I can serve the present state of politics. It may sound like an attack but there is an underlying search for understanding, a search for building a rapport, a search for rationality. So, when somebody says that I have ceased to be angry, that I have receded from the political scene, it pains me, because to reflect or to do a kind of surgical incision in tranquillity is not considered right. It calls for an insistence on my own stand. At one level, we are running away from life while making a film, staging a play or writing a novel—when we try to hinge a story upon a dramatic situation which is nothing but an evasion. In one lifetime, we can have, say, five or ten dramatic events at the most. But every single day I get up in the morning and get involved in a round of activities, like any other person. And fall asleep at night. If I stop to wonder about what I have achieved that day, I will have to confess that nothing of great import has occurred. Nevertheless, I have grown wiser by so many hours. This then is how I grow; my wisdom grows through these inconsequential events. I have begun thinking—why not build my script on these non-essentials or, so to say, non-events which appear at first glance to be insignificant but are actually very much a part of my life, very much my whole existence?

161

Mamata Shankar in *Ek Din Pratidin* (1979).

Q. You mean the mundane?

A. Right. That's what I'm trying to tackle. Take *Ek Din Pratidin*—the happening of a day, the happening of a night, and a young woman lost. It's somewhat in the manner of Ibsen who begins with a big event which in turn sparks off many other incidents and situations. I try to pick out small things from everyday happenings, from daily life, and then try to give those a shape, lead them on to a point. The characters metamorphose and enter into new relationships within the process, resulting in an emergence of new values, which is perhaps one of the hopes for survival—as in *Ek Din Pratidin*, or something of a revelation, as in *Chalchitra*. What I try to show in *Chalchitra* is how, without my knowing it, my lifestyle changes and I become something of a deserter. It is not an accusation; it is a mild warning. *Kharij* also starts with a big event, a death in the family. But the film is not about how the man dies. It is about what happens after the death. So I choose happenings that could have happened and do happen every other day, but the event of the

Young actors in *Kharij* (1982).

death is what lends the situations their difference. I slowly lead them on to a point where things operate on several planes and also serve to define our social positions. There was one spectator who complained, 'This is not a story of class struggle. Then why have you made such a film?' It is not directly a story of class struggle but the story that I have told can happen only in a class-divided society. That's the point from where I proceed, and the point I eventually reach helps us to understand, if even a little bit. This understanding I find significant and politically valid.

Q. What we are realizing more and more is that the quality, the content and the nature of political art is determined primarily by the time. Something that may be intensely political in the situation and time in which the artist works may not be political in another time, or in another country, where the historical situation is different. It may not be political there and yet it can be extremely political here.

A. In this connection, I would like to tell you something from my own experiences. Whenever *Ek Din Pratidin* was screened in different parts of Europe, I found people, especially the women, greeting it with palpable excitement. I once ran into a bunch of girls who hailed predominantly from the Scandinavian countries. I asked them, 'How is it that you get excited over this film? I know your society to be the most permissive of all the permissive European societies. What do you find in the fuss over a young woman not returning home one night?' They told me, 'You have captured your milieu. We accept reverentially this statement of your milieu, for that is the real image of your society. Once we accept the physical reality of your milieu, we are drawn into the universal issue of male chauvinism.' Then I told them, 'Whenever I have shown this film in Calcutta or Bombay or Delhi, the women in the audiences, in particular, have questioned me about what actually happened to the girl. "How did she spend the night?" That's a question I have never faced in Europe nor in the United States. It's quite significant, sociologically, for a woman in Pakistan or Bangladesh, too, would be asking the same question. Even when I tell them I have no right to know what she was doing, that I have no unhealthy curiosity about it, and nor is my story concerned with a young woman's private affairs, they insist upon a man being involved in some way or the other. I would even deliberately adopt an amoral attitude, in this case. Then I remember the gentleman who stood behind me and asked me, "Mr Sen, it is very important for us to know what happened to the girl." I said, "My dear sir, I made the film for you to see and suffer. You'll suffer because you'll never get the answer."'

My Indian audience, living in the milieu of the film, would naturally ask that question for they cannot accept any breach in the norms of existing morality. They have to be reassured that the young woman has not committed any 'wrong', any immoral act—the 'immoral', in its turn exclusively identified with sleeping with a man. Since that is a question irrelevant in Europe today, the European spectator is never distracted by it and can easily recognize the fundamental issue being raised, that of male chauvinism, and along with it, certain other social, moral and economic constraints. While I agree with you that an issue that may be politically true for me may not have the same political significance in another country —perhaps it has crossed the stage politically, socially, and morally—nonetheless, if I am able to successfully capture my milieu (and this is true of every performing art), I can arrive at some universalized truth which people in another milieu should have no difficulty in understanding. It is essential to have an understanding of the experience of Roman Catholicism to enter the milieu of an Italian film, or to be able to see the significance of certain religious motifs in a film set deep in the interior of a Mexican village—or in other words, to intellectually extend our experiences to an understanding of those in different milieus. In the same manner, a spectator set in a different milieu has to intellectually extend his own experiences or recall experiences from an earlier stage in the social development of his own milieu to make an identification, and reach into the more universal dimension of the experience conveyed.

Q. You have been travelling a lot in the last few years to film festivals. Haven't you noticed a change of direction in the international cinema, from the tendency in the 1960s evident in the greats like [Ingmar] Bergman or [Michelangelo] Antonioni to project an almost universal experience in a no man's land or a no man's Europe or every man's Europe, to a concentration on more sharply defined areas, moments, times, situations, in the spirit of intense probing, so that Antonioni's failures stand nakedly exposed and in his latest works, he shows signs of utter exhaustion? In other words, isn't there, more and more, a realization that a good film is made when a director tries to be true, to be faithful to his own milieu, rather than when he tries to be universal?

A. True, that's how I feel. The safest and the most effective way to reach the international audience is to be strictly national in your approach, in the sense of capturing the physical feel of your milieu (though I have my reservations about the so-called 'national cinema', or even about whether there can be any thing called a 'national cinema'). While I can see the soil and the light and the air of a particular country growing, for example in a film from Poland or Hungary, quite often into my own experience, the West European filmmakers suffer from a lack of a national milieu; they don't seem to know what to hold on to. That is

Antonioni's problem too. The latest Antonioni film I have seen—*The Identification of a Woman*—remains a problem for me. He is beyond doubt a master filmmaker; he knows his craft extremely well. But what emerges in the film is only a man in a state of desperation, trying to justify his case. The case. Yes, but what is it precisely? I don't find any experience in the film.

The situation is different in the Third World scene. I sit up and take respectful note of Third World cinema, with its strong evocation of a sense of place becoming physically palpable with its people, with their emotions and attitudes and relationships. At the same time, a new complication is surfacing here. Since you mention the international festivals, you must have noticed how the festivals are becoming accessible to filmmakers all over the world. As a consequence, one often sees a Third World filmmaker, who has made his mark at a festival, showing a propensity to focus on the exotic with an eye on the West, in a desire to extend his audience. In the process, he often plays up or even constructs his film out of elements or rituals externally exotic but not a part of today's reality. I have noticed this tendency in some of our South Indian directors too. I remember coming out at the end of one of these films and telling my foreign friends, 'Just as you were living for these two hours in an alien world, so also, despite the incorrigible Indian that I am, was I. I have my doubts about this being the reality in that particular part of the country.'

At Cannes this year, the new film by the Algerian [Mohammed] Lakhdar-Hamina [b. 1934], who had won the Golden Palm in the early 1970s, was terrible—an accumulation of rituals through which he tries to project himself as a very national director, which he is not. The film betrays an element of cheating even, for when you come to the incidents he portrays, I have my doubts as to how valid they are in his milieu today. The film didn't make any impact at all.

While it is very important to probe, to go deeper into the reality of your own country, your own area, at the same time it is also very important to see that you remain faithful to that area, that you do not invent. When you try to resurrect the obsolete, you merely play to the gallery.

Q. I have noticed a development from your *Ek Din Pratidin* to *Kharij*. As you explain, you have been trying to capture the reality of the mundane, the reality of the everyday, the relationships that work through them, and the hindrances that inhibit the normal development of these relationships—

A. As revelations—

Q.—Through the mundane. Within this process, in *Ek Din Pratidin*, the young woman seemed to stand apart, separate from the rest. At one level, this impression came from the structure of the narrative. She is not there but she is being discussed most of the time. She automatically stands on a different level thanks to the narrative structure. This is something that happens in the theatre when a character not present on the stage is discussed by others and gains an image build-up that is larger than the life, the physical life, of the other characters that appear on the stage.

Q. Didn't you notice that even when I was doing this, I was trying to make a comment on, or trying to project the social scene, the economic reality?

A. I'm not blaming you. I'm not complaining against this. The structure gives her a separateness; it doesn't make her better or worse than the others, but gives her a different level. At another level, from the facts that we get, she is virtually the one person who feeds the family, the family depends on her. In other words, she has a function which is more positive than that of the others who are dependent on her. Obviously, she is different, she stands somewhere else. When she comes back, there is a confrontation between two sections of the same community—the working woman, the breadwinner who is independent in her own way, and yet whose independence is being doubted, being challenged by her community. A dramatic element emerges out of this confrontation. But when you come to *Kharij*, you have succeeded in eliminating, almost

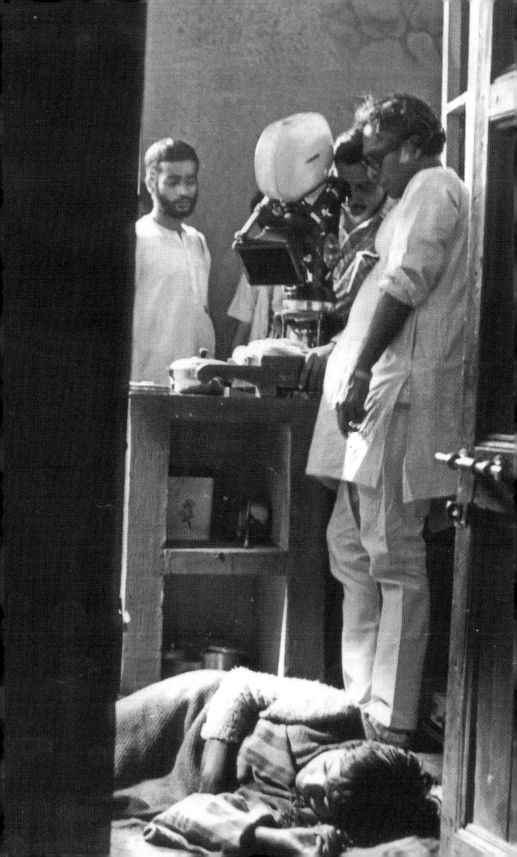

totally, this dramatic element. I would identify this as progress, for here there is no character who has gone out of the situation—for none of us really manages to get out of this situation. The working woman on whom the family depends is pulled down, dragged down in real life, at every moment, in the deadly situation. She is not allowed to stand separate. This is the reality.

Q. Yes, not in a dramatic dimension. It may happen once or twice in a lifetime. It's very rare. In *Ek Din Pratidin* it reaches a dramatic dimension in the confrontation towards the end. The confrontation was inevitable in the whole situation, in the structure. But as I have told you, I am trying to build my scripts out of the apparent non-essentials, or to be more precise, on non-events, on the non-dramatic, on the mundane, everyday experiences of life. Hence *Kharij* is much more difficult, perhaps much more significant. For, at every moment, you feel that a confrontation is inevitable, is imminent, but there is none, which is typical of middle-class life. A kind of escape. And so, I have found it much more challenging, much more faithful to reality, much closer to life. But the confrontation was perhaps logical in the circumstances of *Ek Din Pratidin*. Had I avoided it, the heavens would have certainly not come crashing down about my ears, but I took advantage of the situation to move towards a dramatic point; I couldn't say no to it. But in *Kharij*, despite having the opportunity, I restrained myself. I even provide elements of confrontation, leading perhaps to unrelieved tension at various levels between characters and between situations, but do not allow the confrontation to take place.

Q. Though we speak of the middle class only, perhaps a little too simplistically, in connection with these films, in *Kharij* you very definitely show another class which is lower than the middle class, not a part of the proletariat but lower than our middle class, and that class enters your film quite physically, concretely, substantially. The other young boy, the only person virtually who really did know the dead boy, represents this class. With his looks primarily and with some of his actions,

(FACING PAGE) Shooting *Kharij* (1982).

he is the only person who intrudes upon and embarrasses the couple when they are alone with their guilt. For example, when he brings them their tea. Towards the close of the film, the boy becomes a part of a whole group of servants, most of them young, from the neighbouring homes—the class looks more like a class. There is the subdued threat of a confrontation between these two classes hanging over a considerable part of the film. Anyone from this class could have demanded an explanation, could have asked for something extra, which doesn't happen, which doesn't normally happen in reality. There is a subterranean confrontation between these two classes, always reaching up to the surface but suppressed on the verge of an explosion by the system of our social relationships and social behaviour patterns. You see that whole operation in action. So you have the edge of the confrontation, but you don't have the confrontation itself because everybody virtually exposes himself to everybody else. Nobody is clean and clear in the whole setting.

A. Perhaps, at a certain point in time, they all realize that each one of them has been playacting with the others. The death is just a catalytic agent, as much as is the other boy, the servant boy of the landlord, who appears mute a number of times—and my sole intention behind his appearances is to put my middle-class protagonists to embarrassment, to disturb them. To give them a sense of guilt. So that in an impotent rage and in utter desperation, they try to transfer the guilt to others, and when they realize what they are doing, demean themselves before one another.

Q. When in that scene, one of the characters takes the cup of tea and the other doesn't, I see a bit of playacting in the woman's refusal.

A. Exactly. One tries to score over the other. When I do not know how to face reality, how to combat reality, when I'm consciously trying to escape the confrontation, I tend to playact and enter into a game of win-or-lose with those closest to me. Behind the facade of seriousness, I find all this quite funny. But this is what we do. This is what we hold on to for all of our lives. If I can expose this, if I can bring this to the surface,

I think I serve a valid social or moral or even political purpose. For this is a tendency that touches our political life, our morality, our social life. Incidentally, the servant—the minor working boy—who works for the landlord did not appear in the original story. But I needed him as a catalytic agent. He is not one of my characters, just as the boy who dies or the father of the dead boy are not my characters; they all serve as catalytic agents in the manner of the hobo in [Roman] Polanski's *Knife in the Water*, who does not really take part in the film but hastens the reaction between husband and wife.

Q. I don't know whether I am over-reading, but there is an almost conscious level of playacting, in the ritual that follows when they come back from the cremation of the boy, trying to transfer the tension of the moment to another level, the distance of a traditionally organized ceremonial, trying to draw everything back once again into the rigour of a Law, for everything that has happened so long has disrupted and violated the Law. The death of the boy was a departure from the Law, for the Law had laid down that minor boys working as menials in a middle-class household would be sleeping anywhere in the house, underneath the staircase or in the kitchen, and go on living without much care or even notice. In a sense, the Law was going haywire, everything was going wrong, till at last you try to control or master the situation. You know it's time for the friends of the dead boy to come back with their strain, their suffering, their anger, but you have the tradition of the ritual to cast upon them like a spell or a snare and master the situation. This is also an excellent piece of playacting.

A. I don't think you are over-reading it. Knowingly or unknowingly, I have used the same experiences elsewhere too. In *Mrigaya*, as long as the trial continues, the accused person is news. But the moment the verdict is given, he ceases to be news. But I wanted to carry him along for while more. And I introduced a set of political rituals. That, too, was a sort of playacting. You see a logical extension of the same phenomenon in *Kharij*. Once you recollect the *Mrigaya* sequence, it may help you to reassess the filmmaker. But there is another dimension to it in *Kharij*,

171

for through the process of playacting I am able to reveal to my audience the existence of a whole faceless population, the menials who sleep underneath the staircase or just about anywhere, and go on living, as you say. Their return to the house as a collective, crossing the threshold of the house to come in, as they had earlier gone out with the dead boy, is an assertion of their presence—and I beguile my audience with the false hope that something dramatic may happen. Yet nothing happens, only because nothing like that happens in reality. As you are exposed to this scene, anger ferments within, but it hardly surfaces in reality. I am not one of those who take full advantage of the middle-class existence and then condemn it outright. I believe that the middle class plays a vital role in our social and political structure. I try to concentrate on the middle class to which I essentially belong. I try to show them in their state of crises, in their playacting, in the way they get caught at playacting—and I am interested in them because they are not insensitive. They face a moral crisis only because they are not so. The whole experience of non-communication, on which Antonioni made fantastic films in the 1950s and the early 60s, perhaps begins with this sensitivity, the non-communication between two aware persons growing into a moral crisis. This is where I start.

Q. When you speak of the sensitivity of the middle class, you automatically imply that if you could touch or rub that sensitivity, they would grow aware, and thus you define a role for yourself. When you base your films in this phase to a certain extent on this notion, I find it surprising that you don't seem to touch in your films on the almost institutionalized effort going on to destroy this sensitivity.

A. . . . Organized . . .

Q. . . . Through the glorification of sports and some of the media. Football, with all its excitement, has always been a popular game in Calcutta, but in the last five or six years—coinciding significantly with the years of the Left Front government that we cherish—it has developed into a madness, a frenzy, that can lead to deaths and killings. At one stage, we were quite complacent with the notion that the TV serves only a fringe of the people, only the rich. But it has spread ominously far already. We can't afford to be complacent any longer with the notion that the TV is only a luxury for the affluent, and that it will not affect the community at large. We can notice a tie-in between the TV and the sports madness. Right now as we sit here, a football game is on, and it's being telecast, building up a frenzy. How do you face up to this? In other words, as you try to go to a more probing, in-depth, sensitive position, with a further deepening of the sensitivity between *Ek Din Pratidin* and *Kharij*, aren't you threatened by the institutionalized effort, to destroy the sensitivity or responsiveness of your audience? How do you cope with this? This is a political problem.

A. Of course, it is a political process. This has been worrying me for some time. The TV culture you refer to has spread like contagion all over the country. The TV forces me to watch the kind of films that I wouldn't have normally chosen to watch. When I draw up a balance sheet to determine how such a film could be popular, the fear looms larger. And then I find something dangerous in the very concept of the film as a mass medium. Why shouldn't we treat the film the way we treat the novel, as another art form? Or the way we treat a painting? You need discriminating readers to really appreciate a good work of literature. You need discriminating viewers to appreciate a good painting. So you need discriminating spectators to enjoy a serious film. There is nothing very special about cinema in that respect. The only matter for concern is that filmmaking is much more expensive than any other art. Hence, you have to see how the money comes back. Under the circumstances, I can think of no other way than inculcating in oneself the spirit of how to make a low budget film, how to work under a certain discipline. Filmmaking in the modern world is nobody's monopoly, it is everybody's business, and filmmaking should not be as expensive as it appears to be. Just as the sports and TV culture goes on systematically deadening the sensitivity of the people, so the big budget films with big stars create the same kind of impact. So, when one of our friends, belonging to our community of serious filmmakers, makes a success and takes a leap into a star-studded big budget venture, I tell him, 'You need to be austere, not for the sake of austerity, but to be able to survive, not to be a part of the machinations which they have been systematically practising.' There is no other way to function. At the same time you have to go on trying to locate and mobilize the discriminating spectators spread all over the world. For you have to be in circulation, and you can be in circulation only if your film fetches money. [. . .] The New Indian Cinema has its foothold only in the urban areas and, in addition, perhaps in some semi-urban areas, not anywhere else. I repeat, not elsewhere, certainly not in the rural belt.

Q. Don't you also see the intrusion of obscurantist values in the urban life all the time as another kind of assault on the new values you are trying to explore in your films?

A. Why not look at the city walls carrying posters and hoardings about the ever-increasing miracle men—the *baba*s? We, in Calcutta, never knew of such promotional drives for these *baba*s. These are all recent developments. And now, in the month of Shravan [second month of the monsoon season], alongside political demonstrations, you see young men and young women, many more than you saw earlier, men in shorts and T-shirts, women not, of course, in maxis, carrying pots suspended at two ends of poles on their shoulders, rushing past and chanting 'Baba Taraknath'. True, they were always there, in the month of Shravana, going to Tarakeshwar [town in West Bengal popular for a temple dedicated to Shiva], all the way on foot, performing rituals. But don't you see that the numbers have increased frightfully and that the character of the devotees has also changed? You now find an educated variety among the crowd who indulge more in senseless revelry than in anything else. How will you explain all this? On the one hand, you see the leftist forces steadily growing from strength to strength; on the other, you watch the 'modern' variety among our youth joining the bandwagon and chanting not political slogans but the name of a popular *baba*. And all this is a growing phenomenon. It is a shame. What do they do—the radicals on the political front? I wonder. And look at the growing popularity of the goddesses Shitala [North Indian folk deity] and Santoshi-ma [a Hindu deity whose popular veneration appears to have begun in the 1960s] even in the politically 'hot' city called Calcutta, even among the educated people . . . Incredible!

Q. Some of the new Indian filmmakers have offered two rather simplistic lines of thinking: one, that the industries have reached the villages, there are dams coming up in the villages, thanks to the SALT and the INSAT satellites even the TV has come into the villages, so there is not really very much of a difference between the city and the village; and two, since mainstream Hindi cinema or what is often called the all-Indian cinema, has a mass clientele and reaches the villages and cities alike, it should be our goal to bring the parameters of this cinema and those of ours close together, and that's the way out of the problem. In their elaboration on the second principle, some of these filmmakers adopt a stance that there can be no distinction between the new cinema or the progressive cinema on the one hand and the commercial cinema on the other. These have to come together eventually. How do you react to these positions?

A. I am almost convinced that it is very difficult to strike a balance between the two. How far has science and technology really penetrated into the village? Can we really be effective in the areas where a penetration has been made? Even where a dam is set up, it is inaugurated and decorated with the sacred vermilion. Have we been able to touch and affect the lifestyle there, or are we not functioning within the limits of that lifestyle? There, we justify ourselves by building up myths like upholding the tradition, speaking to the tradition, going deep into the tradition. Even as we accept science and technology, we try to maintain our myths and traditions—there lies the contradiction.

Q. Even in the case of tradition, a changing society draws a distinction between the secular traditions and the religious or obscurantist traditions. But we do not make that distinction.

A. There lies our contradiction.

Q. We'd crack a coconut to launch a ship, made of sophisticated technology carrying sophisticated cargo, out to sea. We tend to conserve the most superstitious of our traditions.

A. Look at our social anthropologists. When they try to build a case for the tribals, on the one hand they attack the 'national-park theory' of Verrier Elwin [(1902–64), British anthropologist who came to India as a Christian missionary and became an tribal-rights activist], yet on the other, they have a religious veneration for their age-old rituals, rituals that are today no better than a sport or a routine demonstration for the tribals themselves.

Q. It can be so economically wasteful, when they have to kill cows or pigs, and spend to an extent that they cannot afford.

A. Exactly. When we were shooting *Mrigaya* in a tribal area near a barrage, beyond two hills, we had to hold up our shooting one day, because they were having one of their festivals. [. . .] This is the contradiction that fosters the culture that assails our sensibilities. I can see the two cultures pitted against each other, and I don't consider a compromise between the two to be a way of popularizing your art—for that can happen only at the cost of the reality. There is no easy way out of this. We have to function within this situation. I have to serve my own conscience as I serve my own time. This is what I am doing.

Q. If we could go back to your earlier film, *Chalchitra*, you will remember that I liked it the first time I saw it, but liked it less at a second viewing, and the more I thought about it. I have since tried to analyze my reactions. The one thing that struck me was that I found it too thin. The other thing, as I look back at *Chalchitra* from *Kharij*, and compare it with *Ek Din Pratidin*, and *Akaler Sandhane*, it looks rather jerky and uncertain in its movement and lacks the relentless logic of the three other films. It jumps from one point to another, making the thinness more obvious. The sense of total milieu that we experience in your other films moves out of the house, the shape of the milieu disintegrates, with the protagonist as an observer moving through things going on, never really belonging to it, never growing into it. Much of the solidity of both

Ek Din Pratidin and *Kharij* comes from the definite setting and the way the action is held within it. It's a house in *Ek Din Pratidin*, and a couple of houses with just the suggestion of the neighbourhood, in *Kharij*. That is what *Chalchitra* lacks. It carries the same point as the other films of this phase, and yet it leaves me somewhat dissatisfied.

A. There is a variation in the income groups of the protagonists between *Ek Din Pratidin* and *Kharij*. In *Kharij*, my characters are a little more affluent than those in *Ek Din Pratidin*. But in both the films I maintained an elliptical approach: I am determined not to go out, but I shall try to project the society in which my characters live and grow. I think I was structurally quite effective in my handling of man and society, in both the films. In *Chalchitra* too, I was aiming at man and society. As long as I was in the interiors, I could not get at society, for I scrupulously avoided anything that could be considered dramatic. While in *Ek Din Pratidin* and *Kharij*, I begin with a big event and then dwell on that which is apparently non-essential, in an Ibsenian manner, in *Chalchitra*,

Mrinal Sen, on location, *Chalchitra* (1981).

I concentrate exclusively on the everyday happenings of a household from the very beginning. As a result, I could not touch the wider world from within the home, and I was compelled to step out. I could no longer be elliptical, as I was in the two other films. I do not know how far I have been able to integrate because several people, whose opinions I value and who have appreciated *Ek Din Pratidin* and *Kharij*, have had reservations about *Chalchitra*. I may have failed to integrate when I stepped out. The structural difference lies in the fact that in the two other films I limit myself to the interior of the household, and suggest the physical world and make comments on the relation between man and society by implication.

Q. Two of the episodes in which you step out of the household in *Chalchitra*—the one in which they run for the cab and the one centring around the palmist—I find independently lively, with their strong physical feel of chaos and helplessness in a big city and the demystification of an apparently prescient character respectively. But what do they really reveal, when you set them against all the revelations, reactions, conversations, even silences and exchanges of looks in *Kharij*—sequences that are not episodically or dramatically as lively as those in *Chalchitra*? The tension, the frustration and the rhythm of trying to catch a taxi in Calcutta has a drama growing out of it all. The palmist, who is a cheat, and has been forced into his role by poverty, and still retains a middle-class pride and egotism, is amusing. But all this remains so thin; merely slices of life, never touching the core of middle-class existence. All that you can suggest of a whole structure of relationships in *Kharij*, at ease with a scrap of dialogue, or characters passing each other, or even waiting, does not build up out of the situations or sequences in *Chalchitra* which are so dramatic, lively, interesting and authentic by themselves.

A. *Chalchitra* was a film in search of a film. So, I have gone into several situations trying to capture the humour, frivolity and frustrations of a city arising out of, for example, the problem of taking someone to a hospital, or through a glimpse of another world, the world of a good man forced to become a cheat, with a direct bearing on our central theme of a young man unknowingly changing his lifestyle. My young friend, film-maker Buddhadev Dasgupta, asked me, 'How does it matter to you or to society or, for that matter, even to me, if I buy for my wife a soap a little more expensive than the one she is used to? Do I do any wrong?' That is not the question. I use the smoke in a certain context, as Gandhi used salt to fight against the British. Churchill asked the same question, 'How does it matter to the British Empire if the half-naked fakir boils saline water on the Indian shore?' But it mattered. As Churchill realized later. I use smoke in the same manner—in my own way, depending on my own experiences.

Q. Symbolically.

A. Symbolically. I do not accuse the young man. I only tell him, warn him, 'You are changing your lifestyle, mind you.' The theme came from an experience. A gentleman came to see me at home one day, with four or five children. I couldn't place him in spite of my best efforts. He looked pretty old. He referred to my village, to my school, to people I had known, but I couldn't place him. Finally, I realized that he had been in school with me, in the sixth standard, many many years ago. The children touched my feet, one after another, before the door. I asked them in, and I started playacting, and honestly, I still hadn't recognized him. He told me about his life, but all that he was really interested in was to prove to his children that he had been in school with an 'internationally famous film director', for that is how he described me repeatedly to them. I acted extremely warm and friendly towards him, offered them refreshments, introduced my wife to them, chatted with him for over an hour, realizing all the while that his world and mine were entirely different. They were using a vocabulary, the man and his children, completely unknown to me. It was very frustrating and tiresome for me to continue the dialogue, but I had to do it. As he was leaving, I asked him to come again, silently cursing him for having wasted my time when I had been busy with work. The moment I shut the door upon them, I burst out, 'The bastard! He had to waste my time.' The moment I said it, I realized that the man must still be on the stairs, telling his children,

'The man hasn't changed a bit.' The thought made me feel so small. I realized how, unknowingly, I was becoming less and less human. That gave me the emotional kick to make this film about how we change ourselves. To establish that, I had to bring different worlds together, bring in a lot of people, and relate the deception of the palmist to the self-deception of my protagonist. The spectator is required to make a cerebral effort, to make the necessary integration of the fragments I offer, and to build a story out of them. Still, on second thoughts, I have a fear that something may have gone wrong somewhere, since people whose opinions I value seem to feel uncomfortable with this film. This happens quite often with me; whenever I see a completed film I have made, I tell myself, 'I wish it had been just a dress rehearsal. I wish I could do it again.' But at my La Rochelle [International Film Festival] retrospective this time, *Chalchitra* was immensely liked by most of the spectators, and they concentrated on this film at the press conference. They found in *Chalchitra* an extension of neorealism. *Chalchitra* remains the search for a story. We do not find it at the end, but we arrive at certain conclusions, certain facts of life, certain new experiences, though they are not necessarily very palatable ones.

Wait a bit before you wind up the tape-recorder. I have told you a lot, said a lot. But I would not promise that what I have said now will be the same when, in future, you and I have another session talking about cinema and myself and about time. Which never stagnates, which moves on.

[*Interviewed and translated from the Bengali by Samik Bandyopadhyay. Originally appeared as 'Dialogue: Mrinal Sen and Samik Bandyopadhyay' in* Cinewave 3, *November 1982.*]

Interview, 1983

1

Q. Would you like to go some day for an open form like [Jean-Luc] Godard or [Alexander] Kluge?

A. I am not too sure. Maybe I'll do that. This is what [Cesare] Zavattini once wanted to do. And he was not very successful. But then it is always good to have a rough idea of what you intend to say, what precisely your objective is in a particular film. And then after that when you go out for shooting, you keep your eyes open, you keep your ears very alert, you hear and see many things around you, and you can incorporate them in the right manner. You may have to reject things if you don't like them, but then it becomes a very expensive proposition, that I know.

Q. But your two latest films look so well constructed that they give the impression that there had been a finished script. How can you manage that when you tell me how you shoot the films and . . .

A. That is perhaps because of my experience. I have been working for quite a long time. Not everything is constructed. Many things are never thought of when I am doing the script, many things. I can give you several instances, tell you a lot of anecdotes about how I thought on the spot of a particular sequence which later proved to be one of the most important sequences of the film. Even in my two last films. And I'll show you the place near Bolpur where I shot *Khandahar*. I have a sequence in the film which to my mind is very delicately built, but it was not there in the script at all. Between two shots I often see something, or something strikes me, an idea comes to my mind, and I immediately feel that I can incorporate it . . .

Q. What does your production manager say when you want to change like that, and maybe change a whole day?

A. Well, when I tell him that this is what I am going to do, and I need this, I need that, he looks at me, keeps quiet for some time. I can see that he gets very annoyed, very disturbed, but then he says, OK. Because he knows me and he knows that this is what I am going to do, he is prepared for any eventuality.

Q. But don't you make the film more expensive going to work this way?

A. No, it doesn't become expensive because I work from my experience, and I have seen that I can keep on taking chances, and the chances work out very well.

Q. Mrinal, how would you describe your kind of realism?

A. It is very difficult to tell you in brief what I mean by realism. But all that I can say is that it is not possible to redeem the physical reality in terms of cinema. What you can do is to project your understanding of the reality. In other words, you cannot project a slice of reality physically on the screen. What you do by the lensing of a particular object, by the tonal and linear compositions that you create, is that you give a very impressionistic impression of the reality. That is what I also try to do. And I can only present my understanding of the reality, which may not be the same as yours. We may be exposed to the same reality physically, but when I present it on the screen, it turns out to be different from somebody else's understanding of the reality. There it is controlled. The physical reality is controlled for me by my own mental make-up.

Mrinal Sen and Reinhard Hauff, Calcutta (1987).

Q. Do you measure your realism against a reality, or you don't need this, like [Rainer Werner] Fassbinder who says, 'The reality is my films. I am not interested in any other reality'?

A. I would put it differently. What I do is that when I come in contact with the reality around me, I sort of personalize the whole thing. And then what I ultimately present is my own reality, which means that it is my own creation. It is not the reality which you objectively see with your eyes. It is a kind of reality which I present, and it has its own logic.

Q. A question about your cultural identity, as a Bengali...

A. I was born of Bengali parents, I married a Bengali, my son happens to be a Bengali, and we live in a Bengali milieu. But I can't forget that we are part of this age of science and technology, where there has been an enormous shrinkage of time and space. And there is hardly anything any longer which could be called truly Bengali or truly Indian or purely German or purely British or purely French. We live in a kind of bastard culture—which is great for me. With the tremendous growth of science and technology, I feel that, sooner or later, we would arrive at a stage where to find a cultural identity, to find cultural roots, will be an exercise in futility.

Q. But at the same time we in Europe, especially the new directors, have been demanding cultural independence from the hold of American culture, the Coca-Cola culture, all over the world.

A. I don't understand what they mean by that, what they call an Americanized culture. Technology is not the monopoly of any particular culture, or of any particular government . . .

Q. But I don't speak of technology. I speak about the influence of a consumer culture and the influence that it can exercise over other cultures.

A. I would leave it to personal choice. If I am attracted by the American culture, well, I have every right to Americanize myself. But the way I look at it, my choice is controlled by the fact of the reality around me.

Q. Good.

A. I have been talking about the crises that have determined the nature of my films. If you look at my earlier films you would see that my concern was predominantly with the physical world and the crisis of physical existence. In my earlier films a physical world dominates the scene, its rhythms, its contrasts, its grimness and humour too, and along with all this the contradictions in which my characters shape themselves, destroy themselves, and reveal themselves. At a certain point of time, I used to do a lot of shouting, talking about rebuilding, about the wonderful future, which I thought must be round the corner. Perhaps it was a simplistic approach, but for me it had its own passion, a very genuine passion. I derived all this from my own time, from the social and political reality which was dominant at that time. It was very much in the air. I have travelled a long way from that point, and I don't feel tired at all. I feel like a full-blooded young man, even at my age. I am like the city of Calcutta, vibrant, full of vitality. I still continue to serve my own time, do a kind of introspection, self-searching, self-criticism to be more exact, pulling myself by the hair, as Peter Weiss said, and making myself stand before the mirror. Will you call it narcissism, masochism? No, never. You can't accuse me of indulging in such things. I look into myself, I tear myself to pieces, I try to bring my inside out. I want to know myself, I am in the throes of that process, to know the society of which I happen to be an integral part. For the last few years, since *Ek Din Pratidin* in 1979, my concern has been with the interior world, to discover its mysteries, its frustrations, its confusions and of course its hidden strength. With that concern at the back of my mind, I focus on the crisis of my characters and that of my own self... Look at my *Ek Din Pratidin*, a friendly family of seven to start with. But as the film grows they start fighting, till they tear themselves to pieces, once they stand face to face with reality. Or for that matter think of *Akaler Sandhane*. While making a film on a gruesome reality of the past, the Famine of 1943, the makers confront the ruthlessness of the present that they had been running away from. Or in *Kharij* where both husband and wife try to turn their faces away from reality, but life is too strong an influence to escape, and I try to talk about this inevitability.

What interests me now is not the physical reality, which to me is soulless. I want to invest the physical reality with my sensibility, my own contemporary sensibility. Reality with a comment. But in its final shape it cannot be subjective. There are various versions of reality. And you have to destroy somebody else's version to establish yours. So with information. Unless information assumes a form, it is just news, ineffective. As a social being I look for effects. Call me a propagandist if you like. When, in my films I try to build cases for some of my characters, and destroy those held up by other characters. I try to present a point of view. And this possibility is not the worst kind of propaganda. When I look back on my earlier films, I find that such propaganda, perhaps subtle and perhaps distant, was not allowed. When I talk about a common culture, what I have in mind, is that with growing organization and with growing industrialization, we are heading slowly but irresistibly towards two cultures: the culture of the privileged and that of the underprivileged. The more regional features of culture are slowly but inevitably disintegrating, disappearing, and new features are coming up. All this is perhaps due to a community of common dangers which the world may not be quite aware of today. The rapid growth of science and technology acts like a catalyst perhaps, hastening the reaction. When I watch your films you remain a German, and I remain an Indian, an incredible Indian. But I think I understand you as much as any German would. I share your views, not that I don't argue with your conclusions, but I also agree. I never fail to identify with your anguish, your crisis. I have the feeling that, sooner or later, the national cinema will cease to exist. There will be two kinds of cinema: a cinema reflecting the views of the privileged and a cinema capturing the world and the views of the underprivileged, and that will be all.

Q. To what class of filmmakers will you then belong? To what group?

A. Well, I identify with the class from which I come. It is the class of the underprivileged. But there again I confront a crisis. I am not the same

Mrinal Sen and Reinhard Hauff, Calcutta (1987).

man today that I was in the beginning. So I have to have a fight within myself. A kind of duality exists in me. If you ask me whether I have changed my lifestyle I would emphatically say: No, I haven't. But then again I know I have changed, perhaps without my knowledge.

Q. You mean your intellectual position has changed?

A. I am not so sure, but then what happens whenever you change your lifestyle is that even without your knowledge, even in spite of yourself, your internal approach to the world undergoes a change. That is what I am scared of. That is why I try to look back. I try not to forget the past, and there I remember what Chaplin had once said. He said, 'I have no humiliation, and humiliation is a thing you can never forget.' I try to remember this line, keep it to myself, so that I don't lose myself, I don't lose my moorings. This is very important.

Q. Some people say, Mrinal, that you are making films for foreign festivals only and not for your country any more.

A. Well, I make films to satisfy my conscience. My conscience dictates to me to make films and I am in love with my content. With whatever I want to say, I feel an intense urge to communicate to the widest range of people. And I am in love with the technique of the cinema. Both in terms of content and in terms of form I feel the urge to reach a world audience. And I send my films to foreign festivals, true. And who doesn't want to send his films to foreign festivals?

Q. Everybody wants.

A. I would like my films to be seen and discussed by people. And that is why I send my films to a foreign festival.

Q. A good friend of mine, the film director Peter Lilienthal, once said: 'To be honest, there is only one possible answer. I make my films for myself first of all, and then for my friends. And if they get a wider audience, I am happy.' But this is his view. What do you think about it?

A. Nobody is happier than the director when he sees that his films have reached a wider audience. Only when it doesn't, does he build a kind of mechanism in himself trying to say that he makes films for himself. But like your friend I too feel that I make films for myself, and when I am satisfied with my film I feel that it will satisfy others too. And talking of sending films to foreign festivals, it is no crime to win an award for a film that you have made. On the contrary, it gives you the satisfaction of having been able to express yourself in the right manner. That must be the reason why the film has been liked at the foreign festival. If it gets noticed you should be very happy for the right reason.

Q. I met your producer today, and he told me that it would make no difference to him if your next film is a failure. He said: When I make friends with someone, it's friends for ever, and if the film fails, well, my friend has done his best, so what's there to say about it?

A. That was very nice of him. But then I have always had the feeling that relations between the director, the producer, the man who puts in the money, will always depend on the dimensions of the balance sheet. If the film does well at the box office, the producer is very happy. If it fails to fetch enough money, well, he naturally doesn't feel too happy.

Q. You have changed your producers very often . . .

A. Previously, it so happened that I never had a second experience with the same producer, unless the producer happened to be myself. But now, once I have access to the minority pockets all over the world, which, taken together, make a sizeable field, I am a more marketable proposition, so I don't have a problem these days.

Q. Your producer told me that he needed twelve million people to watch your film to get his money back. And since he knows that this is not going to happen, he can only expect his money from abroad. Is that right?

A. That's what he thinks. I think he is very optimistic about it. I am not. But in any case let's see what happens. We keep on hoping against hope. And I have been working on a war footing for all these years anyway, as much as you have been, so let us see what happens. And we have to keep on taking risks.

Q. Is it a fact that a lot of Indian directors have a following that surrounds them for many years, which is seldom the case in Europe. Fassbinder had it for some time, but not many others.

A. No, we don't have anything like that here. To start with, we are often together, but the moment I find solid ground under my feet I would isolate myself from others. This is what has been happening with us. When I began, there were a group of us together, who all wanted to make an aggressive infiltration into cinema. We could do it ultimately. But before we could do it, we had a kind of palship among us—fascinating!—when I recall the past, I feel so enthusiastic about it. But the moment we became somebodies in the film scene, we got alienated, we hardly had any dialogue among ourselves. I remember, in 1975 or 1976, I went to Bangalore, and that was the first time I was exposed to the new cinema in Kannada. In the state of Karnataka in the south. I remember, once at about one o'clock in the night I saw a film made by a very young man from the Film Institute [Film and Television Institute of India, Pune] called Girish Kasaravalli [(b. 1950), one of the pioneers of Indian Parallel Cinema], and that was his first film: *Ghatshraddha* [1977]. I told him: this is your first film, and I watched your film like a student, and I learnt many things from your film, but that does not mean that I look upon your film as a spotless one, a flawless one. I have my reservations, but at the same time you have many miles to go. Let us keep in touch and let us have dialogues all the time. I went there three years later, and I found that the dialogue had stopped.

Q. Mrinal, do you have friends or do you have a lot of enemies? Do you sometimes feel lonesome as an artist?

A. Well, I have friends on an enemy's boat. I am in the show business, where as long as I do not become somebody's contender, I can afford to be friendly to him. The moment someone believes that I am his contender, well, something comes between the two. And this is what has happened. And I feel very lonely at times, very lonely, I feel like an island at times. I feel very bad about it. I wish we could talk things over. I remember once to have discussed this problem with a Frenchman, who told me, well it is always there. If you go to Matisse and talk to him about Picasso, Matisse will say, 'Aoh', and if you go to Picasso and talk to him about Matisse, Picasso will say, 'Aoh'. That's how it is. But in India, it is more vulgar, because of the fear of extinction; the kind of animosity we develop is in worse taste here.

Q. A friend told me that he feels that the Calcutta intellectuals are very arrogant, maybe ignorant even about the circumstances, and as you explained to me, it may have something to do with their history, of which they are very proud. Maybe it helps them to forget a lot of things that should be brought to the surface today not only that . . .

A. The intellectuals in Calcutta do not have any special virtue or special vice. It is the same all over the country. But then, whenever I find the Calcutta intellectuals acting arrogant, I take it as a way of hiding one's frustrations.

Q. That would be true for every kind of intellectual arrogance. But the complaint against the Bengali intellectual can be heard from Indians all over the country.

2. At the Cemetery

A. But, Reinhard, the cemetery you see now is no longer the same as it was when I came here in 1978 to shoot *Parashuram*. It was all open then. Now you find structures coming up all over the place, which means that there are more homeless people living here. Homelessness is a part of the Indian lifestyle, or the reality in India.

Q. Do you feel nostalgic coming back to one of your locations?

A. Well, I do, but then I feel very bad when I see that things are not the same as they were.

Q. You think they don't develop in a very positive way?

A. No, not in a positive way. To watch them closely makes you feel worse. But even then, the intensity of living, the urge for life that keeps people living here, is very interesting, and this is perhaps one of the hopes for survival for the people here.

Q. Don't you feel strange that reality changes while the arts remain the same in the museums or archives?

A. Yes, while reality changes, the films go to the archives, which probably only proves that films are not able to do anything positive to change society. Look at the cemetery. It is a cemetery, but people have been living here because they have no other place to live. And mind you, all these people come from the villages. In spite of all the talk of land reforms, little has been done so far. So landlessness remains a growing reality in our country. In the periods between harvesting and ploughing, people have nothing to do, and they come in successive waves to the city. And they live on the pavement, they do odd jobs, but what is most interesting is that they continue to dream, continue to breed children, continue to grow families. That is what fascinates me.

3. At the *Akaler Sandhane* Location

A. There was one sequence which I couldn't do here, which I had to do in the studio. It was the sequence of the paralysed husband in the house, who dies one night during the shooting of the famine film. We had originally thought of shooting that sequence in the house here, in the room here, but then, before that we had to shoot another sequence, in which the widow has to undergo a ritual bath. As we shot the bath near the pond here, I could see that the villagers around, particularly the women, could not take the sequence in the right spirit. For them, with the superstitions, it was playing with death. They felt very bad about it. And immediately I decided that I should shoot the death of the husband in the studio, away from them. They cannot be 'corrected'. They will live and sleep with their superstitions. And then, when you ask me about my responsibility as a filmmaker, my social and moral responsibility, I know I cannot 'correct' the people about whom I make these films.

Q. Maybe not 'correct' them, but correct the situation . . .

A. Yes, exactly, to correct the system, and that through the people who see these films. When I make these films, I make films about certain people, but not necessarily for them. I make the films for people who understand my films. And I make very effort to see how I can make the viewers understand my films. But maybe I do not present the problems

Dhritiman Chatterjee, Mrinal Sen and Smita Patin at the location of *Akaler Sandhane* (1980).

and analyse the problems in the right manner. This goes on as a continuous process. I keep on making films, posing problems, analysing the situations, and trying to keep a perspective. On the other hand I also expect my viewers to realize the situation or to correct me. This is done through their response to my films and also by my response to their response.

Q. But don't you feel it a big problem when after all this you come here and see that nothing has changed for the better, and maybe they are even happy as they are? But you made the film to say something!

A. That's something which intrigues me and makes me sit up, when they feel happy to see themselves on the screen...

Q. But that is no serious point if the village people feel happy to see themselves on the screen...

A. It's not a case with the village people alone. You go to a slum, you make a film about the worker, you make a film about the children of the slum, and they all feel very happy to see themselves.

Q. Of course, but hadn't you started with a different approach? And this is my point. I always start to make a film about something, and if I didn't have a kind of hope that something could be changed, not through the film directly of course, but if the film cannot even influence the attitude of some people at least, the more responsible people, for the system to . . .

A. Possibly it influences by creating a climate.

Q. I have another question. This little girl, Arati, whom we met just now, asked you whether you could take her home or not. What did you answer?

A. The moment I came here she asked me whether she could come with me. I said: 'What would you do? She said that she would like to act in films. So she was not interested in what I am trying to say through my film but she was interesting in acting in the film.

Q. But she wanted to come to your place to work.

A. Yes. To work as what? I asked. And she said, 'Well, you tell me whatever I have to do, I would like to act in your film.' And do you know what happened? Once when I was making another film, the father of this girl came to my house in Calcutta and started crying. He told me that the girl was missing for two months. And he had moved heaven and earth to find the girl, but the girl couldn't be traced. It took six months to trace the girl. With something like this, I feel I have a responsibility, when I have her in a small sequence in my film, and she is fascinated by this game called cinema. And that is what makes her run away from the house. That's all the change that happens, a change for the worse.

4

Q. How would you describe what you consider your main difficulties as an artist?

A. When I started my career, my main difficulty was to organize money. But now organizing money is not that difficult. With subjects I have become very choosy these days. This is due to the fact that human

193

relations have become much more complex now than when I had started my career. My difficulty now is in choosing the subject. What shall I focus on? What do I say to my audience? And what do I project in my films? Every time I start a film, I undergo a crisis. I feel I am in a vacuum. And I feel perhaps this is the end of my creative activity. Possibly I won't ever go any further. This has always been the case with me, for the last few years. I find the money-backers at my door. But then I ask them to wait. But how long can they wait? Then there are the very practical problems of the members of my unit. As long as I do not start a film they are out of employment. That is another reason that worries me. And that makes my confusion worse.

Q. Mrinal, maybe I could put my question a little differently. Do you as an artist have the feeling that maybe your main talent is in storytelling and not in building up images, or any such feeling?

A. Well, I always feel that I have to start with an idea, with a concept. The concept comes first to me, not as visual, not as image. An image or a sound can give rise to a concept within one. But it is the concept that you start with. That is the take-off point. The concept. From there you keep on growing. You think of the images, you think of the sound, you think of the music and then you think of the tools that are employed in the making of the film.

Q. So it will never happen to you that you go to a location, and maybe you find a house, and you think, Oh, I have to build a story around this? That's something you think will never happen with you.

A. I don't get your point there.

Q. Maybe if you go to a location . . .

A. . . . To make a film?

Q. . . . To make a film, and then you get influenced by this location and then you decide to make a film around it. Could it happen?

A. Yes, it happens. I see something. I hear something. A sound. I see visually. And that provokes an idea. That may be the starting point for a concept. But it is the concept which you start with. When I go to a particular place I look at something. And I can say I must make a film here. But what about? That is the point. Or I read something in the newspaper, and I think: Why don't I make a film on this? But the main point is to evolve a concept. What are you precisely interested in and what are you going to do? That's the beginning, and it comes to me in many ways. For instance, there is the story that I had read a long time ago. Maybe I didn't like it or I liked it and forgot all about it, till suddenly in the middle of the night I just pull out a book, and there is the story that I had read ten years ago, and hadn't found that exciting, and now find a lot of meaning in it. And then I start on it. And that becomes the starting point for a film. This is how it happens. I think of the technicalities later on.

Q. Has it ever happened to you that you have nearly finished a script and then decided not to do it?

A. Never. I can never write a script without knowing that I am going to make a film of it. Once I choose a story and start writing the script, I often feel like a fool and think I shouldn't have chosen it at all. There is a tension. But I love tension. Tension keeps me young. Tension becomes a challenge. And that is how the script grows till ultimately it comes out to be something quite interesting. I keep on changing the script which merely serves as a guideline.

Q. I guess you believe in a dialectical style of filmmaking.

A. You can't escape dialectics, it is embedded in your thinking. As for the formal aspects of the cinema, I believe in trying it out with my tools, I mean the camera, the recording machine, and the subsequent post-shooting operations, including the montage, the mixing, and a whole lot of things. Well, I believe in trying it out with all this, the way a child does with his building blocks, the way a poet does with his words, the way a footballer tries with the football, the way a painter tries with the brush. That is how I would like to work with my camera and the sound.

Q. But what I found out is that you are quite precise as to your meaning, even though you are always speaking about spontaneity, and toying around with all these tools.

A. The precision comes later ... I believe in a kind of madness. But there should be a method in this madness. I had once even thought of taking credit for direction, script and gimmicks—all by Mrinal Sen. In a highly conformist country like India, where people do not want to go beyond the experiences of their predecessors, it is important to release a little bit of madness. I have done my bit of that. But now I have arrived at a stage when I talk about the interior world where I feel there is no place for my earlier staccato cutting. The montage now becomes different from what I had been doing earlier. It is the content which determines the style.

Q. Could you ever think of making a film without content, a film as film?

A. The film has to have a content. By a film as film, do you mean the abstract film? Even the abstraction has something to say. Abstraction too is derived from one's experience of life.

Q. But there are a lot of people now who don't trust the language of film editing itself because it is always expected to say something and carry a message.

A. I am not against it at all. But personally I'll not make that kind of film. But if I see something which exists as a formal exercise. I wouldn't say 'no' to that. I'd love to see it. To be able to communicate more effectively I wouldn't mind picking up some of the techniques used in such a film. Think of Norman McLaren [(1914–87), Scottish Canadian animator, director and producer], for example. Well, he has made many films with very rich themes, but he has also made films that do not try to convey any idea, but just certain patterns. I find these patterns fascinating. I feel ecstatic about all these films.

Q. And now a personal question. I found you quite nervous when we started to do this film. And everybody in your circle told me, Oh, he is very nervous. Was it so?

A. I have never faced a camera before. When you ask me questions I don't know how to organize my thoughts. That is why I possibly felt nervous. I fumbled a lot. And my answers were not always the right answers. After the shot was done I would feel I could have put it in a different manner.

Q. Don't you think it is a good test to be once in front of the camera?

A. That's true. I thought I knew how one should behave before the camera. But when I do it myself I fail. I think it is also true of many other people. I don't really know. My problem is what to do with my hands, when I stand before the camera.

Q. You have made several provocative films. Even today you are fond of provoking me on a different level. Do you think that a film should provoke the audience, and at what level?

A. The film does provoke. There was a time when I called myself an agent provocateur. It is not necessary for my audience to agree with me. My business is to provoke them. My business is to disturb them, my spectators, and to start a dialogue, if not between the spectator and myself, then between the spectator and his fellow-spectator. I made a film called *Padatik*, the third of a trilogy on Calcutta. While I was very critical of the movement led by the Marxist–Leninists [i.e. the Naxalite movement], I made sure that I didn't indulge in slandering them. The line between self-criticism and slander can be a very thin one, and I was fully aware of that when I made this film. Many of the Marxist–Leninist activists in Bengal did not like the film at all. They hated it. Yet some of them found it to have some substance, politically speaking. For me that is good enough, for the film can then provoke a discussion of a political nature. Whether you like this film or not, whether you accept my point of view or not is another matter. But the very fact that my film acts as somewhat of an agent to provoke a dialogue on political issues, that is where I feel I succeed.

Q. Mrinal, do you like to put questions to the audience?

A. Yes, I do that. But I also give the answers or suggest some answers. My films contain questions to the audience. What I have been doing for some time now is to keep an open ending. I don't want to rush to conclusions, because I find life to a large extent inconclusive. All that we can do is to analyse the situations so that the audience starts asking questions till they find an answer.

Q. I find a difficulty when you use such an approach in a narrative, storytelling form. The way it is used, it comes to have an end, even if the end is not a conclusion; for there is an end to the storytelling. So there is a contradiction.

A. You mean, structurally. That does not mean that you have to find a conclusion. You may have an end, but you can leave it open-ended at a certain point of time.

Q. At the level of thought I think they will agree to have it open-ended, but at the level of emotions I guess they will always want to have some kind of end.

A. But you can suggest an end, and leave it at that. In your *Knife in the Head* [1978] and *Man on the Wall* [1982], you suggest an end, you suggest a conclusion, but it still remains open-ended. One is free to interpret it the way one feels one should.

Q. This is the problem with the audience, for they want an end . . .

A. . . . And end with a conclusion. The audience would always like to be spoon-fed. They don't want to think.

Q. Yes, but maybe we should bring them to think about our film. We should give them an end. That is a better way than to leave it open. I guess.

A. The film ends somewhere. That is true. The film ends somewhere, but not always with a conclusion.

Q. No final conclusion. Maybe it's only the conclusion of the story, but it should go further.

A. Yes, it should go further. It should stay with the audience. That is why I feel that it is very important for the audience also to take part in the creative activity. The director making a film should keep in mind that he has to give some clue to the spectator to help him to relate the situation to his own experience. That is how in the theatre he becomes a creative agent. If a condition like that can be created—that is possible only when we make that kind of film and also when we find that kind of spectator—when a communion can be established between the creator and the spectator, then something else comes up. Then you present something to your spectator and the spectator also tries to relate it to his experiences, and the spectator may come to a certain kind of conclusion which may not be yours . . .

Q. Of course, it must be possible . . .

A. . . . and that, I think, would be very good. That to my mind is the ideal situation, when you can bring your audience into creative activity, when you can provoke him to be a creative agent. That is why I try to provoke the audience.

Q. It all depends on how intelligent we are in manipulating them.

A. And how intelligent they are in reacting to the manipulation.

Q. Yes. But do you like to be a manipulator?

A. Why not? I am a manipulator, so are you.

Q. Yes. But I like to get manipulated only up to a certain level. If it gets more I don't like it.

A. There was a time when I used to be very didactic, it was a time when all of us suffered from an infantile optimism. We thought there was something called hope just round the corner. That was what our political leaders had taught us, and I caught the contagion. That was the time when I used to make very didactic films, and I went about saying that I am not ashamed of using my film as a propagandist pulpit. To a certain extent it was true but it didn't help much. For it can neither project the reality in its proper perspective nor can it be effective as a moulder of human aspirations. I have learnt better since.

[*Interviewed by Reinhard Hauff. Originally appeared as 'Conversations' in* Hauff on Sen: Ten Days in Calcutta; A Portrait of Mrinal Sen (*Calcutta: Seagull Books, 1987*).]

A World Built or Gained Is but the World Lost . . .

More than three years ago, an incorrigible Indian living in Calcutta, a non-too-innocent abroad, was summoned by the French minister of culture whose first name, when spelt, looks and sound English. A proposal for the co-production of a film was placed across the lunch table in the Indian capital. Two years later, a protocol was signed by the Indian and French governments. Operating within the framework of this official protocol, a French company felt inspired, a Swiss group was involved and a Belgian party quickly extended its helping hand. Thus, a team was formed consisting of Indians speaking different languages and Europeans with diverse national identities.

Soon afterwards, the team invaded the ruins of an abandoned village somewhere in India. No signs of life; only the broken walls jutting out of the debris and looming above us almost like ghosts. The only inhabitants (going into periodic hibernation) were the snakes. Although quite a large number of scorpions were also seen scurrying about. Neighbouring villagers warned the team about this place: the haunted ruins, the cursed zone, God's wrath falling on it for reasons unknown to man.

The team defied all that was said about the area and braved all that was seen. The film was shot both under the blazing sun and in the freezing cold, all in that 'damned' area, with a four-member cast which spoke Hindi.

The filming, as planned, was completed in two months. As usual, problems cropped up at every stage—before shooting, while shooting and also while transporting the crew and materials by road and air to the 'undefined' locale. Such problems, threatening at times to escalate into crises, were of various kinds; occasionally, they even affected the life of our commune. The project, however, absorbed all the shocks and jolts, mastered the occasional daunting threats of collapse and survived. What was more, coupled with all these hazards, both the unpredictable and the foreseen, there was the constant fear of God's wrath descending on the team, the like of which, so the villagers believed, fell long ago on this once-prosperous land.

Strangely enough, that is precisely what seemed to have happened one day; it was quite an event occurring just two days before we wound up our shoot. Elaborate arrangements were made for a massive explosion; TNT was requisitioned and more than a dozen smoke bombs were collected. The utmost precautions were taken, and each member of the team as well as all visitors, were alerted. The explosion was planned and executed under the direct supervision of the Border Security Force [BSF] and was also meticulously photographed. The walls were razed to the ground, debris flung up into the air and thick smoke enveloped the sprawling ruins. An hour later, however, in the midst of absolute stillness, a bomb suddenly burst, injuring only three people. But who were these three? The one who brought the team here—the incorrigible Indian, the French cameraman who photographed the explosion, and the Flemish sound-recordist who captured the deafening explosion. This was not sabotage nor terrorism, nor callousness on the part of the BSF.

The nearby villagers were unshakeable in their belief about it being an act of God. Some of the God-fearing members of the crew nodded their agreement about this being decreed by an angry deity. Said a tur-banned octogenarian who lived in the neighbourhood and who was not unfamiliar to the team, 'We warned you. We asked you to offer prayers. You didn't care. So now you suffer.'

'How can God be so vengeful?' wondered an innocent member of the crew.

Soon afterwards, the scene shifted to Europe where we completed the post-production work.

According to the contract, France allowed a part of its money to be spent outside the country. Switzerland, being more generous, set no such specifications about the investment of its share of the capital and the manner in which it had to be spent. But Belgium, like India, made it a point to confirm that all its money had to be spent entirely within its territory. As a result, quite a substantial bit of the post-production work was done in Paris and Brussels. So those who worked had no choice but to shuttle between the two European capitals. Being a habit-ual globetrotter, this incorrigible Indian did not mind the travelling but he did have problems of another kind—that of communication. Having absolutely no flair for foreign languages, he took recourse to gesticulation as often as was required, and with courage but hardly any conviction, punctuated his English with his tentative French and perhaps even Flemish, at inappropriate places.

The film nevertheless was completed on schedule and, one hopes, as planned. It turned out to be a product of cross-fertilization. An attempt to capture history in its broadest shape, and for what it is worth, in a capsule.

The experience has been stupendous, both for this non-too-inno-cent abroad and for his European partners as well, those who worked incessantly for three months. What the Indian succeeded in doing was nothing short of incredible: snatching away all possibilities of boisterous Saturdays and sleepy Sundays from the occidental crew and making

Directing *Genesis* (1986).

them work almost round-the-clock and for every day of the week. And he has, in the course of this three month exile, been part of an immensely rewarding experience.

Now, on his way back to his El Dorado, the wandering Calcuttan looks back in excitement and wonders if this Indo-European project can really be called a piece of history worth storing in memory, or, to put it pompously, as a drama enacted by a horde of absurdists.

Talking about the absurd, the same Calcuttan recalls a story which, while travelling from Brussels to Paris, his friend Jean-Jacques Andrien [b. 1944], the Belgian filmmaker, had once pulled out from an ancient book of Belgian folklore and narrated to him. It was as follows:

Some day, some time in the small town of Liege. I was standing on the bridge looking down at the river. I saw a huge stone floating down the river and noticed four men standing on it. One had lost his eyesight and another his legs. The third, his hands, and the fourth, his clothes.

A bird flew by. The man without eyes saw the bird, the man without legs chased it, the one without hands promptly caught it, and the fourth without clothes hurriedly put the bird into his pocket.

One is free to read the story as one will. But there is no denying the fact that the international team worked non-stop for five months and succeeded in putting *Genesis* into six large cans.

Finally, a transit passenger at Frankfurt. The Calcuttan is now homeward bound. With some time to rest and recline and perchance even to dream. He thinks of the man without whose 'irresistible persuasion' the film would never have been made at all. He is the man with an English *prenom*, as they say in France; one who then walked into active politics and became the minister of culture of the French Republic. One who still retains his seat as a deputy but whose party recently lost the election by a very narrow margin.[1] Before boarding the Air India flight, the homesick Calcuttan scribbled a parting note to him, acknowledging his gratitude for the wonderful support lent to the international team and, remembering the recent election reverses, added a postscript:

It happened this morning, in my Brussels apartment. My wife was packing up things in great haste and I was helping her. A phone call. A journalist asking if I could make a short statement about the film. I said, 'A world built or gained is but the world lost, to be rebuilt or regained. Genesis, all over again.'

[*Originally appeared as 'Genesis: Rebuilding a Lost World' in the* Sunday Statesman, Miscellany, *25 May 1986.*]

Note

1 In the 1986 election to the French National Assembly, President François Mitterrand's Socialist Party lost its majority, and Jack Lang [b. 1939], who had served as minister of culture since 1981, lost his position at the ministry.

Apu, Eternal Apu

*We make things spectacular not by their exceptional qualities
but by their natural qualities.*

Cesare Zavattini

Jotting idly. Scribbling aimlessly. Crumpling up the half-formed thoughts and tossing them away. And trudging back. To the beginning. Time after time. Every time. I return to Apu. There is no way to leave him out. For me or for anyone else. It is as though our collective beings have been smeared and stained with the very essence of Apu. We are his prisoners, irrevocably bound, and he remains firmly ensconced in the treasure trove of our hearts. If we delve a little deeper, spend a few moments with him, get to know him intimately, it is suddenly so simple to understand Satyajit Ray. And besides, it is with Apu that Satyajit began his journey; Apu helped him take the first few steps and Apu helped him conquer the world.

Apu. Apurba Kumar Ray. Created by Bibhutibhushan. And imbued with a radiant tenderness by Satyajit who then introduced him to the rest of the world.

Apu. Eternal Apu. Ever-familiar Apu. He is born, is rocked in the cradle and then, passing through childhood, now verges on adolescence; hand-in hand with Didi [elder sister], he gambols about the neighbourhood and then moves further to explore the woods and thickets until he finally stumbles into the *kaashbon* [wilderness of kaash grass]. He discovers a completely new universe; he holds his ear against the telegraph pole, listening, and then runs far beyond the kaash flowers until he is beside the railway tracks. He sees the train belching thick black smoke as it disappears to the end of the horizon and his small world is shaken by its thunder. He does not know where it is going and neither does Didi. In the still waters of the pond, tiny creatures wriggle in natural restlessness; alongside, the siblings carry on with their playfulness, their pranks, their endless devilry. They are unaware of and their minds are untouched by the grim reality of their impoverished circumstances. They don't have to worry about it at all—neither Apu nor his Didi. Then . . . one day . . . he loses his Didi for ever and is suddenly and completely, alone. Almost immediately, almost overnight, Apu grows up. The family moves away.

Is this it? Is that all that *Pather Panchali* has to say? Is there nothing more?

There is plenty more. There is the all-enduring Sarbojaya and Harihar and Indir Thakrun. There is the beauty of nature's lush and abundant bounty cheek-by-jowl with the loud laments of the poor and the starved; there is the mean and narrow mind existing side by side with the great and the generous. Of course, there is definitely room for debates and differences of opinion regarding the question: Who is the main character of this film? Nonetheless I will emphasize that it is Apu who is everywhere and in every moment; even his absence is a kind of presence. It is as if this is a mere prelude to a journey that will probably be without end. And also something else; something unknown, unprecedented, ineffable.

The train hurtles over the Ganga with a tremendous display of strength and vigour, making the very foundations of the universe tremble. On the other side lies Varanasi—Kashi.

Apu moves to Kashi with his parents. His father dies there. The mother-and-son pair seeks refuge under the aegis of an affluent family; Sarbojaya works there as a cook and Apu as an errand boy. She notices that in his spare time, Apu is made to pluck out the householder's grey hairs. She begins to fear for her son and, at the first possible opportunity, returns to Bengal. To Monshapota. There are no *kaashbon*s here. Instead, there are vast fields of paddy. In the distance, where the blue of the sky and the green of the fields coalesce, are the rail tracks. A train chugs past. Apu points it out to his mother. And along with the two of them, perhaps the viewer too succumbs to a moment's lassitude.

Will Apu then become a priest? Pursue his father's profession? He tries it out for a few days but it holds no appeal for him. No, Apu must educate himself. Balanced between adolescence and youth, Apu suddenly matures into an adult. While still in Monshapota, his universe begins to expand, his horizons begin to widen. He cannot resist the call of the 'greater' world beckoning to him and gradually the familial ties begin to loosen. But that may not be the only reason. Perhaps the adult Apu is finally coming into his own. The mother–son relationship now becomes inexorably entangled.

Apu moves to Calcutta and his mother remains in Monshapota. He is restless; she, calm and unperturbed. The eternal complexities of the human mind now attain modernity.

His mother doesn't tell him that she is unwell. She doesn't wish to do so. The mute tangles of human relationships are represented anew. Momentarily, somewhere in her eyes, in her face, in her very being, we glimpse the traces of a revenge shorn of rancour or guile.

Nonetheless, Apu does get word about his mother. He rushes back. This is the same Apu who hadn't gone home to his mother; hadn't wanted to go home to her. Excusing himself by saying it would impair his studies, he had 'managed' the situation by sending her a paltry sum of money. This is the same Apu who was so worried about missing the train that he had quarrelled with her and rushed off to the station long before the train was due. When it finally arrived he had hesitated for a few moments and then, yielding to an irresistible and indefinable emotional bond, had traced his footsteps back home.

Apu returns to Monshapota. It is as if the entire house is being devoured by a terrifying silence. Apu cries secretly to himself. Though in the background, his mother's death evokes excruciating, heartrending grief. The next day, at the crack of dawn, he gathers up the few odds and ends—memories of his mother—and heads for the station. All we come to know is that he will perform his mother's *sraddha* [funeral rites] in Kalighat. In Calcutta. This is the moment when, for the rest of his adult life, Apu becomes truly alone. He is now completely unfettered, truly a free man. He is alone but strong, firm, unflinching. The unvanquished. Apu.

Calcutta. The city that Apu must come to grips with today.

Apu, waiting on the threshold of adulthood. Unable to pursue his studies further because of financial constraints, Apu sets off on his struggle to survive armed with a certificate from his teacher. The world is full of students assembling in protest marches, screaming out their rights and demands. He succeeds in getting himself some sort of a job but still, remains poor. He works, sometimes succeeds in paying the rent and sometimes doesn't, and daydreams continually. He dreams of being a writer, of penning a novel. There may even be a few snatches of autobiography in it, who cares! It would be about life, about surviving and staying alive; not about escaping and running away from the fight. In his little room, Apu plays the flute and begins work on his novel. He also pegs away at a small job in order to subsist.

And he keeps dreaming. Endlessly. And mulls over so many many things in his mind. Once, late at night, returning home from the theatre with a friend of his, Apu suddenly smashes the silence into smithereens by screaming at the top of his voice, 'I am Mainak, son of the Himalayas. My wings are hidden deep in the oceans.' Then equally suddenly he says,

'Goethe, Dickens, Keats, Lawrence, Dostoevsky . . .' He comes back home. A small room up on the terrace. Apu. Alone.

The events that follow seem to occur without any preamble whatsoever, swiftly and abruptly, almost without Apu himself knowing of their occurrence. Apu's marriage—an unexpected marriage. The tense excitement of a brief spell of married life, the death of Apu's wife at the moment of his son's birth, his aimless wanderings, the hurling of his entire manuscript into the air, watching it sink into the water and then finally, one day, coming home to his son. Kajol was, by then, about four years old. (A few days after their marriage, Apu had stared deep into his wife's eyes and asked her, 'Tomaar chokhey ki?' ['What's that in your eyes?'] and she had whispered, 'Kajol.' ['Kohl.'])

One day. There was no one around. An extraordinary relationship begins between Apu and Kajol. Apu stretches out both his arms. Kajol takes a few tentative steps towards him and then rushes into his father's embrace. Apu swings him up and places him on his shoulders. And begins to walk. As though he has finally discovered the direction of his destiny.

Apu walks, hugging the bank of the river. Kajol sits atop his shoulders. But where is Apu going?

The river flows on. And Apu keeps walking. Carrying the little boy Kajol. The son of the girl with the *kajol*-lined eyes.

From the moment of its creation, *Pather Panchali* has been a ceaseless journey, an extraordinary chronicle. One that has a beginning but no end. The journey is not just Apu's nor simply that of rural Bengal; it is of undivided Bengal, of India and of the rest of the world. And finally, it is a journey of all humanity.

[*Originally appeared as 'Apu-r Antaheen Jatrapathey' in* Ananda Bazar Patrika, *14 April 1992. Translated by Sunandini Banerjee.*]

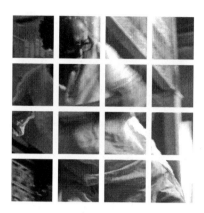

Chaplin's Odyssey

Like every year, this year too the Cannes Film Festival was abuzz with excitement. Every day there were films—competition entries—to be watched. Three a day, or sometimes two. We had to sign our names in the register before each screening. That is, leave behind proof of our having actually been present. I watched the films, attended frequent meetings of the jury, exchanged and verified opinions with the rest. And throughout all this there continued the attempts at mutual understanding; there were some that we rejected absolutely while others we lauded to great heights. And there were some others about which we simply made some conciliatory noises and then set aside. And then we would set out again to watch more films or to simply chat with each other. Or get back to the hotel for some rest.

In-between this daily dichotomy of work and leisure, I remember, one day, after watching a film, the three of us stepped out. My wife Geeta, Geraldine and I. By Geraldine, I mean Chaplin's daughter. We strolled down to a restaurant on the beach. Geraldine had already threatened me in advance. 'No film talk. Anything but.'

We talked of many things for a while. Very naturally, the topic of Chaplin occupied the greater portion of our time. At one point, I brought it up. I asked her, 'Do you remember that story? The one about the civil war in Spain?'

She looked questioningly in my direction. And said, 'Civil war?' I replied, 'Yes. A great story. The moment I read it, I wanted to translate it into my own language. Into Bengali. I've done it too. After all, how many of the world's writers have managed to come up with a similar story? So deeply committed against war?'

Geraldine asked me, 'A story by Father? Written by him? Where did you get it? When did you read it?'

Geraldine really had no idea about the story. And I was genuinely surprised at discovering that fact. The very same daughter who had turned everything upside down and inside out to track down the coffin with her father's body, and had finally managed to excavate it from a cornfield beside Lake Geneva, almost entirely through her own efforts knew absolutely nothing about this story. I narrated it to her. I recounted most of it exactly the way in which it had been put down by Chaplin; I knew it almost by heart. The very words which he had used. And in just the manner that he had arranged them, one after another, to ultimately create a particular setting. Perhaps I managed to convey these to her. It was a very short story. Just like his short films. But not enough for a film to be made out of it. So it didn't take me more than a few minutes to tell. By the time I neared the end, I saw her eyes shining with unshed tears. I understood, and perhaps rightly too, that she was overcome by a certain amount of guilt.

She hadn't known this fact about her father. She had had to hear it from me. Someone whom she had known for only seven or eight days and whom she would continue to know for as many days more.

I told her, 'I am proud to be the one who first narrated this story to you. If only I could tell it to you in my own language, in Bengali.'

'Will you send it to me?' she asked. 'Have you got it written down?'

I said I would. But I didn't. I had wondered, what would Geraldine do with the translation? She would keep it with her for a few days after which it would perhaps be left lying around somewhere. Or it would be sent to Oona, to the village in Switzerland where she lived. But today, at this very moment, I am thinking of those who read only Bengali and are thus unable to read Chaplin's original and am overcome with a desire to share this extraordinary story with them. I want them to know about those terrible days, when, according to Rabindranath, 'barbarism, with its fangs bared and claws unsheathed, was spreading horror all across Europe', 'when the very air above the earth reeked with the stench of the abuse of human souls'. When he had replied to Japanese poet Yone Noguchi's [1875–1947] letter by writing: 'I wish your countrymen, whom I love so much, not success but remorse.'

The story was called 'Rhythm'. And the subtitle read 'The Story of Men in Macabre Movement'. Which, in Bengali, I had translated into 'Jantra-Chhanda' [Machine-Rhythm].

The outskirts of Madrid. A prison. A vast courtyard at the back. Hemmed in by high walls. A Loyalist stands at one end of the courtyard. Opposite him is the firing squad. Six soldiers. Beside them, the squad leader. The Officer-in-Command. Standing some distance away from them is a small group of officers. Waiting eagerly to witness the execution. Everything is as quiet and as still as death itself. And the day inches closer, dragging its feet. Dawn breaks.

One still believes, hopes, that ultimately, things just may turn out differently. At the last moment the powers-that-be will withdraw the death sentence. No matter that he is an Oppositionist, a Loyalist (anti-Franco). In reality, however, he is no ordinary person. He is a great man, whose name is known to almost everyone. No one can write stories as funny as his. And to top it all, he is an old friend of the squad leader. They have grown up together, studied together, spent time together, chatted together. They have spent day after day arguing, fighting, debating.

There have been differences of opinion, even mutual conflicts with regard to the politics of the country. The same politics that has today assumed terrifying proportions and is being manifested through violence and terror and civil war. Today, they are standing face to face. Between the walls of this prison courtyard.

Memories of their past come back to the officer. But what is the point of remembering? Today, there is no need for their arguments and debates. The war has rendered all that futile. The past is null and void, their friendship is annulled and only the future stares them in the face. The same future has goaded the country into civil war.

The two friends are meeting today after what seems an age. On this terrible morning. There is silence all around them. They look at each other, and smile slightly. Not a word is spoken. Quietness. Only the morning light slowly spreading over the courtyard. A cold stillness.

The rhythm of silence. Almost like the beating of one's heart. And every single person present there is trapped inexorably in that rhythm. The firing squad, the squad leader, everyone.

The squad leader's voice suddenly rings out into the silence. 'Attention!'

Six rifles shift into place. Six soldiers tighten their grip on their respective weapons. Strong. Firm. A firing squad tuned to that peculiar rhythm.

Something occurs then with the swiftness of a flash of lightning. The young Loyalist coughs slightly. Clears his throat for the last time.

At once, the rhythm snaps. The beat falters. The entire atmosphere jars. Discordant. The rhythm of silence is splintered, irrevocably.

And it is as if the squad leader is hurled aside. Flung away. At a loss. Trying to clutch momentarily at something that floats away. Into the air. He looks towards the prisoner. In case the man says something.

The prisoner, the young Loyalist, stands absolutely still. His back to the wall. His eyes ask no questions, his demeanour demands no explanations. The firing squad? The leader looks towards them. Six armed soldiers. Set to an unyielding tune.

Waiting patiently, obediently for the next order. For a few moments the squad leader loses 'consciousness'. He stands there, seeking desperate resort in his sense of sight. He can see a man, standing with his back to the wall. Standing still. Six armed soldiers stand facing him. A few more people, a short distance away. An extremely ordinary sight, without meaning, without relevance. As though a clock had been ticking through eternity and now, suddenly, the throbbing has petered out and died into silence.

A few inert moments pass by, thus.

Then, 'consciousness' returns ever so slowly. The squad leader realizes that he has just barked out an order and that there are a few more to complete. He tries to give himself a mental shake. Tries to come to grips with himself. And simultaneously yells out to the best of his ability, 'Shoulder arms!' Realizes immediately that it doesn't quite ring true, not even to his own ears. Irrelevant. Out of tune. Out of rhythm.

Tries to find his footing. Restore the rhythm. He yells, 'To aim!'

The six soldiers are ready. Fingers poised on the trigger. Waiting. For the final command.

Just then, footsteps break the silence. People seem to be running in their direction. Has the sentence been repealed, then? Finally, the powers-that-be have paused to change their mind?

In utter desperation the leader screams, 'Stop!'

Six men. Poised with their rifles.

Six men. Caught in the rhythm.

Six men, when they hear the scream to stop, f-i-r-e.

A short story. One that leaves you breathless. A mere fragment. But possessed of a terrible horror and an incredible helplessness. These two elements assume a grotesque physicality before the eyes of the reader. The discerning reader will of course recall Dostoevsky. And a heartless cynicism will assume prominence from beneath this horror and helplessness. One that does not weaken men nor crush their spines beneath its feet. One that does not numb the mind nor destroy their will to live. This is the sort of cynicism that forces man to be still, for a few moments. And in the next instant, provides him with a belief, with a confidence as strong as though crafted from steel and which, even today, even now, provides him with the inspiration to resist the senseless chaos of the times. Instead of false assurances of hope, it gestures towards an honest conviction and faith. All this in the guise of cynicism. It is as if Chaplin was talking about this very cynicism, a couple of years later and in his very own beautiful style, at a discussion following the completion of his film *The Great Dictator* [1940].

The ending of this movie was not his usual tongue-in-cheek happy ending but one that made a certain category of people distinctly uncomfortable. He said, 'It would be much easier to have the barber and Hanna disappear over the horizon, off to a promised land against the glowing sunset. But there is no promised land for the oppressed people of the world. There is no place over the horizon to which they can go for sanctuary. They must stand and so must we too.'

He had expressed this undeniable truth, somewhere in the mid-1930s, when he had begun work on *Modern Times* [1936]. During a time when the entire world was obsessed with an inhuman war. After completing *Modern Times*, while in conversation with Robert Payne, he had mentioned, as though reasoning out things to himself, 'In my new film, he will not be quite so nice. I am sharpening the edge of his character so that people who have liked him *vaguely* will have to make up their minds.'

It seemed to be at the same time a conviction and a complaint. As though he wanted to say, quite happily, that at least a fraction of the international popularity received by his creation—the little tramp— had been like an unexpected windfall. And had remained largely unclear. Which is why, 'vaguely' wouldn't do, any longer.

Chaplin felt the need to delineate the edges of this character more sharply. And that is what happened, too. The character was rendered more sharply although none of his individuality was lost in the process.

It is not as if the danger of losing individuality was not pointed out. But I will say, on the basis of all my thoughts-ideas-discussions on Chaplin, as of the Jewish barber in *The Great Dictator* or in *Monsieur Verdoux* [1947]—it is not difficult to chart the progress of that character from time immemorial, that is from the 'conception of the average man'. It is all present in the persona of the Jewish barber and in his extremely commonplace yet explosive dialogues.

Let us think of that scene. The Dictator's goons attack the helpless barber. One of the Dictator's high-ranking officers rushes to the spot and rescues him. Saves his life. The man gets back on his feet. Just as he has always done, from the beginning. The officer says, 'I thought you were an Aryan.' And the instantaneous riposte, 'I am a vegetarian, sir.'

Or the comment made by Chaplin when he was about to start work on *Monsieur Verdoux*. He had said, 'There are situations when even murder becomes comical.'

Comical! A murder is committed. And the hall is filled with the sound of laughter. Just as it used to be heard or still is, when the audience is confronted with the ridiculous activities of the little tramp. That is the only difference. The tramp has mimicked the millionaire in various ways, and in the process has embarrassed himself. And others too. And here, dressed up as Monsieur Verdoux, it seems he has crossed the borders of particularity and mimicked the totality of a class—the class that specializes in genocide. Comical, laughable.

I have seen Chaplin in the flesh just once. On 3 September 1972. On the stage of the famous opera house Le Venetia, in Venice's Saint Mark. The last day of the 33rd International Film Festival. They had been running a Chaplin retrospective.

All the boats going in the direction of Saint Marc were full that day. The Opera House too was brimming over with people. I was among the lucky ones—I had gone to collect my award and I had a seat on the stage. There, accompanied by two accomplished assistants, that legend of a man walked onto the stage. I was incredulous when I saw him. It was almost impossible to recognize Charlie. The Derby was gone as was the moustache and the tight buttoned-up coat was missing too. The stick was nowhere in sight. Not a single trace of his defining persona was present.

He sat there, in the middle of the stage. An assistant on either side. Ailing. His skin now wrinkled. I shall never forget that evening. It was certainly a day to remember.

The festival was at Lido. I watched him there, on the screen—'a fallen aristocrat at grips with poverty'. He has had to tolerate many insults. He knew that 'humiliation is a thing you cannot forget'. His has been a very long journey; his experiences have been varied and often, amusing. He has faced the world and its challenges with courage, and often, even met with defeat. But he has never lost his sense of the humane. With brave Quixotic steps he has constantly moved towards a new horizon. *The Great Dictator* is, of course, an exception. There, he and his beloved do not drift off into their dream world. In the role of the Jewish barber, he uses the assumed identity to place his impassioned plea before the world—'to create happiness, to make life free and beautiful, to make life a wonderful adventure.'

For those two weeks, all I had done was rediscover Chaplin's odyssey. This undaunted progress of his, through troubled times. This unflagging search for man's compassion despite social injustice and political treachery. He was not schooled in politics and its protocols but his ear was set to the tune of the passing of time.

His reactions were always spontaneous and he never tried to conceal this. The film *Shoulder Arms* was made in 1918—an unknown soldier of the Allies, Kaiser, has been arrested. The audience doubles over with laughter. Kaiser is taken to the nearest camp. And in the very next moment, the following line appears across the screen—'And peace to the world'. This simple view of life, in today's complicated world, assumes a kind of Shavian wit. That was the time when genocide was prevalent in the world around us. When Monsieur Verdoux, the murderer of twelve women, is being taken to the guillotine, he says only this: 'War, conflict—it is all business. One murder makes a villain, millions a hero. Number[s] sanctify.'

Watching him on the screen for that entire fortnight in Venice, I loved him, laughed at him, thought about him and somewhere along the way, my own mind and thinking moved ahead a bit more. *The Great Dictator* and *Monsieur Verdoux*—these were all inevitable developments of his own creation of the 'ordinary man'. Not exceptions at all. It was society and its conditions that effected this transformation.

After watching him on the screen for fifty years, I finally got to see him, that day, in the flesh. Amid the crowds at the Opera House. Everyone went berserk and broke out in deafening applause. The man who had spent his entire life expressing a wealth of emotions on his face and later, talking in plenty, was strangely silent that day. He simply threw a few kisses at the enthralled audience. The curtain dropped. I was standing just behind him. I realized that the end of his life was imminent.

The next year, in Teheran, while my wife and I were lunching with the famous French director René Clair [1898–1981], one of the luminaries of the twentieth century, we heard that he and his wife had come via Switzerland where they had visited Chaplin. His condition had deteriorated further, he said. Clair was almost the same age as Chaplin; a decade or so separated them. At times, though, other differences have rendered them apart. That day, at the lunch table, he talked only of Chaplin. And of Oona, Chaplin's last wife, daughter of the famous playwright Eugene O'Neill. He spoke of how she stayed by him constantly, like the eternal mother who guards her foolish son. He had to be bathed and dressed and fed. She was an extraordinary woman, this Oona, and extraordinary was her love.

But in 1974, in London, during the release of his book *My Life in Pictures*, Chaplin said it was not possible for him to take a break because his mind was besieged by ideas.

Man's thinking can never come to an end. It is only his life that must draw to a close. In three years, everything was over. On 25 December, Christmas. Many many years ago, Christ was born on this day. In accordance with his wishes, Chaplin's last rites were performed without any fuss or grandeur. He was laid to rest, quietly and peacefully. Suddenly, two months later, his coffin went missing. Finally, twenty kilometres away from Lake Geneva, the coffin with his body was discovered in a cornfield. He was buried for the second time. And the offenders were duly punished.

In that cornfield, the farmer placed a simple wooden cross upon that spot. And hung a cane from it, in memory of Charlie.

I wonder, if he were to make a film about this stealing of the coffin, how would he make it? I have a whim—to be the owner of that cornfield. I would have done exactly as he did. And I would have also placed a scarecrow upon that cross. It would be a beautiful gesture—a sweet revenge upon the enemies of men and humanity. Of course, I would express this in true Chaplinesque style—that of 'inspired nonsense'.

And then? I would engrave his unforgettable words upon that cross. 'The birds will sing tomorrow'.

I saw Chaplin in 1972. He lived for five more years. I have heard that with an unflagging zeal for life, even the year before his death, he had said, 'To work is to live, and I love to live.'

Today, on his centenary, it is those words that ring in my ears. I recite them almost like a mantra. 'To work is to live, and I love to live.'

2

The millionaire tosses away the burning cigarette. The homeless little tramp immediately pounces upon it, as though it is his own. He places it between his lips, takes a puff, and then lets out a cloud of smoke. Just like the millionaire. And at the same time, puts on an air of almost philosophical detachment. Simple. Effortless. Easy.

We laugh. We laugh and think. And our minds grow.

The vagabond, the little tramp saunters on. Right through history. On . . . and on. And somewhere along the way, he becomes a part of history himself.

The wheels of history keep turning. Film after film is made. Various sorts of experiences occur in the tramp's life. He lampoons himself. Pities himself, slightly. But he meets the world head on. Recklessly. Throws a challenge at everything that comes his way. And then at a particularly terrible moment in time, this fearless tramp suddenly stops in his tracks. Tosses away his bowler hat, flings off his coat, trims his moustache. Although his persona remains largely unchanged. He turns towards his inquisitors. And says, 'Genocide! The whole world is party to it. Compared with the rest of them, I am a mere amateur.' The masters of the farce find him guilty and condemn him to death. He tells them, with a quiet and unshakeable conviction, 'I shall see you soon, very soon.'

Man laughs. He laughs and thinks. And his mind grows.

In his new incarnation, regardless of age, he indiscriminately plays lover to an assortment of wealthy women. This sport has fatal consequences for the other players because he begins to kill them off, one by one, and steal their wealth. Man laughs and thinks to himself, and his mind takes a leap forward as he hears the following words—spoken by the murdering man to his crippled wife. 'These are desperate days . . . millions are starving and unemployed . . . It is not easy for a man of my age.'

Shakespeare said, 'Genius is to madness alike.'

And Chaplin perhaps believed, 'Ruthlessness is to comicalness alike.'

The ruthless and the comic.

In this way, having established a link between these two extremes, Chaplin became an outstanding example of an essential creativity. One that transcends all conceivable absurdities and yet emanates a tremendous wisdom. So that in the world of cinema, he can be compared to no other but himself. [Federico] Fellini comes to mind. He had remarked, about Chaplin: 'He is a kind of Adam from whom we are all descended.'

3

Of late, a lot has been written about Chaplin. There is more that is still being written and even more that will be. Different people have regarded him from different points of view. Both from within his films and without.

The inquisitive reader reads everything avidly and tries to come to terms with his own mind and its ability to understand.

Debates have arisen and continue to do so. But that is all centred around analyses. There has never been any question about his immensity. Even when a smattering of questions have raised their heads they have all been in a particular context and only when the egos of some weighty faction have been trampled upon. But those too have been quashed, in the long run. As Chaplin had known they would be. When he was forbidden by the government to return to the United States, much to the loud dismay of the rest of the world, and British reporters hounded him for a response, he had answered briefly: 'I have countless friends in America. Only a handful of enemies.' As though nonchalantly sweeping aside a mere triviality.

All of this has been spoken about at length, written about and read. And today, celebrating his centenary, the newspapers and magazines brim over with all this anew. Seminars and symposiums will witness more discussions. And perhaps most of that will adopt a certain religious fervour, of course under the guise of 'duty'. Therefore this moment finds me deep in thought. What do I write about? What do I say that hasn't been recounted a million times already? What is there to say?

Let me put all else aside and recount a simple incident. Far removed from his films. A very personal little moment. Written in an account by one of Chaplin's sons. While writing about his father, he says, 'I was going through a difficult patch with my wife. Divorce seemed the only solution. Which meant legalities and huge expenses. So I wrote off to father. Told him everything. Asked him for some money. He sent me the money; as much as I had asked for. But he wrote something for me—'I have met your wife only once. Having met her and spoken to her, I quite liked her. How did this happen so suddenly? I hope you are not doing something on a whim? You must keep one thing in mind—there comes a time in every person's life when he thinks to himself, "I wish my life had an anchor." I too have felt that lapse. Oona is the anchor I was so in need of.'

Oona. Chaplin's fourth wife. Eugene O'Neill's daughter. The person who, despite riding the crest of success has had his personal peace disrupted continually by intrusions and invasions, most of which he invited upon himself, that fifty-four-year-old man married a young girl who had just crossed her eighteenth year. And he came to understand and learned to perceive that Oona was his anchor. And any compassionate man will realize and confess that this was a tremendous realization on his part. And this realization befits him—the man who walked hand-in-hand with time, who altered himself to suit time's needs and demands, and sharpened the edges of his persona, responding always to time. And who moved forward, from one new experience to another.

In later years, at the other end of his advanced years, Oona was his only companion. He spent hours sitting silently, holding her hand. And referring to Chaplin's anchor, his son has said, 'She was able to share a part of his incredible loneliness.'

[*Edited version of 'Charles Chaplin: A Tribute' which appeared in* Nandan's *Charlie Chaplin centenary issue, and 'To Laugh, to Think, to Grow' which appeared in the* Sunday Statesman, Miscellany, *16 April 1989.*]

Cinema Par Excellence: Films from Latin America

It was rumoured that finally, [Michelangelo] Antonioni was coming to Calcutta, and bringing his wife along with him. Antonioni turned eighty only a couple of years ago. Now a world-weary and exhausted man, ill and wheelchair-bound, despite various physical complaints, he was still risking the trip to Calcutta. This was a matter of pride for the city, in fact for the entire country. The artist, the magician of cinema—Antonioni. In whose words, 'We know that underneath the revealed image there is another that is more faithful to reality, and beneath this still another, and again another under this last. And so on up to that true image of that absolute, mysterious reality that nobody will ever see. Or perhaps up to the point at which every image, every reality, decomposes. Abstract film would in this way have its own reason for existing.' He has been speaking nothing else but the language of cinema all his life. Cinema occupies every part of his consciousness, every part of his being. Even the simplest things are refracted through the lens of cinema.

A journalist had once asked him: 'Won't you ever make a film about New York?' The reply: 'Yes I will, when the screen is no longer horizontal but vertical.' Here too, through the language of the cinema, he immediately projects the city of New York before one's eyes. Amazing!

But today, ailing as he is, I am not sure of how much he will say. Perhaps this time round he is coming only to listen, and to watch.

James Lester Peries from Sri Lanka is also coming. Our neighbour, one of our very own. Whose film *Gamperaliya* [1963] won the Golden Peacock at the New Delhi Film Festival in 1965. And Argentina's Fernando Solanas, also accompanied by his wife. This will be the first time he visits India, and the first time he sees Calcutta. Along with other famous personalities. Well-known and venerated members of the international film community.

The name Solanas throws up a thousand memories. The 1960s and 70s when all of Latin America was in turmoil; filmmakers and cinema workers restless and distressed. When courage and confidence smoked against the air and across the skies in rapid bursts of gunpowder. When, like many others, Solanas too was a spark from the same fire. The same time when Glauber Rocha of Brazil wrote his *Aesthetics of Violence*.

Fragments come back to me.

The October of 1972. The small town of Nyon, in Switzerland. A small film festival had been organized. Nominated as a member of the jury, I was watching film after film, from various parts of the globe. The festival drew to a close. The participants were returning home, to their respective countries. We, the members of the jury were also making preparations for our homeward journeys when, the morning after, I was suddenly awakened by a telephone call. From the festival director. Moritz Hadeln. 'I have to discuss something important with you. I'm coming to your hotel.' He arrived in a little while accompanied by Henri Stork—a close friend and co-worker of Joris Ivens. Moritz gave me a letter to read. From Colombia, Latin America. It had been smuggled through. Secretly. It was from the Latin American director, Carlo Alvarez. He had written it from prison, and to many places in the world, including Nyon. This is what he had to say: 'The military government has imprisoned me, my wife and many other artists. We have been charged with indulging in illegal and destructive activities. We will have to stand trial and if we are proven guilty, then the punishment will be severe. Our plea: please save us.'

Under the circumstances we did what it was possible for us to do. We drew up a draft, in the intricate rhetoric of a communiqué. And it was immediately translated into various languages, typed out, and dispatched to several places, with the aim of forming public opinion. In fact, we even sent it to the Colombian government, to the UN and to the UNESCO. This petition representing the barbaric attacks against members of the cultural community was signed by a whole host of luminaries in the film world. And many others as well.

Next year. Again in October. In Mannheim, Germany. There too, due to various circumstances, I was once again heading the jury. On the last day of the festival, another petition was read out to those invitees who were present, on behalf of the jury. Its statement: that the Chilean filmmaker Patricio Guzmán had been imprisoned. Its plea: to free him immediately. And at the very same festival, despite Guzmán's absence, his film *The First Year* received an award.

Nineteen seventy-six. Leipzig. I was among those invited. I was standing in the foyer of the hotel that morning. A small throng of people moved over in my direction. They had no difficulty in recognizing me because I was clad in my usual kurta–pyjama–jahar coat, etc. And the colour of my skin no doubt also aided recognition. They introduced themselves, one by one—Alvarez from Colombia, his wife Julia, and a few others. And the Chilean Guzmán. Oh, such happiness, such love, such affection. And that's when I heard, about Glezier in Argentina. He had been dragged off by the police. And until then, no one knew to where he had been taken. In other words, he had fallen victim to a process by which 'difficult' people in Latin America were 'removed'.

I had seen this Glezier only once. And been introduced to him just that one time. In 1973, at the Berlin festival. He had been distributing handbills personally, running from person to person. He came up to me. Pushed one into my hands, and waited. It was a handbill on behalf of the trade union, mentioning some important facts about the necessity of the union. I asked him: 'Being a part of the business of cinema, did you really need to take on this additional responsibility?' He replied saying this was the kind of work that he really enjoyed. I watched one of his films at the Berlin Forum—*The Traitor*—about a certain politician who betrays the cause of the Union while pretending to be working in its best interests.

Is Glezier still alive? Perhaps not. Just like Brazil's Glauber Rocha. Wanted on six counts of alleged sabotage, he fled his native land and travelled from one foreign country to another. Finally in Africa he made a film—*The Lion Has Many Heads*—and then moved to Paris. And from Paris to Berkeley, California. Rocha wrote a letter to one of his American friends. The day the friend received that letter was the very same day I arrived at Berkeley as his guest. Rocha's friend was my friend too—Tom Ladi. Tom handed the letter over for me to read, along with a handwritten filmscript, also by Rocha; he was simply waiting for the chance to make a film based on that script. In his letter Rocha mentioned that it had become impossible for him to carry on. Bit by bit, his life was being eaten away. All he wanted to do was make the film the way he had envisioned it—he needed money, the right atmosphere, and people who thought the way he did, with whom he could share his thoughts and his conversations.

Tom was unable to do anything for Rocha. There was nothing he could do. And one day Rocha returned to Brazil. And wasted away slowly and finally, died.

Miguel Littín. Of Chile. Another remarkable person. Extraordinary. He spent almost twelve years running from one country to another, living the life of an exile. Then, after many secret plans and conspiracies, after much thought of the pros and cons, after changing his name, age and physical appearance, he finally sneaked back into his country for six weeks. And returned safely to Spain after filming in very dangerous circumstances. That footage resulted in two films and two shorter documentaries. And later, when Gabriel García Márquez wrote *Clandestine in Chile* based on Littín's six-week secret stay, Littín mentioned, 'It may not have been the most heroic action of my life, but it was the most worthwhile.'

Sometime around the middle of 1986, I happened to meet both of these men. In Munich, I met Littín and in Cuba, I met García Márquez. And I chatted with each of them, at each of these places. But neither of them even breathed a word about the Chilean experience. Despite their maintaining a safe distance, both of them still had to be incredibly careful and cautious. Because the book still hadn't been published. In case word got out and reached a certain group of people. Then the entire plan would come to nought. And truth to tell, this fear wasn't unwarranted at all. Because when the book was released, somewhere towards the end of 1986, 15,000 copies were burnt in one of the Chilean cities, on order from the Government. Which explained the caution. And the secrecy. Today, Littín has returned to his homeland. And returned to a safe homeland. Just like Solanas too has gone home to Argentina, after having been on the move constantly, from one place to another. To the very same Argentina, where, during a terrible time in the 1960s, he had made his film *The Hour of the Furnaces*. An extraordinary film.

Let me tell you about that film. Strangely enough, within a few days of my writing about it in one of our newspapers, my film *Oka Oorie Katha* was shown somewhere abroad, and at Cannes too, and Solanas came to me. And said, of course speaking through an interpreter, that this film had reminded him of his own country.

That was the first time I was seeing him, so there was no way of recognizing him. The interpreter hadn't introduced us either. Perhaps to surprise me, he did so, a while later. I asked him, 'Are you a foreigner?' He replied, 'Yes.' I asked, 'Where are you from?' He answered, 'Argentina.' 'Do you make films?' 'Yes.' At that moment, and I remember this clearly, the interpreter clapped each of us on our backs and said, 'This man's name is Solanas!'

Solanas!

Solanas' *The Hour of the Furnaces* is a manifesto. It is unabashed propaganda from the first shot to the last. It is didactic, it is agitational, it acts like a detonator. It is, in essence, a guide to militant action.

It is a film made in Argentina. It was made secretly, it was shown secretly, also discussed secretly. It was part of the guerrilla movement shaking up all of Latin America. Much later, after hundreds of clandestine screenings, the film was legalized by Juan Perón. Understandably, immediately after it obtained the certificate, the film was circulated world wide.

It is a shame that this gem of a film could be made available to the Indian audiences only after such a long time and that too, for not more than, alas, a dozen showings. *The Hour of the Furnaces* is a feature-length documentary. It was made to sharpen one's understanding of the reality that struggled to grow under the constant pressure of the physical and psychological violence of the neo-colonial system. The film is a trenchant attack on the politics of neocolonialism and an indictment of its terrible system.

The system, as the film ruthlessly exposes, manifests itself on various levels in the society of the industrial belt, in the urban milieu, in the agrarian base. With militant fury, the film shows the ugly face of the system which, under the guise of social respectability and radicalism, beguiles the people with very many false beliefs. Bit by bit, it unmasks the lies and hypocrisy behind the façade and then in unambiguous language, asks the people 'to learn to hate'.

The film is full of such explosive lines. A people without hate cannot triumph, the film says in a certain sequence. In another sequence, it makes a categorical statement that colonial education is just an attempt to legalize dependence. And it does not fail to comment on the field of mass communication, which is where the 'intellectuals' are seen to be quite active. Mass communication, according to the film, is more effective than napalm.

All this and many more lines and words, punctuated by hosts of images—both moving and still—passing across the screen at a rapid pace and that is how Solanas, the director, constructs his film. Solanas addresses his spectator directly. He tells him the real truth behind the external calm of the neo-colonial system. And, as the film reveals this truth, Solanas says, 'We fear peace more than war.'

This 'peace' must be combated. Solanas names his spectator as 'the humiliated'; he asserts that his condition is 'rebellion'. The film asks the spectator to organize revolution.

The people must react. To be able to react in the most revolutionary manner is magnificent. Since the people are not allowed to between life and death, only by choosing death can they choose life.

And instantly we see Che Guevara on the screen. Dead.

Each and every detail, thus, speaks of political sagacity, of ideological depth.

Brick by brick, the film, through consistent analysis, redefines the history of Argentina, of 'balkanized' Latin America which, in a broader political context, can rightly serve as a model for all of the Third World. And here lies the universal significance of this stupendous document called *The Hour of the Furnaces*.

Structurally the film is one hundred percent cinema. As I watch it, I can unmistakably see a glowing tribute being paid to Dziga Vertov who, many years ago, propounded the theory of Kino-Eye.

And who, in his manifesto, asked the future filmmakers to organize revolution.

The film, in a way, also pays homage to Sergei Eisenstein who, during his lifetime, could not fulfil his desire to film Karl Marx's *The Capital*. Lastly, here is a film which, with remarkable accuracy, juxtaposes image and sound in apparent contradiction and in the process, presents a brilliant case for the aesthetics of the audio-visual montage.

The last shot, the long close-up of Che and the percussion beats on the soundtrack. You look deep into Che. You too remain unmoved.

The revolution germinates within you. It spreads its contagion. It grows around you.

This is cinema par excellence.

The exiled Peron came back to his people after twenty-one years. When he assumed power, he legalized the film. Peron, then lost his lustre. But *The Hours of the Furnaces* is still with the people.

It belongs to the people, to the persecuted, to the humiliated, to all those whose condition is 'rebellion'. To all those who have nothing to lose but their chains.

[*Edited version of* '*Shekol Bhanga Chalacchitra*' *which appeared in* Aajkal, Robibashor, *9 January 1994 (translated by Sunandini Banerjee) and* '*Combating Peace*' *which appeared in* Ananda Bazar Patrika, *14 January 1994.*]

A Funny, Bitter Allegory: Lindsay Anderson

One must read the man and the film together. Only then can you, or so I think, really 'see' the film and not just view it. In the 1960s, there were the three greats in England—Lindsay Anderson (*This Sporting Life, Thursday's Children, If. . .* , *O Lucky Man, Britannia Hospital*), Tony Richardson (*The Loneliness of the Long Distance Runner, Tom Jones*) and Karel Reisz (*Saturday Night and Sunday Morning*). They created a wonderful climate for British cinema and gave a new look to it, both in terms of content and form. The movement, however, if at all it could be called a movement, was short-lived. Richardson left for Hollywood via New York only to get lost amid an unfavourable crowd, and was finally elbowed out. Karel Reisz, remaining an Englander as always, eventually lost his bite. The only one left at the post, to quote the man himself, was Lindsay, standing on the burning deck, fighting Putnam and his kind.

A sequence in *Britannia Hospital* [1982]: the hospital staff is on strike but the Queen Mother has to visit the hospital. The agitated staff cannot be cowed down, so the Queen Mother has to be brought in, concealed in a coffin. Sacrilege! Blasphemy!

An afternoon in Calcutta. A telephone call. A voice that was a bit on the loud side and a trifle flippant.

'Could I speak to Mrinal Sen?'

'That's me.'

Instantly the voice assumed a tone that was distinctly superior.

'Who am I?'

A few seconds passed as I ransacked my memory, fumbled a little and then answered confidently, 'Who could it be other than Lindsay Anderson?'

'You are great!'

'Would you then recommend me to Scotland Yard?'

'Yes, I will. I must. But right at the moment I badly need your help. Save me, Mrinal—I am in prison.'

'Prison?'

'Yes, prison. I mean, I'll be taken there soon.'

'Where are you?' I asked, intrigued.

'At the Calcutta Airport, sitting before a Customs high-up, claiming to be your friend. I am a trespasser, he says.'

'What does he mean?'

The story is simple but funny. Lindsay was under the impression— and he was right—that anyone holding a British passport did not need a visa for India. But it so happened, due to circumstances beyond his control, that he was born in India. So, being the holder of a separate passport because he was born outside the Queen's land, he was possibly a little less than a complete Britisher, and hence needed a visa.

Lindsay explained it all on the phone and asked me if I could put in a word or two to the local authorities and organize his clearance, even if for a few hours, if not a week.

Happily, Lindsay was cleared in two hours. The stupid law was also withdrawn not much later. And when he died a sad death in the early 1990s, he died a British citizen, plain and simple.

Anderson was a courageous man, unusually so, and he paid heavily for remaining so all his life. With every act of courage, his enemies multiplied although he made friends too. In his own country he was both loved and maligned. Maligned for various reasons and in abundant measure. Which was why he was never the media's blue-eyed boy. But he never cared, never. That was why he said, 'Stand up, stand up!' Perhaps he believed that the one who stands alone is the strongest.

Once I called him 'un-British' because his life was a consistent violation of the Anglo-Saxon understanding of the British code of ethics.

Did he take it as a tribute? I do not know. But years later he gave me a book, a book about John Ford written by him, and wrote in it:

For Mrinal...
Are we intelligent enough to survive?
(And thank you for understanding)
Salut!

This was in 1982. Twelve years later, I now say, 'Salut to Lindsay.'

Lindsay Anderson died recently. Not in his own country but in France where, reportedly, he had gone for a holiday. And coincidentally, it was ten years ago in France that we had last spoken. When we parted, I still remember him saying, half-jokingly, 'Today's fantasy will turn out to be tomorrow's reality.'

Remembering him, I now pull out from my old file a rather small piece which, long before our last meeting, I had written for a radical political weekly. The piece was about a queer fantasy of Lindsay

Anderson's—*If*... [1968]. It was Lindsay's all-time best. And this was what I had written:

Enough! Enough of bad films that have been filling the air. For a change now, let us find a good film to talk about.

If... is the film of my choice and one that I saw for the second time in Delhi during the festival, last January. My first viewing was at Venice where, unconnected with the festival programme, a very private show was quickly organized in an exclusive and private theatre. It was an after-dinner show. The fashionables, among others, visiting the festival and holidaying at the Riviera, hustled together, all garbed in their formals and mouthing the customary how-do-you-dos.

As a contrast, the director was dressed informally; he paced up and down, squatted on the floor for brief moments, stretched his legs every now and then, yawned without offering any apology and generally outraged the fashionables' sensibilities at every moment. A vicarious thrill, indeed!

Lindsay Anderson is the name of the director, born in India and made in England; angry, intolerant, intense and yet endowed with an inimitable sense of humour.

In Delhi, three months later, the film was presented at the festival outside the competitive section and, as a condition for all festival showings, it was untouched by the Censor Board.

In May 1968, the students at Sorbonne erupted in a huge fuss over it and soon it grew into a major national event; a kind of 'mini' revolution attracting worldwide attention. In May 1969, *If*... got the Grand Prix at the Cannes Film Festival where, exactly a year ago, Godard and his colleagues had rushed to the big screen of the festival theatre and created a scene, militantly chanting 'Mao' and bringing the traditional ceremony to a standstill.

I can see a connection between the two: the ferment in 1968 and the verdict of the international jury of the 1969 festival at Cannes.

The script, I am told, was written before the May 1968 events in France. But changes were made, changes that made the connection more obvious. 'The story of the film, if it is to be called a story at all, is all about a juvenile attack on the establishment.'

From the beginning to the end, *If*. . . is an outrageous protest, absurdly funny on the surface and bitter to the core. In its overall structure, its thematic exploration, the use of tools and in its attention to the minutest of details *If*. . . defies all conventions. It aims, at times, at the ludicrous, sometimes at the grotesque, but is always dangerously rebellious. And nowhere in the film has anger said goodbye to humour, which, to my mind, has lent Lindsay Anderson's film a fascinating extra dimension.

The silent protest of the students, the ferment, even the fun and violence of the inevitable sex act among the adolescents, and ultimately the resistance and the crusade—all this is the story of *If*. . . . A kind of wish-fulfilment. Queer, youthful and vibrant, totally dream-like in form and in content.

The students of the public school pursue a lovely dream—that of putting an end to the hateful business of 'licking the frigid fingers' of the caretaker for the rest of their frigid life in that establishment. While, in essence, the message of the film goes much beyond the frontiers of the school premises, it is interesting to note that the director, in order to find a 'model' school, did not have to cross the English Channel. The area of operation is a typical British public school.

A duty-bound, discipline-ridden school inspector walks into a room. The inspector smells alcohol. The students feign innocence. Silence: awkward and amusing. Fuming within, the inspector walks out. Quietly, the boys pull out their bottles from under the pillows and cushions.

'In Calcutta,' says one, an expert among the students, 'there is one death from starvation every few minutes.' The 'warring' boys perform a ritual, pledging revolution. And thus, 'through wisdom' the students 'get understanding'.

Chargesheets are framed against a few boys for breaking the moral of 'the house'. They are punished, reminding you of the horrors of the concentration camp. While you see the law-breaking juveniles being caned mercilessly and in the process getting steeled, the camera surreptitiously captures another boy in another room looking through the microscope, doing his 'practical'-s. The bacteria spreads. So does anger and violence.

The establishment continues to function with apparent efficiency and considerable tact. There is no end to the empty boasts about the loyalty-bound public school nor to the tall promises about producing supermarket managers.

But the boys refuse to be beguiled any more. In utter desperation they rise in revolt. They take a pledge: Death to the oppressors. Resistance, they say. Liberty, they promise.

Everything moves on a war footing. They call it a 'crusade' and the visuals and the soundtrack are largely reminiscent of modern warfare. And then, in the midst of sound and fury, the film ends abruptly. Not with the customary 'The End' but with a big 'if'.

If . . . is a funny, bitter allegory of an unusual kind where the implications of words and visuals are as familiar and evocative to a Calcuttan as they are to a Parisian or a Londoner or a New Yorker or, for that matter, to anyone who lives and grows in the contemporary climate.

If . . . is a sharp note of defiance. And a dream.

[*Originally appeared as 'A Defiant Dream' in* Gentleman, September 2000.]

This Space of Silence: Andrei Tarkovsky

A field. A vast expanse of emptiness. A stretch of water. The sky, overcast. Tall trees like haphazard signposts across the landscape. Trees that are possessed with enough daring to try and touch the sky. An old man drags a huge, bare tree into this space. This space of silence that the noisy world seems to have flung away from itself. The little boy helps him, wordlessly, with hands that are unused to the task. The old man makes the tree stand upright, underneath the sky. The boy, though still unsure, continues to help him. The tree will remain thus, standing tall. Soon its bare branches will sprout new leaves. So the old man says, as the two of them work side by side. And he begins to tell the boy a story. A story about a monk. Once upon a time, near the foothills of a mountain, a monk planted a dry tree in this very same way. He would water it every day and then set off for the fields. Coming back to it only at the end of the day. One day the tree blossomed into life, its branches bearing fruits and flowers. The old man keeps working and talking to the boy. He says,

'If only everyone would do the same . . . if they worked away at just one thing ceaselessly . . . at the same time . . . in the same way . . . every day. Perhaps the world would have been different. Perhaps it would still have the capacity for change.' This is how the film begins. *Sacrifice* [1986]. Andrei Tarkovsky's last film. A postman on his bicycle, and a few other characters slowly collect at this same spot. A doctor, a husband-wife pair and another and finally, a solitary servant-girl. As though they have swept aside all the world's clutter and wiped off the layers of accumulated grime, and have come here to this space of silence, temporarily freed from all their burdens. In search of respite. And, unknown to themselves, in search of a confrontation with their own souls. The entire film lasts for almost two and a half hours, during which very little actually occurs by way of physical action. At the apparent level, these occurrences seem extremely insignificant, but at the heart of the film there is the silent preparation for a particular emotion. An emotion that arises from the fear of the 'end of the world'. And this emotion culminates in a terrifying explosion. When it seems as though the entire universe has been swallowed up in flames and burnt down to a fistful of ash. And the few characters and the members of the audience wait patiently for a new world to be born. Once again, there is the space of silence, the solitude that soothes the soul, the tranquillity. We see the little boy— unworldly and uninitiated in the ways of the world, and speaking not a single word—at the end of the film, at 'the end of the world'. He walks towards the tall bare tree. Waters it, as he was supposed to everyday. Then he lies down, flat on the ground, staring at the sky overhead. Or perhaps he stares at the branches of the tree which spread out above him, stretching out in various directions. Branches which will be, one day, covered in fresh green leaves. Across the stillness and from the depths of this boundless silence, the innocent little boy asks a question. Slowly. Quietly. Perplexedly. 'In the beginning was the word. Why?' This is followed by a few moments of stifling silence. Then the camera moves away from the little boy's face and turns to the sky and then, to the branches of the tree. Its gaze is fixed. Ever so slowly, through the carefully modulated background music, a small thought of Tarkovsky's appears on the screen: *Dedicated to my son Andriushka, who has hope and confidence.*

I, and many others besides me, firmly believe that Tarkovsky knew this was his last film. He knew he would not live for very much longer. That day at Cannes, when the auditorium was overflowing with his fans who had come for the film's premiere—14 May 1986—it had been impossible to bring Tarkovsky down from Paris. He was fighting for his life in a Parisian hospital. A week or two later, on the 22nd or the 23rd, at the glittering award ceremony, again before a packed auditorium, Tarkovsky's name was announced. And a fourteen- or fifteen-year-old boy walked up from among the audience—the young Andriushka to whom his father Andrei Tarkovsky had dedicated his film *Sacrifice*. That was a truly memorable moment, a moment capable of filling even the sternest person's soul with an unbearable lightness of being, overwhelming him completely.

At that moment I too was grappling with an extraordinary sensation. And it was not just then, but at every moment as I watched the film. Although as soon as it was over and its spell loosened its hold on my mind, I must confess that I experienced a severe sense of discomfort as I analysed and dissected the film.

On the one hand I was overwhelmed by the force of the tremendous passion present in every moment of the film. I have been defeated in my attempts to test the unshakable foundations of my innermost convictions. I have been plagued with the urge to cleanse my soul of its vicious torments. And I have been rendered speechless in admiration at the harmonious arrangement of image and sound and the extraordinary precision of its rhythm.

On the other hand, having cast aside my bewilderment and amazement, I have stopped short to ask myself this question: For the already exhausted, tormented and helpless man, further weighed down by the gradually increasing intensity of the technological age accompanied by various inequalities, differences and an overwhelming emptiness, is suicide the only escape to freedom? Or can it be achieved through a philosophic self-disciplining? This question and many others have risen in my mind. I have mulled over them in moments of solitude. There have been doubts too. I have thought to myself, that perhaps all his life Tarkovsky had experienced a terrifying loneliness and the burden of a tremendous hopelessness, which hung over him like a cloud and threatened to consume him completely towards the end. Which is perhaps the reason he opted for this profession. At least, this is how it seems to my mind and reasoning. Or maybe I am making a mistake somewhere? And perhaps it is because of that mistake that even at this very moment I remain an obnoxious agnostic, a confirmed materialist, a victim of the excesses of logic.

[*Originally appeared as* 'Hoyto Pritthibi-ta Paltey Jeto' *in* Ananda Bazar Patrika, *19 February 1988. Translated by Sunandini Banerjee.*]

Shards of Sound and Scraps of Seeing

Clatter-crash.

The crossroads of a busy street. Traffic rushed past in a blur of trams and buses. I was sitting in a little teashop by the wayside. People talked in raised voices and tables were thumped emphatically and liveried waiters continuously bustled to and fro. The air was full of sounds; crockery clinked and furniture scraped and bumped and people hurried in and out. The busyness spilt over to the street outside where buses and trams trundled past noisily and more streams of people flowed on their way. In-between these two scenes of hectic activity, the owner of the teashop sat silently behind the counter, leaning against the wall and wearing an expression of studied formality. In the heart of this teeming city, in the cocoon of the shop's sounds and sensations, everyone suddenly started.

Clatter-crash.

It was the sound of breaking china, slipping out of the hands of some harried waiter and crashing to the floor. At once, heads turned in

241

that direction. I turned too, not to look at what had been dropped but at the waiter who had dropped it. However, at that very instant the man had bent over to quickly collect the broken bits off the floor. As a result of which my gaze travelled straight to the opposite wall, to a portrait of Mahatma Gandhi. He was smiling—a small smile, with his head bent slightly to one side. It was uncanny; as though he was softly chiding the waiter and saying, 'Now look what you've done!'

The entire situation had taken only a few moments—the crash (of breaking china), my turning to look over my shoulder and my gaze passing over the man's bent back and stopping short at the picture of Gandhi on the wall. It was only a moment, but what a moment. Shards of sound and scraps of seeing came together to make such a perfectly rounded whole. For a brief moment in time, that single sound had risen above the prevalent hubbub of these surroundings and held its own. *Clatter-crash.* Almost immediately a few obvious images had flashed before my eyes—the pieces of broken china lying scattered on the floor, the irate owner's tirade and the frightened waiter's helpless look. These scattered images—which will always be inextricably linked to that sound and that setting—did not really appear as individual pictures in my imagination. They crowded upon my mind in a rush, which is the way these thoughts usually do. Immediately, my mind sought a reaction. That was the exact same moment when I turned and caught sight of the picture of Gandhi on the wall wearing that particular expression. And I instantly felt that instead of being a framed portrait on the wall it was actually the man himself. Who was perfectly in tune with these surroundings and events and thus was smiling gently and saying, 'Now look what you've done!'

Of course, this was only a momentary perception. The very next instant Gandhi returned to his lifeless existence of a framed picture upon the wall and the waiter was duly harangued for his clumsiness by the angry owner. But the fact that Gandhi seemed to emerge into the real world for a moment and that I perceived him as a participant in the ensuing scene of action and reactions—this is tremendously significant as far as the art of cinema is concerned. Ordinarily, this is what is meant by an 'illusion'. But if we delve a little deeper it will be evident that 'illusions' such as this are responsible for steering the art of cinema in a whole new direction.

In the early days of Soviet cinema, Russian director Lev Kuleshov [1899–1970] discovered a most interesting phenomenon while experimenting with the visual aesthetics of the form. Immediately after a scene of chaotic activity, he added a close shot of an expressionless man and this was followed by another close shot of a scene of absolute desolation. The shot of the man seemed to complement both with equal effect—the one of chaos and confusion and the other of silence. Although the image was the same—a close shot of a man wearing a vacuous expression. Between two absolutely opposite settings and two mutually uncomplementary moods, the placing of a neutral and otherwise lifeless shot resulted in infusing it with a certain significance and poignancy and it simultaneously became a part of both the shots, although obviously in two different ways. Of course, removed from its position it would once again revert to being exactly what it was in the first place—a shot of an expressionless man.

This shot remained the same—it was only due to the influence of the atmospheres that one momentarily felt the frenzy of the chaos and the despondency of the silence. Just like the framed picture of Mahatma Gandhi at the roadside teashop. There too, a sudden sound had given rise to a series of events and caused a shift in the atmosphere which in turn had effected the illusion that Gandhi had stepped out of the picture frame and actually participated in the goings-on like any other flesh-and-blood personality around me. As soon as the atmosphere loosened its grip upon my mind he went back to being a picture on the wall. Therefore what is most important—whether it be amid the throng at the restaurant or on Kuleshov's table—is nothing other than establishing an atmosphere. If done skilfully, something totally lifeless can be rendered meaningful and relevant. Under the influence of this particular atmosphere even a detached object may be imbued with an animating effect.

What we have to now ask ourselves is, whether in reality this skill is important to the art of cinema. And if so, then how important is it? Or is it the very nature of this art to imbue indifferent impassive objects or scenes with life and significance?

Actually, this phenomenon that Kuleshov stumbled upon and that I experienced unexpectedly for myself at the café is not an unknown device in other forms of art and artistic expression. Through the works of various artists down the ages this device has been responsible for effecting successful transformations. Through this, authors have found one of the strongest methods of self-expression which helps them articulate their feelings, their vision, their deepest emotions. This is how they have tinted their environments with the colours of their thoughts and instilled life into objects that were lifeless and dull. This is how the effects of establishing atmosphere have been used by artistes and writers through the centuries to achieve their primary aim—that of expressing themselves.

A look through either older or recent works of literature will provide us with ample examples. But instead of dragging out the heavyweights, a very ordinary instance will suffice to illustrate this point:

Late one night. The discordant jangling of the alarm clock roused me from deep sleep. I was to travel abroad, on work. The taxi waited at the front door. Describing a similar wintry night, Rabindranath had penned the following lines:

The taxi at the door, calls out,
Like a man, roaring loudly. The neighbourhood, still with
     sleep,
Remains oblivious.
In the guards' rooms, far away, the clock strikes half past
     three.

'Gharchhara' (Leaving Home)

The taxi. An inanimate metallic vehicle. Not human, just a car, without any feelings and sensations whatsoever. Nevertheless, in the silence of the night, when a man leaves home to set forth upon a journey, at that very moment the taxi seems to be a living presence, as though infused with life. All the emotions which seem beyond the poet's reach now seem to acquire an almost 'physical palpability' and leap out of the page to greet the reader's mind. And the poet is therefore able to express himself in a beautiful way—one that is partly fantastic and yet rooted in stark reality.

Let us continue with the object of the taxi. This heap of metal has been depicted in another sort of way by Eliot who used it to express a different kind of emotion:

> When the human engine waits
> Like a taxi throbbing waiting.

T. S. Eliot, The Waste Land

Taxis like the one described by Eliot can be seen daily at the three-point crossing of Park Street–Chowringhee–Red Road or at the intersection of Dalhousie Square and Council House Street [busy Calcutta intersections]. During the evening rush hour, countless such cars stop at the red lights, one after one another, in endless rows. As though they are lying in wait, throbbing in tense anticipation for the light to turn green. An unbearable and restless throbbing.

I have come across this same car in Jibanananda Das' [(1899–1954), modern Bengali poet] poetry too. Again, the scene is set in the dead of night. Not a night like the one described by Tagore but a night when the silence seems to stifle and the air seems heavy with ghosts:

> The last hours of the night crowd in upon the city
> A stupid car lumbers past, coughing
> Spitting out a stream of restless fuel.

'Ratri' (Night)

Here too the car is attributed with human qualities and behaviour; here too an emotion that was apparently beyond the reach of the poet thus gets life breathed into it and appears as much of a flesh-and-blood entity as the reader himself.

The same taxi—a lifeless and inanimate object—but transformed by three different settings to communicate three different emotions. These emotions or effects are, of course, results of the atmosphere that has been earlier established. And that is the phenomenon which Kuleshov brought to light.

Therefore why can't this effect, which is such an important rhetorical device in poetry for the purposes of self-expression, be equally important for cinema as well? And it is eminently possible for an emotion that is clearly evident or perceptible in the case of poetry to be the same in the case of cinema also. Especially in the three examples cited above, where the qualities attributed to the inanimate taxi are all fragments of visual and auditory sense impressions received by the human mind. 'Roared loudly' (Rabindranath), 'throbbing' (Eliot) and 'coughed' (Jibanananda)—all three consist of visual or auditory stimuli. What is interesting is that both may be captured and therefore represented through the medium of cinema because the two primary tools of this medium are the camera and the sound-recording equipment. With the aid of the camera, it is not only possible to capture the tempestuous waves of the sea but also the faint tremor of a child's lips and to then project them upon the screen at the desired dimensions. With the aid of the sound recording equipment, the audience may be made to hear anything from the loudest explosion to the soft ticking of the clock with equal ease and clarity. Therefore, it is not impossible to believe that the emotions which the writers and the artists express and infuse with life, aided by the animation of their form and their imagination and the use of fragments of sense impressions, may be made even more real and perceptible on the screen with the aid of the camera and the sound equipment.

Beyond the world of cinema, in the other arts and in literature, there are innumerable variations on this, scattered throughout the genres. All it requires is a little patient reading and keeping one's mind alert, one's ears pricked, as it were, for the nuances. The stock is limitless. Examples? Where do I begin? For the time being let us take the case of Subhash Mukhopadhyay's 'Micchiler Mukh' (Faces of the Procession), and the phrase which reads thus: 'haather aranya' or 'a wilderness of hands'. Thousands of people shouting slogans, clenched fists raised in the air. Irrespective of what they may be clamouring for, one gets an extraordinarily beautiful image of the procession in those few words— 'a wilderness of hands'. The language of pictures.

There is an even more effective example in Tagore's 'Achalayatan' where a group sings and dances in the fields while sowing crop. They sing:

We work in the fields, happily
It is here that we spend our time, from morning to evening
The sun shines overhead, showers of rain burst upon us
The air is laden with the smell of the soil
Our souls are heady with these songs of the earth
They are coursing though our veins
And its rhythm even excites the young poets and inspires new
    verses
The stalks of corn glow with life
And all earth seems to explode in joyous laughter
Under the golden sun of Aghran [the last month of autumn],
    and bathed in the silver of its full moon.

Every word of their song seems to be embellished with happiness and a spirit of celebration. 'The leaves whisper in the bamboo grove', 'The stalks of corn glow with happiness'. When the entire song is suffused with the spirit of sowing the new crop, when clumps of fresh earth are thrown up on both sides of the plough—happiness then, captured by the camera and represented on the screen, seems to be arrested within an extraordinary physicality.

We can even look at *Mother* [1906] by Maxim Gorky [1868–1936, Russian writer, founder of socialist realism in literature]. The police have arrested Pavel, and his mother spends sleepless nights waiting and worrying. An immense emptiness, a vast meaningless silence seems to be wrenching her apart from within. Everything seems shrouded in desolation and despair. According to Gorky:

> The cold sighed and rustled against the walls, the wind whistled down the chimney and something scuttled under the floor. Drops of water dripped from the roof, the sound of their falling merging strangely with the ticking of the clock. The whole house seemed to be softly swaying, while grief had turned familiar surroundings into something alien and lifeless.

The peripheral physical details provided by Gorky in order to communicate the mother's state of mind—the unceasing rain, water seeping through the cracks and dripping slowly, the ticking of the clock and various other things—can all be captured by the camera and/or the sound equipment. Gorky uses his words to arrange a series of images alongside each other, imbuing the atmosphere with a certain emotion. Then, is it not possible for an actor to utilize his acting skills and project that emotion even more realistically on the screen?

Or, consider another instance from the same book, where Gorky describes in detail the huge crowd gathered in front of the hospital gates. People have collected there to form a procession that will carry away the dead hero Iogor's body. They wait, impatient and restless. A sea of grief- stricken faces. Every now and then, within the throng, a comment or two is spoken out aloud. The crowd is unarmed. And the police have arrived amid them to maintain peace.

. . . The gate swings open. The corpse is brought out. Decorated with garlands and festooned with red ribbons. Gorky writes: 'The waiting people immediately lifted their hats, giving the impression that a flock of black birds had suddenly taken wings.'

Thus, an emotion of great magnitude that would otherwise have remained inaccessible to the reader and which wells up from the depths of the public heart at the sight of the hero's body assumes tangible proportions through Gorky's description. Having created a complex atmosphere, Gorky introduces the hero's dead body at a crucial moment, and immediately they respond by raising their black hats skywards—like so many birds spreading their wings and taking flight. Gorky had imagined such a scene and then drawn it for the reader with the help of words and the reader too must visualize it for himself in his own mind. But in cinema, doesn't this very same image lay claim to a greater degree of realistic representation? And won't the emotion prompted in the reader at this imagined raising of those black hats be intensified at least a hundredfold when confronted with the same scene on the screen? There, ordinary vision will be narrowed down by the camera to focus on countless hands and countless hats and the blue sky in the background.

The protagonist of Richard Aldington's [1892–1962] English novel *All Men Are Enemies* [1933] is a man called Antony. He is on the verge of losing faith; his soul is restless and tortured. He avoids his friends and relatives and roams about alone, thinking strange thoughts to himself. At one such moment, at a loss, Antony stops for a moment on a busy London street. The author writes:

> Antony stood alone on the pavement outside the National Gallery, feeling the inhuman loneliness of a great city. It is not solitude because it is inhabited; it is not inhuman because all these passers are anonymous, self-absorbed, indifferent . . . stilled with people, arid swarms of indifferent people . . . This inhuman humanity was terrifying . . . The streets were all familiar streets, but to Antony desolatingly melancholy.

The scene which the author has described here is nothing more than a busy street corner in any large metropolitan city. Like Esplanade, in Calcutta, for example. But Antony was not content to view the London street so plainly and refracted its busyness through the prism of his own state of mind at the time. In his *Jeebansmriti* [Remambrance of Life (1912)], Rabindranath has elaborated on this same technique. While living on Sudder Street, beside the Indian Museum in Calcutta, Tagore stood on the balcony one day, staring out at the busy streets of the city. In his words, 'Since my childhood it seems I have been seeing only with my eyes. Today, for the first time I felt as if I was looking at the world with my entire consciousness.' The vision he perceived with his entire being was, of course, not as terrible and unbearably heartless as Antony's. He observed in the throbbing restlessness of the city 'the unending carnival of the flavours of life that ripple into cascades of laughter all around, in the unfathomable depths of this world'.

Irrespective of how and what either Antony or Tagore happened to see, the important point is that of perceiving reality with one's entire consciousness instead of merely viewing it through one's eyes.

And this is what has been described by Eisenstein as *intellectual* perception. The key to the world of emotions, according to him, lay through *visual* perception. He has explained the whole concept very simply in one of his essays using a rather commonplace example. Say, it is three o'clock. When you look at the clock, what is it that you see? You see two hands—one large and one small—at right angles to each other. Nothing more. That is, you see only so much with your eyes—only the two hands of the clock at a right angle. That is the visual perception. You exercise your intelligence over it and conclude that it is now three o'clock. You are able to realize the true significance of the fact that it is three o'clock only through your Intellectual perception.

In that same piece, Eisenstein defines Intellectual perception even more clearly by citing an example from Tolstoy's *Anna Karenina*.

Vronsky comes to know that Anna is pregnant. Vronsky's world is suddenly turned upside down. The ground seems to be shifting from under his feet. He is completely bewildered. He stares into space. Gazes fixedly at the church clock, in the distance. He is unaware of the time. All he can see before him are the two hands of the clock.

A tremendous shock has resulted in Vronsky losing his Intellectual perception. Or, in Rabindranath's terms, Vronsky has temporarily lost the ability to see the world with his 'entire consciousness'.

Although, it is only normal not to lose this kind of vision. On the contrary, its absence denotes an abnormality, almost an inhumanity. And man is a rational being because of this very ability of being able to transform a Visual perception into an Intellectual perception.

Like Aldington's Antony in a particular state of mind or Tagore on that particular day, the cinematographer may also view the inanimate objects and surroundings through his entire consciousness. And this in turn is made possible not through the use of words but through the camera and audio technology. For example, if the actor was made to stand at Esplanade [a busy Calcutta intersection] one evening. At a glance, what would he be seeing before him? Countless images—trams and buses, crowds, bright lights, neon lights glowing and similar odds and ends. The camera sees the same thing. And there is plenty to be recorded by the sound equipment too. But the actor, with the use of his acting skills, aided by the intelligent selection and arrangement of sounds and images and by the construction of the event, may be able to impart a different meaning altogether to whatever is being shown on the screen. He may imbue the entire atmosphere with a particular feeling or emotion. Thus, the scene is looked at by first encountering it at the superficial level and then seeing it through our entire consciousness.

As far as cinema is concerned, one highly successful film in this regard is the Italian film *Bicycle Thieves* [(1948) by Vittorio de Sica (1901–74)]. The hero's hopes, desires, despair and other emotions are all expressed most effectively through his surroundings—be it the streets of Rome, the marketplace, the cafes, the fortune-teller's room, the stadium. Everything seems to be animated with a vitality, a liveliness. And that is why this film is so alive, so intimate. And this is why every emotion the hero experiences seems to reach out and touch the viewer's heart. And so the film remains one of the finest forms of artistic expression in this age.

A friend and I were having a discussion about *Bicycle Thieves* a few days ago. According to him, the hero Antonio's acting is flawed by a certain degree of under-acting. Although almost immediately he also confessed to the fact that the film had moved him deeply. Despite the acting of the principal character not being up to the mark, the film had nonetheless overwhelmed him. This seemed a strange reaction. I realized my friend was 'dramatic' to a terrifying degree. Possessed with a singular vision, even at the cinema he would be thinking of and making comparisons with the theatre. To the extent that he mentally removed Antonio from the screen and placed him upon the stage and then judged his acting skills accordingly. It is true that, had Antonio acted the way he had on screen on the stage, it would definitely have been considered under-acting. But that is no reason to expect him to perform theatrically in the complicated setting of the film. And had he done so, would the final product have really been desirable? Wouldn't it have seemed grossly exaggerated? Although acting is one of the primary tools of cinema, it is not the only tool. If it was, then what value would Kuleshov's discovery have for us? And how significant would my experience at the restaurant be? If a close-shot of an otherwise expressionless man or an inanimate portrait of Gandhi can, under the influence of a particular atmosphere and setting be transformed into a flesh-and-blood entity, then it is hardly likely that despite being flawed by under-acting, a film may still be capable of influencing my friend so deeply. The close shot seems uninteresting and insignificant when removed from its position between the two different scenes and Gandhi returns to being a picture on the wall once the atmosphere of the teashop loosens its grip upon the mind. So also when my friend removes Antonio from the distinctive setting of the film and regards him thus isolated and only within the purview of his imagination, the actor seems to have been under-acting. Thus, my friend's observation carried the ultimate proof of the success of establishing atmosphere in the art of cinema.

The good thing is that even in our country, a few people have begun to realize the importance of this aspect, of late. And some have used this to make the impossible possible as well. Although I feel that I must mention that most directors seek their 'art' amid clouds-moonlight-rain-birds' nests and other typical scenes from nature along with various apparently poetic phenomena. And they have not been able to move beyond this. They are unable to understand that the days of clouds and rain and flowers are now over; perhaps they are incapable of progressing in another direction due to an incomplete grasp of the true nature of the art itself. Which is why I notice that in their creations, plot, events and character are all irrespective of setting and situation. There is no sign of 'typicality' anywhere. And there are no indications whatsoever of the inner consciousness anywhere in the setting, although the opportunities are endless. The result is that they are clinging to some outdated notions and concepts, having denounced the newer ideas and trends and those who follow these more recent practices, and now wait for their 'enemies' to face financial ruin and disaster. It is not that the newer generation is not facing financial misfortune. New experiments, new forays—it is difficult to say for certain that these will always be successful. And these opportunities are not missed by the older lot. Not only are they venting as much malice as possible but at the same time also capturing a large section of the commercial audience. This in turn puts obstructions in the path of the newer filmmakers. A full-scale war is being waged. And so in our cinema, today, there is tremendous conflict—between the new and the old. A conflict of souls, of art, of existence.

There is, however, room within this conflict for new attempts, new experiments. Everyone is clamouring for new stories—stories that are alive, that are real. That the plot is terribly important is true. But that is not all. A story needs to be shown on the screen with due attention paid to its various elements and nuances. Therefore just as there is paramount need for good storylines, there is an equally urgent need to weigh each of the elements of the cinematic art and then use it skilfully and adeptly. And the one element that needs special attention, an element which has already been noted by many filmmakers of today, is that of establishing atmosphere.

In his *Japan Jatri* [A Traveller to Japan (1919)], Rabindranath referred to an ancient Japanese poem while discussing Japanese poetry. A three-line poem:

An old pond.
A frog leaps,
The water splashes.

While painting a picture of silence, according to Rabindranath, 'not only is there a harmony of words but also that of thought. This harmony of thought is not disturbed at all by the restlessness of spirit. This may be called the heart's frugality.'

While establishing atmosphere in cinema, what is required is this 'frugality of the heart' along with a tremendous passion.

['*Paribesh Nirmaan: Film-ey o Shahity-ey*'. *Translated by Sunandini Banerjee.*]

Cinema and Literature

There is something that we have more or less acquiesced to in the present day and age: cinema must cultivate an attitude of reconciliation to literature and not one of competition. This is the only way to preserve its own standard and form and succeed in carving out its own distinct niche among the other arts. Of course, this does not apply to films that are not based on literary works. Although we may well wonder whether or not they too should possess some literary qualities. And if they are present, then by what method we can ascertain their presence.

That is a lengthy debate in itself. For the time being, we will limit our discussion to those films that are based on, or are adaptations of, literary works.

What is the form of the 'reconciliation' I have just mentioned? If such a form does exist, is it possible to define it clearly? Using such terms and logic that it will not give rise to further debate and differences of opinion? And will be sanctioned by every faction? And be unanimously agreed upon?

That is not possible. Innumerable examples may be trotted out to illustrate the fact that any easy or simplistic definition will not suffice. The discussion may only be taken so far and the debate may heat up only to a point, but there they must come to a standstill and progress no further.

Let us take the example of Bibhutibhushan's *Aparajito*. And those of Satyajit Ray's *Aparajito* and *Apur Sansar*. Or Rabindranath Tagore's 'Nashtaneer' [The Broken Nest (1901)] and its cinematic version *Charulata* by Ray. While critiquing Ray's *Aparajito*, a senior film director wrote in a huff: 'Bibhutibhushan is dead, long live Bibhutibhushan.' Similarly, the film editor of a renowned weekly raised certain questions about *Apur Sansar*. And later, there was quite an upheaval among the intellectuals while discussing a piece by a writer of great erudition who had initiated a debate about Tagore's 'Nashtaneer' and Ray's *Charulata*. It was responsible for a great deal of bitterness; the outrage spilt over into newspaper columns and magazine articles, seeped into discussions and conversations and trickled its way into cultural circles as well.

I too have been subject to similar reactions. And not just once but almost every time that I have directed a film based on some reputed literary work. Although they have never been that virulent or widespread. This is because no one—especially those who are accomplished writers or speakers—has at their disposal large stretches of undisturbed leisure in which to enthusiastically analyse or discuss either someone like me or my films in every last detail. However, questions and debates that arise tend to stick in the mind and can ultimately be dragged under the greater purview of the problematics of the form itself. So, I shall speak about myself.

Premchand. In my opinion and in that of most others, he is one of the greatest Indian writers of our age. 'Kafan' is one of his stories, written towards the end of his life. I had used 'Kafan' or, rather, to make myself even clearer, I had used the characters from 'Kafan' to make a Telugu film. It was called *Oka Oorie Katha*. Translated into Bengali, it reads *Ekti Gramer Golpo* [The Story of a Village]. In English, we had found a rather fitting subtitle—*The Outsiders* or *The Marginal Ones*.

Premchand's son, the widely renowned Amrit Ray, scholar and Premchand's biographer, watched the film. I went up to meet him as he emerged, after the screening. He said, 'It is a shattering experience and a shattering film, although I do not agree at all with your interpretation.'

I had, of course, anticipated this difference of opinion. So I spoke up with a certain amount of courage and said to him, 'I cannot be absolutely sure that, had your father been alive today, his reaction would have been any different from yours. But tell me, at this particular moment, are you regretting the fact that you let me make a film based on this story?'

He almost shouted his response, 'Not at all. Why don't you tell me when you'll be using another story for another movie!'

I was greatly reassured.

Let me begin our discussion from this point. And let us limit our discussion to the screenplay of 'Kafan'. Let us examine the relationship of reconciliation between cinema and literature from here.

An unknown village in Uttar Pradesh. A bitterly cold night in winter. Having stolen some potatoes from the zamindar's fields, the idle father–son pair sit roasting them around a fire in the front yard. Famished and now greedy at the sight of food, they continue trying to hoodwink one another in the hope of bagging the lion's share. A one-roomed hut that looks as if it will fall to the ground at any moment. Inside, the pregnant daughter-in-law is in the throes of agony. Despite her condition, she is the one who has worked excruciatingly hard to feed herself and the two men. On days when she could not bring anything home or when the men were unable to either do some odd jobs or steal from the neighbouring fields, all three of them went hungry. This is the way they have managed to survive until this awful night. And it is here that the story of 'Kafan' begins. The men gorge on the potatoes, roasting them in the fire, and sometimes shifting uncomfortably as the piteous wails of the woman reach their ears. After their impromptu meal, they fall asleep out in the open. The next morning they discover that the woman is dead. The villagers visit, make a few comments, and then return to their own lives. The father–son pair set out, begging. They need money to perform the last rites. All the villagers contribute something or other, partly out of pity and partly in the hope of increasing their own piety. Having collected money in this manner, the men can no longer contain themselves and promptly rush to the local hooch den. They guzzle vast quantities of booze, discuss profundities of philosophy, and then lurch about obscenely, singing and dancing.

We—Mohit Chattopadhyay [(1934–2012), Bengali playwright, screenwriter and poet] and I—had the impudence to write a full-length screenplay based on this story. During this process we maintained our loyalty to three things in particular. First, to the original idea which the writer wished to convey through his story. Second, to the form of artistic expression known as cinema. And third, to the time of the present day and age. Keeping this triadic scheme of loyalties in mind, we internalized the original story and began our screenplay from a much earlier point on the imaginary graph of the storyline. Also, our screenplay ended in a manner very different from the original story. And somewhere about the middle of our screenplay, we made the characters come into conflict with one another, especially the old man and his daughter-in-law. There may have been subtle indications about this in the original story but no evident elaborations were made. In fact, we even invented certain incidents of which there were not the slightest hint or trace in the original. All this was done in order to cater to the needs of our art; it was all prompted by instinct and after a great deal of introspection. And most importantly, in order to heed the dictates of time. What became increasingly urgent with regard to our thoughts, ideas and actions while reconstructing the story thus, was the need for some new perceptions, some new questions. These perceptions or thoughts were of course not meant to insinuate our lack of faith in the writer but arose from a restlessness to re-explore and perhaps rediscover the original, refracting it through the lens of a new age and a new experience. While creating the screenplay and, later, while filming the movie itself, we have had to constantly grapple with all these various stages of creation and with these questions which kept occurring, to the best of our ability. The reconciliation between all these factors could never be an artificial or forced one; this was a truth which we always kept in mind.

Let me illustrate with an example. A concrete instance. The descriptive passages in the story vividly recreate Uttar Pradesh, in North India, for the reader. Our film was shot in Telengana, in South India. The harsh winters of Uttar Pradesh must have added to and enhanced the harshness of the quality of life. That cruel winter was an absent season in Telengana, as well as in our screenplay and ultimately in the film. And if someone decides to raise this point, I am done for. Our logic, our understanding was such: the despicability of poverty and the terror of exploitation are brutal realities, irrespective of seasonal changes. Therefore, the relevance of 'Kafan' is not dependent on any time of the year in particular but is true for all times. This is what we believed.

We have heard many people, including many erudite people, make the observation that in an exploitative society, savage oppression has often prompted otherwise innocent men and women to gradually descend to a level of existence and of being that can only be described as non-human. 'Kafan' is an awful representation of this observation. My question of course would be: Is this explanation one that is universally applicable? Is it an absolute?

In our opinion, the aged father of 'Kafan' is not a negative character at all. According to our reading of the story, he is an extraordinary 'iconoclast'. He has seen the world through the eyes of disillusionment. He is acquainted only too well with those who wield power in society. And having heard and seen and experienced so much, now, at sixty, he appears at once eccentric and omniscient. The son has grown up as his devoted disciple. We regard both of them as restless rebels. This rebellion appears before us in a form that is grotesquely physical; through

distortions and parodies, through derisions and contempt, through cruel actions and also through apparently cynical behaviour and speech. Skirting the edges of society, the old man stays on the fringes and remains an 'outsider'. And that is where he prefers to be. Along with his son, his initiate. He disclaims all social norms and customs with tremendous disgust and scorn; he considers all social value systems defunct and unnecessary. Therefore in our screenplay and in our film, when we are confronted with these two men who are unshakeable in their determination to steal, we are also suddenly aware of the spirit of brave rebellion underlying this apparently anti-social act. In the original story by Premchand, when we see the father and son pair blow up the money they have managed to collect as alms for the funeral on cheap country liquor instead, it is then that we realize how deeply they have struck at the very foundations of the oppressive social system and how easily they have succeeded in bringing to the ground, the immovable edifice of social 'good' and 'bad'. In this way we see the old man, in Premchand and in our screenplay, in various settings, bizarre mindsets, a destructive intensity. We see a rebellious sannyasi who is intent upon conquering the body's hunger. Who has renounced all the desires of life and lives supported only by a terrifying viciousness and endless scorn. The same hatred and scorn that we find in *Monsieur Verdoux* at a different level.

This is where we differ from the erudite 'pundits' and with the inflexible readers. I have noticed that they evaluate Premchand's 'Kafan' using the yardstick of the prevalent value-system; they have placed the events and the characters on the weighing scales of a society that believes in oppression. This is why they have interpreted the men's reluctance to work as the Indian philosophy of inaction. And in the opinion of many of these people, Premchand has represented these facets in his story with an air of disgust and disrespect; he has lampooned them with tongue firmly in cheek.

Let us now return to the triadic scheme of loyalties which cinema must bear to literature. There must therefore be a reconciliation not only with literature but also with the time, with the present. And the effect of these loyalties is not an easy one to swallow. It is extremely hazardous. And despite treading that difficult path, it is still not possible to arrive at any certain conclusion. Which is why the questions and the debates will remain, will continue. As they do in history, in philosophy, in the realm of science. Differences stubbornly rear their head out of attempts at understanding. And reconciliation occurs out of arguments and oppositions. It is not possible to avoid this. There is no way in which an easy solution can be made available. Nor should there be.

[*Shahitya, Cinema aar Shomoy'*. Translated by *Sunandini Banerjee*.]

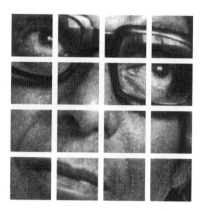

'The Time of the Prologue Is Eternity'

A desperate interviewer, having had a trying encounter with me, asked a not-too-typical 'last' question. 'If you are marooned on, or exiled to, a godforsaken island, with not a single neighbour to communicate with and hardly any chance of returning, name ten films which you would love to carry along with you.' 'Not one,' I said, refusing to explain.

Whether or not I could baffle my interviewer is immaterial. What is important is why I said it. I paused, and after second thoughts, said again, 'Perhaps I shall carry only one—*The Passion of Joan of Arc* [1928], which old story of the remarkable country girl, the Maid of Orleans, who saved France from the English in the first half of the fifteenth century and was later burnt at the stake in Rouen as a witch and a heretic.'

Is it really the best film I have ever seen? I can never be absolutely sure and hence shall not make any impetuous statement for precisely that reason. It could simply be the one that, at a particular point of time and because of my particular frame of mind, left the most memorable impression on me. Which it most certainly did, and does even now. Now, pulling myself together, I begin to realize that I had thought of it not necessarily because it is my most favourite film, one that is closest to my heart, but possibly because whenever I watch this film, and I have seen it more than a half-a-dozen times already, I find it stunningly original and astonishingly modern.

Indeed, every time I watch this film, I undergo a shattering experience, both emotionally and intellectually; I feel refreshingly animated. And to think that it is a film without a single spoken word, made in 1928 before the advent of sound by the Danish director Carl Dreyer who, fifty-five years ago, could never dream of using the technology that is now readily available to all practitioners of cinema. And it is precisely this that brings me close to my understanding of contemporary cinema.

For all that we know, the methodology of cinema is determined, by and large, by technological devices. Born out of the performances of the tools employed, these devices manifest themselves in diverse ways. The growth and development of technology coupled with the creativity of the artist contribute to the diversification of such applications. Thus, with this continually developing technology being put to creative use, the language of cinema is a continually evolving process. This naturally results in expanding cinema's area of operation and lends newer dimensions to its anatomy.

These are the external aspects of cinema and, for what is it worth, a modern phenomenon. But the truth of the matter is that, in essence, the modernity of a cinematic feat or, in other words, cinema's contemporaneity lies not just in its bare externals but in its totality, its inner strength. Which is why I am so irresistibly drawn towards the story of Joan of Arc as retold by Carl Dreyer.

Externally, *The Passion of Joan of Arc* attains a colossal stature by what, in visual terms, it captures and what it does not. It captures faces; faces in groups and in close-ups—the face of the accused and those of the accusers, of the furious and the anguished, of the tyrants and the defiant—all of them in sharp contrast with each other, punctuated by a sense of oppressive void and a feel of space. What it does not capture is splendour, which is always regarded as a necessary adjunct in any period piece. The scrupulous absence of medieval pageantry is precisely what lends the film a certain distinction. Hidden behind such external austerity lies the inherent strength of a film which defies the temporal limits of history and connects past with present.

At a certain level, the film documents history; at another, it leaps out of its physical bounds and transcends into a concept. The concept, thus born, lives in eternity. And it is no wonder that Eisenstein, working on the draft of his script for ¡*Que Viva Mexico!* [1930s, released in 1979] said: 'The time of the prologue is eternity.'

What is important, therefore, is to understand one's own time and to project it within the framework of the story's material, and at the same time to always maintain a perspective. The language, of course, is no mean job, but as in other arts, it is the means to an end and not certainly an end in itself. Tarkovsky's *The Stalker* [1979] uses a similarly appropriate language, enriched with a perfect balance of visual and aural designs. Here, the language of cinema has been rightly used to serve the film, to speak of the confusion and the crisis of the filmmaker's own time, a time which is the dominant reality of the world he lives in. *The Stalker* is a film reflecting the crisis of modern times.

In contrast, I present another example. Francis [Ford] Coppola's *Apocalypse Now* [1979], laden with high-flown language growing out of sophisticated gadgets, products of the most recent technology. It is a film that consists of a world of superb technical innovations and one that is inordinately dressed with sound and visuals. By providing the film with a certain superficial gloss and over-burdening it with technical sophistry, he claims to project the contemporary world. Beneath the surface and at the heart of the film, there is very little substance which may be mistaken as contemporary.

Coming to the Indian scene, take, for instance, several of Satyajit Ray's major works, from *Pather Panchali* to *Sadgati* [1981], including, of course, his films on contemporary life. Which among them is the most contemporary? Which one projects the most subtle nuances of contemporary sensibility? Could it be the ones (or one) set against a contemporary backdrop? A difficult question, indeed, sounding somewhat like a puzzler on a popular game show. I confess that I shall choose none of his works on present-day themes but instead settle undisputedly for *Aparajito*, the second in the Apu trilogy, dating back to the pre-war period in Bengal.

In *Aparajito*, the focus is on the slow but inevitable disintegration of a seemingly unalterable relationship, with constant stresses and strains acting within, and the eventual discovery of the son's new moorings in a metropolitan setting. The entire process, as I watch the film, has its ups and downs, its complexities, its ruthless inexorabilities which are so much an integral part of us and of our time. The whole gamut has been explored in its most intricate details, bit by bit, following the characters and the story to their ultimate destinies.

When, at last, Apu comes back to the village, he is benumbed by a sense of desolation. He comes to know of the death of his mother, has a word with the old man sitting on the porch, turns his back to that fading world which once was his childhood and sets off to another world, to a time which is changing and more challenging than ever. Quiet on the surface but intense throughout, the ending shakes me from within, forces me to face my own time—intimidating, infernal and yet not so unfriendly. None of Ray's films have left as indelible an impression upon my mind as has *Aparajito*. It did so when I watched it for the first time. It continues to do so even now.

Having watched and made so many films over the years, I realize now that a passionate cineaste capable of responding to modern sensibilities does not necessarily, unlike his literary counterpart, have to speak only of his anxiety to change society, of his protest, of the challenge he faces from an unsympathetic world, but must also include the confusion, the anguished questing, the inherent contradictions which are beyond easy solutions. A brilliant example of such tortuous quests and of human situations in total disarray is Robert Bresson's *Four Nights of a Dreamer* [1971]:

One clear, frostless night a young woman is about to commit suicide by jumping from the rooftop. A young man, not known to her, watches her from a distance and rushes to save her from disaster. He succeeds in foiling her attempt at suicide although she herself barely resists his help. The just-rescued woman and her saviour spend some time in a lonely park. After a long silence they begin to talk, groping for words, articulating in broken sentences and even in monosyllabic words. She tells him she has been betrayed by her lover. He feels sorry but does not approve of her action. She is touched by his kindness and he makes note of it. As they part, they promise to meet again.

Next day and the day following they meet again in the same park, at around the same hour. Three meetings on three consecutive days, always in the same park and all of the three nights similarly clear and frostless, build a certain familiarity. From familiarity there evolves a mute understanding. The fourth night. She arrives at the park. Waits for him and finally decides to go to his apartment. As she stands before the closed door of the apartment, she begins to feel diffident. She remains thus for a long time and then, in utter desperation and perhaps a sudden sense of urgency, rings the doorbell. The door opens and there he stands, begging silent apology.

Soon afterwards, the two of them are seen walking triumphantly along the crowded road, hand in hand. Letting the world know that they are in love. As they stroll through the crowds, the man who betrayed her walks past them. She stops, looks back, asks the man beside her to wait a moment, and rushes to the other before he gets lost in the crowd. They meet, they embrace, they kiss passionately. Left alone, the young man who, one clear frostless night, rescued the distraught woman, looks reverentially at the couple embracing. After her initial moments of excitement and ecstasy, she remembers that someone is waiting for her. She excuses herself and rushes to the man-in-waiting. Experiencing a peculiar combination of gratitude and joy, she hugs him, gives him a parting kiss and joins the man who she thought had betrayed her.

The three go their own ways—the woman and her lover in one direction, and the one who saved the woman in another. Soon they pass out of the viewers' sight. The drifting crowd fills the screen.

Marked by profound economy and precision and a high degree of sophistication, *Four Nights of a Dreamer* is a film that speaks of human situations in distress, of confusion and, of course, of human dignity. Sensitively made, it is a film which is compassionate to the core and yet shattering in its ruthlessness. Structurally, it has hardly any parallel: hidden behind the external façade of a disarmingly simple fable-like narrative lie several layers of complex relationships. *Four Nights of a Dreamer* is the most contemporary film I have seen in recent years. I remember having seen the film more than five years ago but it still haunts me.

I wonder why I did not tell my interviewer that I would like to carry this gem of a film with me were I ever to be exiled or marooned upon that deserted island.

[*Originally appeared in the* Sunday Statesman, Miscellany, *6 November 1983*]

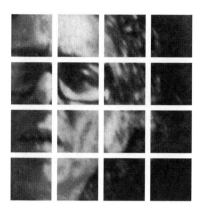

Filmography

Ratbhor (Night's End)
1956, *Bengali,* Black-and-White

Based on a story by Swaraj Banerjee

Photography: Ramananda Sengupta

Music: Salil Chowdhury

Editor: Ramesh Joshi

Produced by: S. B. Productions

Screenplay and direction: Mrinal Sen

Cast includes: Chhabi Biswas, Uttam Kumar, Chhaya Devi, Sabitri Chatterjee, Sobha Sen, Manik Chatterjee

Nil Akasher Niche (Under the Blue Sky)
1958, *Bengali*, Black-and-White

From a story by Mahadevi Verma ('Chini Pheriwala')

Photography: Sailaja Chatterjee

Music: Hemanta Mukherjee

Editor: Subodh Roy
Produced by: Hemanta-Bela Production
Screenplay and direction: Mrinal Sen
Cast includes: Kali Banerjee, Manju Dey, Smriti Biswas, Bikash Ray, Ajit Chatterjee, Suruchi Sengupta

Baishey Sravan (Wedding Day)
1960, *Bengali*, Black-and-White

Based on a story by Kanai Basu
Photography: Sailaja Chatterjee
Music: Hemanta Mukherjee
Editor: Subodh Roy
Art director: Bansi Chandragupta
Produced by: Kallol Films
Screenplay and direction: Mrinal Sen
Cast includes: Madhabi Mukherjee, Jnanesh Mukherjee, Umanath Bhattacharyya, Anup Kumar

International Festival of Cinematographic Art, Venice, 1969

London Film Festival, 1969

Punashcha (Over Again)
1961, *Bengali*, Black-and-White

Based on a story by Asish Barman

Photography: Sailaja Chatterjee
Music: Samaresh Roy
Editor: Gangadhar Naskar
Produced by: Mrinal Sen Productions
Screenplay and direction: Mrinal Sen
Cast includes: Soumitra Chatterjee, Kanika Majumdar, N. Viswanathan, Shefali Banerjee, Kunal Basu, Pahari Sanyal, Kali Banerjee
Regional Certificate of Merit, President's Award, India, 1961

Abasheshe (At Last)
1963, *Bengali*, Black-and-White

Based on a story by Achintya Kumar Sengupta

Photography: Sailaja Chatterjee
Music: Rabin Chatterjee
Editor: Gangadhar Naskar
Art director: Bansi Chandragupta
Produced by: Skups Films
Screenplay and direction: Mrinal Sen
Cast includes: Sabitri Chatterjee, Ashit Baran,Utpal Dutt, Robi Ghosh, Bikash Ray, Sulata Chowdhury, Pahari Sanyal, Chhaya Devi, Anup Kumar, Tarun Kumar

Pratinidhi (The Substitute)
1964, *Bengali*, Black-and-White

Based on a story by Achintya Kumar Sengupta

Photography: Sailaja Chatterjee
Music: Hemanta Mukherjee
Editor: Gangadhar Naskar
Art director: Bansi Chandragupta
Produced by: Ellora Productions
Screenplay and direction: Mrinal Sen
Cast includes: Sabitri Chatterjee, Soumitra Chatterjee, Anup Kumar, Satya Banerjee, Prasenjit Sarkar, Jahar Roy

Akash Kusum (Up in the Clouds)
1965, *Bengali*, Black-and-White

Based on a story by Asish Barman

Photography: Sailaja Chatterjee
Music: Sudhin Dasgupta
Editor: Gangadhar Naskar
Art director: Bansi Chandragupta
Produced by: Purbachal Film Producers
Screenplay: Asish Barman and Mrinal Sen
Direction: Mrinal Sen
Cast includes: Aparna Sen, Soumitra Chatterjee, Subendhu Chatterjee, Haradhan Banerjee, Sobha Sen, Sati Devi, Profullabala Devi

Silver Medal, President's Award, India, 1965

Maitra Manisha (Two Brothers)
1966, *Oriya*, Black-and-White

Based on a story by Kalindi Charan Panigrahi

Photography: Sailaja Chatterjee
Music: Bhubaneshwar Misra
Editor: Gangadhar Naskar
Art director: B. Kalyan
Produced by: Chhayabani Pratishthan
Screenplay and direction: Mrinal Sen
Cast includes: Prasanta Nanda, Sarat Pujari, Dukhiram Sain, Bhanumati, Ram Mania, Bhim Singh, Sujata

Silver Medal, President's Award, India, 1966

Moving Perspectives (Documentary)
1967, Colour

Photography: Sailaja Chatterjee

Music: Vanraj Bhatia
Editor: Gangadhar Naskar
Produced by: Films Division, Government of India
Screenplay: Khwaja Ahmad Abbas
Direction: Mrinal Sen

International Film Festival, Pnom Penh, 1968, Silver Trophy

Bhuvan Shome
1969, *Hindi*, Black-and-White

Based on a story by Banaphool (Balaichand Mukherjee)

Photography: K. K. Mahajan
Music: Vijay Raghav Rao
Editor: Gangadhar Naskar
Produced by: Mrinal Sen Productions
Screenplay and direction: Mrinal Sen
Cast includes: Utpal Dutt, Suhasini Mulay, Sekhar Chatterjee, Sadhu Meher, Rochak Pandit, Punyadas

Gold Medal, President's Award, India, 1969

Best Director, President's Award, India, 1969

Best Actor (Utpal Dutt), President's Award, India, 1969

International Festival of Cinematographic Art, Venice, 1969

Directors' Fortnight, Cannes, 1970

Icchapuran (Wish Fulfilment) (Children's film)
1970, *Bengali*, Black-and-White

Based on a story by Rabindranath Tagore

Photography: K. K. Mahajan

Music: Aloke Nath Dey

Editor: Gangadhar Naskar

Produced by: Mrinal Sen Productions on behalf of Children's Film Society

Screenplay and direction: Mrinal Sen

Cast includes: Sekhar Chatterjee, Surajit Nandi, Sobha Sen, Nemai Ghosh, Sadhu Meher, Keya Chakrabarty, Manika Roy Chowdhury

Interview
1970, *Bengali*, Black-and-White

Based on a story by Asish Barman

Photography: K. K. Mahajan

Music: Vijay Raghav Rao

Editor: Gangadhar Naskar

Art director: B. Kalyan

Produced by: Mrinal Sen Productions

Screenplay and direction: Mrinal Sen

Cast includes: Ranjit Mullick, Karuna Banerjee, Sekhar Chatterjee, Mamata Chatterjee, Bulbul Mukherjee, Umanath Bhattacharya, Amal Chakrabarty, Tapan Dasgupta, Bimal Banerjee, Girindranath Das, Satyen Ghosh, Kshudiram Bhattacharya, Sujit Basu, Almo Marris, Rabi Chakrabarty, M. Subramanium, Asoka Chawla, Patricia Denet

Critics' Award and Special Mention of Festival Directorate, Sri Lanka Film Festival, 1972

Best Actor (Ranjit Mullick), Karlovy Vary Film Festival, 1973

Ek Adhuri Kahani (An Unfinished Story)
1971, *Hindi*, Black-and-White

Based on a story by Subodh Ghosh

Photography: K. K. Mahajan
Music: Vijay Raghav Rao
Editor: Gangadhar Naskar
Produced by: Arun Kaul Productions
Screenplay and direction: Mrinal Sen
Cast includes: Vivek Chatterjee, Arati Bhattacharya, Utpal Dutt, Sekhar
Chatterjee, Shyam Laha, Sobha Sen, Sadhana Roy Chowdhury, Ajitesh Banerjee,
Jnanesh Mukherjee

Special Award, Mannhein Film Festival, 1971

Calcutta 71
1972, *Bengali*, Black-and-White

Based on stories by Manik Bandyopadhyay, Prabodh Sanyal, Samaresh Basu,
Ajitesh Bandyopadhyay

Photography: K. K. Mahajan
Music: Ananda Shankar
Editor: Gangadhar Naskar
Art director: Bansi Chandragupta
Produced by: D. S. Pictures
Screenplay and direction: Mrinal Sen
Cast includes: Ranjit Mullick, Suhasini Mulay, Utpal Dutt, Devraj Roy, Satya
Banerjee, Sadhana Roy Chowdhury, Madhabi Chakrabarty, Sucheta Roy, Binata
Roy, Ashoke Mukherjee, Debatosh Ghosh, Geeta Sen, Surajit Nandi, Ajitesh
Banerjee, Ajay Banerjee, Manik Roy Chowdhury

Silver Medal President's Award, India, 1972

Silver Medal, Best Photography (K. K.Mahajan), President's Award, 1972

International Festival of Cinematographic Art, Venice, 1972

Padatik (Urban Guerrilla)
1973, *Bengali*, Black-and-White

Based on a story by Asish Barman and Mrinal Sen

Photography: K. K. Mahajan

Music: Ananda Shankar
Editor: Gangadhar Naskar
Produced by: Mrinal Sen Productions
Screenplay: Mrinal Sen and Asish Barman
Direction: Mrinal Sen
Cast includes: Dhritiman Chatterjee, Simi Garewal, Bijan Bhattacharyya, Jochhan Dastidar, Prabhash Sarkar, Dhruba Mitra, Ashima Sinha, Kamal Kidwai, Farida Kidwai, Tapan Das

Best Script, President's Award, India, 1973

Director's Fortnight, Cannes, 1973

Chorus
1974, *Bengali*, Black-and-White

Story by Mohit Chatterjee, Golam Kuddus and Mrinal Sen

Photography: K. K. Mahajan
Music: Ananda Shankar
Editor: Gangadhar Naskar
Produced by: Mrinal Sen Productions
Screenplay: Mrinal Sen and Mohit Chatterjee
Direction: Mrinal Sen
Cast includes: Utpal Dutt, Sekhar Chatterjee, Haradhan Banerjee, Abhijit Mukherjee, Ajay Banerjee, Dilip Roy, Nirmal Ghosh, Satya Banerjee, Geeta Sen, Surajit Nandi, Robi Ghosh

Golden Lotus, President's Award, India, 1975

Silver Lotus (Music), President's Award, India, 1975

Silver Medal, Moscow Film Festival, 1975

FIPRESCI Award, Berlin Film Festival, 1975

Mrigaya (The Royal Hunt)
1976, *Hindi*, Colour

Based on a story by Bhagavati Charan Panigrahi

Photography: K. K. Mahajan
Music: Salil Chowdhury
Editor: Gangadhar Naskar

Produced by: Uday Bhaskar International
Screenplay: Mrinal Sen and Mohit Chatterjee
Direction: Mrinal Sen
Cast includes: Mithun Chakrabarty, Mamata Shankar, Jnanesh Mukherjee, Ajay Banerjee, Sajal Roy Chowdhury, Reba Roy Chowdhury, Gita Karmakar, Samit Bhanja, Sadhu Meher, Asit Banerjee, Anup Kumar

Golden Lotus, President's Award, India, 1976

Silver Lotus, Best Actor (Mithun Chakrabarty) President's Award, 1976

Oka Oorie Katha (The Outsiders)
1977, *Telugu*, Colour

Based on a story by Premchand ('*Kafan*')

Photography: K. K. Mahajan
Music: Vijay Raghav Rao
Editor: Gangadhar Naskar
Produced by: A. Parandhama Reddy
Screenplay: Mrinal Sen and Mohit Chatterjee
Direction: Mrinal Sen
Cast includes: Vasudev Rao, Mamata Shankar, Narayan Rao, A. R. Krishna, Lakshmi Devdas

Silver Lotus, President's Award, India, 1977

Director's Fortnight, Cannes, 1978

Special Jury Award, Karlovy Vary Film Festival, 1978

Special Award, Carthage Film Festival, 1978

London Film Festival, 1978

Parashuram (Man with an Axe)
1978, *Bengali*, Colour

Story by Mrinal Sen and Mohit Chatterjee

Photography: Ranjit Ray
Music: B. V. Karanth
Editor: Gangadhar Naskar
Produced by: Government of West Bengal
Screenplay: Mrinal Sen and Mohit Chatterjee

Cast includes: Arijit Guha, Arun Mukherjee, Sumati Guhathakurta, Neelkantha Sengupta, Bibhas Chakrabarty, Reba Roy Chowdhury, Nemai Ghosh, Radharani Devi, Sajal Roy Chowdhury, Arati Das. Anuradha Dev, Abhijit Ghosh, Jayanta Bhattacharya, Sreela Mazumdar, Shailen Gangopadhyay

Special Mention, President's Award, India, 1978

Silver Lotus, Best Actor (Arun Mukherjee), President's Award, 1978

Silver Medal, Moscow Film Festival, 1979

London Film Festival, 1979

Ek Din Pratidin (And Quiet Rolls the Day)
1979, *Bengali*, Colour

Based on a story by Amalendu Chakraborty ('*Abirata Chenamukh*')

Photography: K. K. Mahajan
Music: B. V. Karanth
Editor: Gangadhar Naskar
Art director: Suresh Chandra
Produced by: Mrinal Sen Productions
Screenplay and direction: Mrinal Sen
Cast includes: Satya Banerjee, Geeta Sen, Mamata Shankar, Sreela Majumder, Tapan Das, Tupur Ghosh, Kausik Sen, Nalini Banerjee, Arun Mukherjee, Umanath Bhattacharyya, Biplab Chatterjee, Gautam Chakrabarty

Silver Lotus, President's Award, India, 1979

Best Director, President's Award, India, 1979

Best Editing, President's Award, India, 1979

International Film Festival, Cannes, 1980

London Film Festival, 1980

New York Film Festival, 1980

Akaler Sandhane (In Search of Famine)
1980, *Bengali*, Colour

From a novel by Amalendu Chakrabarty

Photography: K. K. Mahajan
Music: Salil Chowdhury

279

Editor: Gangadhar Naskar
Art director: Suresh Chandra
Produced by: D. K. Films
Screenplay and direction: Mrinal Sen
Cast includes: Dhritiman Chatterjee, Smita Patil, Dipankar Dey, Rajen Tarafder, Jochhan Dastidar, Biplab Chatterjee, Samaresh Banerjee, Paresh Ghosh, Neelkantha Sen Gupta, Devika Mukherjee, Sreela Majumder, Jayanta Chowdhury, Geeta Sen, Radhamohan Bhattacharya, Promode Ganguly

Silver Bear, Berlin Film Festival, 1981

London Film Festival, 1981

Golden Lotus, President's Award, India, 1981

Best Director, President's Award, India, 1981

Best Script, President's Award, India, 1981

Best Editing, President's Award, India, 1981

Calcutta, My El Dorado (Documentary)
1986

Chalchitra (Kaleidoscope)
1981, *Bengali*, Colour

Story by Mrinal Sen

Photography: K. K. Mahajan
Music: Aloke Nath Dey
Editor: Gangadhar Naskar
Art director: Suresh Chandra
Produced by: D. K. Films
Screenplay and direction: Mrinal Sen
Cast includes: Anjan Dutt, Geeta Sen, Utpal Dutt, Paresh Ghosh, Purnima Dutt, Radharani Devi, Kalpana Mukherjee, Rekha Chatterjee, Arati Chakrabarty, Kakali Bose, Rupa Barman, Mithu Mukherjee, Ramen Roy Chowdhury, Dilip Bose, Debapratim Dasgupta, Riddhipratim Dasgupta, Kausik Sen, Sekhar Das, Sujit Ghose.

International Festival of Cinematographic Art, Venice, 1982

London Film Festival, 1982

Tripura Prasanga (About Tripura) (Documentary)
1982

Kharij (The Case is Closed)
1982, *Bengali*, Colour

Based on a story by Ramapada Chowdhury

Photography: K. K. Mahajan
Music: B. V. Karanth
Editor: Gangadhar Naskar
Art director: Nitish Roy
Produced by: Neelkantha Films
Screenplay and direction: Mrinal Sen
Cast includes: Anjan Dutt, Mamata Shankar, Sreela Majumder, Debatosh Ghosh, Neelotpal Dey, Bimal Chatterjee, Indranil Maitra, Debapratim Dasgupta

Silver Lotus, President's Award, India, 1982

Best Editing, President's Award, India, 1982

Best Art Direction, President's Award, India, 1982

Second Best Film, President's Award, India, 1982

Special Jury Award, Cannes Film Festival, 1983

London Film Festival, 1983

Golden Spike Award, Valladolid Film Festival, 1983

Bronze Hugo, Chicago Film Festival, 1983

Khandahar (The Ruins)
1983, *Hindi*, Colour

Based on a story by Premendra Mitra (*'Telenapotar Abhiskar'*)

Photography: K. K. Mahajan
Music: Bhaskar Chandavarkar
Editor: Mrinmoy Chakrabarty
Art director: Nitish Roy
Produced by: Jagadish and Pushpa Chowkhani (Shree Bharat Lakshmi Pictures)
Screenplay and direction: Mrinal Sen
Cast includes: Shabana Azmi, Naseerudin Shah, Geeta Sen, Pankaj Kapoor, Annu Kapoor, Rajen Tarafder, Sreela Majumder

Best Director, President's Award, India, 1984

Best Actress (Shabana Azmi), President's Award, India, 1984

Best Editor, President's Award, India, 1984

Gold Hugo, Chicago Film Festival, 1984

Silver Award, Montreal Film Festival, 1984

International Film Festival, Cannes, 1984

London Film Festival, 1984

Kabhi Door Kabhi Paas (Far and Near) (13 telefilms)
1985-86, *Hindi*, Black-and-White

Photography: Sambit Bose, Shashi Anand
Music: Chandan Roy Chowdhury
Editor: Mrinmoy Chakroborty
Art director: Gautam Basu
Produced by: Mrinal Sen
Screenplay and Direction: Mrinal Sen

1. *Das Saal Baad* (After a Decade)
Based on a story by Achintya Kumar Sengupta
Cast includes: Aparna Sen, Girish Karnad

2. *Ravibar* (Sunday)
Based on a story by Achintya Kumar Sengupta
Cast includes: Mamata Shankar, Dhritiman Chatterjee

3. *Saalgiraa* (The Anniversary)
Based on a story by Achintya Kumar Sengupta
Cast includes: Dipti Naval, Dhritiman Chatterjee

4. *Do Bahen* (Two Sisters)
Based on a story by Narendranath Mitra
Cast includes: Anita Kanwar, Neena Gupta

5. *Aina* (The Mirror)
Based on a story by Dipendra Nath Bandyopadhyay
Cast includes: Neena Gupta, Pankaj Kapoor

6. *Jit* (The Victory), Part I
Based on a story by Moti Nandy
Cast includes: Dipankar De, Surekha Sikri

7. *Jit* (The Victory), Part II
Based on a story by Moti Nandy
Cast includes: Dipankar De, Surekha Sikri

8. *Aajkaal* (Modern Times)
Based on a story by Ramapada Chowdhury
Cast includes: Manohar Singh, Lily Chakroborty

9. *Aparajit* (The Unvanquished)
Based on a story by Mrinal Sen
Cast includes: Manohar Singh, Uttara Baokar

10. *Ajnabi* (The Stranger)
Based on a story by Dibyendu Palit
Cast includes: Neena Gupta, Dilip Dhawan

11. *Shaal* (The Shawl)
Based on a story by Dibyendu Palit
Cast includes: Priya Tendulkar, Dilip Dhawan

12. *Swayamvar* (Marriage by Choice)
Based on a story by Mrinal Sen
Cast includes: Suhel Seth, Nikhil Bhagat, Aparajita

13. *Kabhi Door Kabhi Paas* (Far and Near)
Based on a story by Ramapada Chowdhury
Cast includes: Anil Chatterjee

Genesis
1986, *Hindi*, Colour

Based on a story by Samaresh Basu

Photography: Carlo Varini
Music: Ravi Shankar
Editor: Elizabeth Waelchli
Co-produced by: Scarabee Films (France), Mrinal Sen-PLRT Productions, Les Films de la Dreve (Belgium) and Cactus Films (Switzerland)
Screenplay and direction: Mrinal Sen
Cast includes: Shabana Azmi, Naseeruddin Shah, Om Puri, M. K. Raina

International Film Festival, Cannes, 1986

London Film Festival, 1986

Ekdin Achanak (Suddenly One Day)
1989, *Hindi*, Colour

Based on a novel by Ramapada Chowdhury

Photography: K. K. Mahajan
Music: Jyotishka Das Gupta
Editor: Mrinmoy Chakrabarty
Art director: Gautam Basu
Produced by: National Film Development Corporation
Screenplay and direction: Mrinal Sen
Cast includes: Shreeram Lagoo, Shabana Azmi, Uttara Baokar, Aparna Sen, Roopa Ganguly, Anjan Chakrabarty

Best Supporting Actress (Uttara Baokar), President's Award, India, 1989

International Festival of Cinematographic Art, Venice, 1989

London Film Festival, 1989

Mahaprithivi (World Within, World Without)
1991, *Bengali*, Colour

Based on a story by Anjan Dutt

Photography: Shashi Anand
Music: B. V. Karanth and Chandan Roy Chowdhury
Editor: Mrinmoy Chakrabarty
Art director: Gautam Basu
Produced by: Goutam Goswamy
Screenplay and direction: Mrinal Sen
Cast includes: Victor Banerjee, Soumitra Chatterjee, Aparna Sen, Geeta Sen, Anjan Dutt, Anasuya Majumdar, Abhijit Mukherjee, Nilotpal Dey, Asit Banerjee, Kumarajit Chatterjee, Soumyen Bose, Santosh Haldar, Mukul Chowdhury, Utpal Chakrabarty

International Festival of New Cinema, Berlin, 1991

Antareen (The Confined)
1993, *Bengali*, Colour

Based on a story by Saadat Hasan Manto

Photography: Shashi Anand

Music: Shashi Anand
Editor: Mrinmoy Chakroborty
Art Director: Gautam Basu
Produced by: NFDC
Screenplay and Direction: Mrinal Sen
Cast includes: Dimple Kapadia, Anjan Dutt, Tathagata Sanyal

International Film Festival, San Sebastian

National Award for Best Bengali Film

Show Goes On (Documentary)
1995

Aamar Bhuvan (This My Land)
2002, *Bengali*, Colour

Based on a story by Afsar Ahmed

Photography: Avik Mukhopadhyay
Music: Debajyoti Mishra
Editor: Mrinmoy Chakroborty
Art Director: Gautam Basu
Produced by: P. D. Gupta
Screenplay and Direction: Mrinal Sen
Cast includes: Nandita Das, Kousik Sen, Saswata Chatterjee, Sreejata Bhattacharya, Bibhash Chakroborty, Arun Mukherjee, Sayan Kundu, Subhanwita Guha